erica hannickel
july 09
for revising dissertation

- Turner a product of his place & time
- bourgeois culture dominated the midwest
  since late 18th c (middle class
  capitalist success story, Turner copies it)
- midwest a lab for Am. cult at large

THE MIDWEST
AND THE NATION

Midwest History and Culture

GENERAL EDITORS
James H. Madison and Thomas J. Schlereth

THE MIDWEST
AND THE NATION

Rethinking the History
of an American Region

ANDREW R. L. CAYTON

AND

PETER S. ONUF

INDIANA UNIVERSITY PRESS

Bloomington and Indianapolis

Manufactured in the United States of America.

Library of Congress Cataloging-in-Publication Data

Cayton, Andrew R. L.
The Midwest and the nation : rethinking the history of an American region / by Andrew R.L. Cayton and Peter S. Onuf.
p.   cm. — (Midwestern history and culture)
Includes bibliographical references.
ISBN 0-253-31525-5
1. Northwest, Old—History. 2. Northwest, Old—Historiography.
3. Middle West—History. 4. Middle West—Historiography. I. Onuf, Peter S. II. Title. III. Series.
F479.C34 1990

977—dc20

89-45479
CIP

1 2 3 4 5 94 93 92 91 90

For our daughters—
Elizabeth Renanne Cayton
Hannah Kupiec Cayton
Rachel Kathryn Onuf
Alexandra Kirkman Onuf

CONTENTS

FOREWORD

Bernard W. Sheehan

As the republic in 1987 commemorated the bicentennial of the Constitution, it seemed appropriate that the states between the Ohio and the Mississippi should direct attention to those ordinances that had been so significant in the creation of what has come to be called the "heartland" of the nation. As a result, in early September 1987 Indiana University played host to a traveling exhibition of historical materials concerning the Northwest ordinances and the Constitution culled from the rich resources of midwestern libraries and historical societies. In addition, beginning in the fall of 1986, conferences were held throughout the region bringing together scholars to speak on the formative years of the republic. Although designed mainly for popular audiences, the conferences enlisted the participation of major historians in the field. Convincing evidence of the high quality of these gatherings can be found in the papers delivered at the Indiana University conference, which were published later as a thematic issue of the *Indiana Magazine of History* (March 1988).

Historians have, one supposes, the same craving for immortality that afflicts other human beings, and it is only partially assuaged by the appearance of their work in print. They would like the assurance that their research and writing will decisively affect the scholarship on a critical subject. Should their labors stimulate a major reconsideration of some thorny problem or mark a significant turn in interpretation, they at least have reason to be grateful. By the last years of the 1980s the opportunities in regional history had become evident. The Northeast (usually more New England than the middle Atlantic region) and the South had long engaged the attention of generations of historians. The rest of the country—before the Civil War that meant the Midwest—plainly warranted deeper examination. Thus, as part of its commemorative activities the History Department and the Alumni Association of Indiana University with a grant from the National Endowment for the Humanities proposed to assemble a symposium of scholars interested in the subject. Andrew R. L. Cayton and Peter S. Onuf prepared a manuscript on the state of scholarship on the ordinances and the northwestern region that served as the basis of discussion. In two long sessions over the Labor Day weekend some dozen experts on various phases of midwestern history conferred, debated, and thrashed over the principal issues. The sessions were a testimonial to what serious and civil conversation can be for the life of the mind. Armed with the results of these deliberations, Cayton and Onuf returned to their studies and made their manuscript into a book. In the end, of course, the work could not be a communal project. The conception and the language belong to the authors.

It remains only to record the pleasure of the sponsors in presenting this volume to the interested reader. Though we have no doubt that it will stand on its own as an essay in historiography and regional history, its ultimate justification will come from the work it stimulates from future historians.

PREFACE

Our intention in *The Midwest and the Nation* is to analyze recent work by historians of the Old Northwest in the nineteenth century and to suggest interpretative frameworks for future study of this important American region. Based on our readings of historical scholarship completed for the most part in the last two decades, this book was neither conceived nor written as a definitive study. We have not consulted primary sources beyond those we have used in our previous work on the Old Northwest. *The Midwest and the Nation* is not a monograph or a textbook. Indeed, it is a book that one of our undergraduate professors would have described with more than a hint of disdain as "imprecise."

In brief, what we have attempted to write is an extended and often speculative essay. We have deliberately rejected the caution and qualification which pervades most of contemporary historical scholarship. We hope to provoke, to stimulate, and above all to encourage more study of the Midwest by providing a consciously argumentative point of departure.

To be sure, *The Midwest and the Nation* offers a model for understanding the economic, social, and political development of the Old Northwest in the nineteenth century. But our subject is less the actual *history* of the region than *historians'* interpretations of it. In these pages the names of historians appear constantly. At times, the frequent invocation of scholars may give the text the tone of what a friendly reader of an earlier draft half-jokingly called a cocktail party. But we are not intentionally engaged in some form of intellectual name-dropping. Rather, we want explicitly to associate *specific* historians with their *specific* views on what happened in the past. We do not offer interpretations as anonymous, authoritative statements whose provenance can only be traced in footnotes. Historians appear frequently in this book because their *individual* efforts to make sense of the past and the intersection of their efforts with those of other *individuals* are our major concerns. We are, in short, investigating the ways in which historians have constructed the history of the Midwest.

American historians are often reluctant to drop the veil of authorial objectivity and to examine what they write as one story within a larger set of tales about the past. As a whole, they tend to resist analysis of their work as the product of a context informed by their particular temporal and geographic location, as well as by their gender, race, and class. We admit to a good deal of self-consciousness about the subject ourselves.

After much debate about how we should refer to our own work, we have decided to do so on a limited basis and in the third person. We do not intend to sound self-serving. But to use the first person plural when referring to a work by either one of us would clearly be incorrect, and to use the singular would be confusing and send the reader to the inevitable endnote. While we are clearly going to agree with most of what we have written elsewhere, our intention is simply to integrate our arguments with those of other students of the region.

Our debt to the many fine scholars who have worked in various aspects of the histories of Ohio, Indiana, Illinois, Michigan, and Wisconsin is obvious. (We have provided extensive endnotes to guide interested students to the many excellent books and articles about the region published since 1950.) For the most part, we have tried to avoid pronouncements about the quality of a book or article. But a word of warning is in order here. Since our major interest is to see how individual studies fit into the larger story we believe recent historians are developing, we may at times have inadvertently caricatured subtle arguments. Some historians will no doubt take exception to our summary of the thrust of their work. While we fervently hope that this is not the case, it is perhaps inevitable given our agenda. We hope that any "spin" we may have put on an individual's interpretation will be understood in the light of our larger arguments. As is true with all scholars, the kinds of questions and assumptions we brought to the project have informed our readings of the many historians we have consulted.

If nothing else, *The Midwest and the Nation* should encourage historians to think about the region in more systematic ways than they have in the past few decades. Many historians of the South have made it their business to demonstrate that nineteenth-century America was not simply New England writ large. We strongly endorse such sentiments. But our larger desire is to suggest that the Old Northwest was more than a generic frontier or a cultural crossroads or a meeting ground of North and South. If the region was all of those things to one degree or another, it was also a place with a distinctive character of its own.

Our underlying assumption, in sum, is one we share with a Wisconsin-born historian whom we take to task for a multitude of sins in the following pages. We disagree profoundly with many of the conclusions of Frederick Jackson Turner. But he was surely right to insist on the centrality of the Midwest in the history of the United States of America.

Our work began with Bernard Sheehan's inspiration to convene a symposium on the historiography of the Old Northwest. Under the generous sponsorship of the Big Ten Universities' Project to Celebrate the Bicentennial of the Northwest Ordinance of 1787, a distinguished group of scholars gathered at Indiana University on September 6 and 7, 1987, to discuss a preliminary draft of this book. The symposium was part of a larger bicentennial conference hosted by the Indiana University History Department and Alumni Association. The indefatigable Frank Jones, former president of the Alumni Association, was the guiding genius behind the Big Ten Project and, with the assistance of Mary Helm, made us all feel welcome in Bloomington.

The symposium participants included Joyce Appleby, Robert Berkhofer, Jr., Rowland Berthoff, Mary Kupiec Cayton, Don Harrison Doyle, Robert R. Dykstra, Don E. Fehrenbacher, Paul Finkelman, Elliott Gorn, John L. Larson, James H. Madison, Robert McColley, Donald J. Ratcliffe, Malcolm J. Rohrbough, Bernard Sheehan, and David Thelen. We thank them all for their stimulating commentary. We are particularly grateful to professors Berkhofer, Finkelman, and Rohrbough for their written comments at the Bloomington meeting and to professors Dykstra and Larson for their useful criticisms of a revised manuscript that we presented to the Society for the Historians of the Early American Republic in Worcester, Massachusetts, in July 1988.

We benefited immeasurably from literally hours of discussion about the theoretical assumptions of this project with members of the Ball State University History Department—especially Richard Aquila, Mark Fissel, John Glen, Dan Goffman, and Susan Lawrence. George Billias also gave the book good critical readings at various stages of its development. We are grateful as well to Dedman College and the History Department at Southern Methodist University for bringing us together at a crucial stage in our collaboration. Of all the people who read drafts of this book, none gave us a more thorough or thoughtful critique than Michael Bellesiles; we are deeply appreciative of his interest and his help. We also wish to thank Fred Anderson and Lee Chambers-Schiller of the University of Colorado and John L. Thomas of Brown University for stimulating us to think about many of the issues we attempt to address in the following pages.

Our most valuable critic was Mary Kupiec Cayton. She read several drafts of each chapter, offered specific suggestions for improvement, and consistently demanded that the larger significance of our points be stated as clearly and forthrightly as possible. Without Mary's advice and encouragement, we could not have written the kind of book that follows.

Finally, we happily attest to the intellectual benefits and personal satisfactions of collaboration. Working together has been a pleasure. Our hope is that our readers will find that it has been profitable as well.

INTRODUCTION

"The advance of the frontier has meant a steady movement away from the influence of Europe, a steady growth of independence on American lines," Frederick Jackson Turner asserted in his famous lecture of 1893 on "The Significance of the Frontier in American History." "And to study this advance, the men who grew up under these conditions, and the political, economic, and social results of it, is to study the really American part of our history."[1]

Modern readers are properly skeptical of Turner's bold claims; in many ways, the "advance" of historiography has been "away from the influence" of his frontier. But it would be a mistake simply to exchange the "frontier" for "Europe" and so remain imprisoned in the cultural and historiographical dichotomy that Turner identified and exemplified. If we are to move beyond Turner's thesis, it must be incorporated into a larger, more inclusive narrative framework. This is our goal in *The Midwest and the Nation*.

We suggest that Turner was interpreting American history from a distinctly regional perspective.[2] For many midwesterners, abundant "free land" had indeed meant unprecedented economic opportunity. Traditional patterns of social order and political authority were not easily replicated in the new societies that quickly emerged on the frontier. Responding to these new opportunities and appealing to the American revolutionary legacy, settlers proclaimed their right to govern themselves and shape the course of the region's development. The result was something very much like Turner's "democracy." In short, Turner's version of the American story was powerfully appealing because it seemed so true to the experience of so many Americans.

But what are we to make of Turner's story today? First, it should be emphasized that Turner offered his interpretation, in the proper scientific spirit, as a "thesis." For most of his audience, if not for Turner himself, the plausibility of the interpretation depended as much on its "fit" with other narratives as with its fidelity to the unmediated "facts" of historical reality. Turner may have challenged the fashionable academic wisdom—"too exclusive attention has been paid by institutional students to the Germanic origins"—but his theme was a familiar one, particularly in the Midwest. Turner declared the primacy of "American factors" over European influences, as had a long succession of cultural nationalists. But he also insisted on the leading role of the Old Northwest, the first great national frontier, in the development of America's democratic civilization. The cultural and historiographical significance of Turner's thesis was that it marked a decisive shift to the West, and away from the original colonies and states where European influences were most pronounced. In effect, Turner asserted the identity of western and national history, an identification that dominated professional thinking until the revival of colonial history after World War II.

Historians' changing assessments of the relative importance of the different periods and places they study reflect the fashions and prejudices of their own times. What is most remarkable about Turner's frontier thesis is that professional historians took so long to recognize and articulate a widely shared popular understanding of the progress of American civilization. Turner was hardly the first commentator to identify America's distinctive character and promise with the spread of new settlements and the founding of free institutions on the western frontier. As we will show in the following pages, such visions of expanding freedom and prosperity inspired the American founders as they sought to organize the national domain and secure a "more perfect union." The same themes were appropriated and elaborated by midwesterners themselves, particularly in the years leading up to the Civil War. In these earlier formulations, policymakers, polemicists, and regional patriots had forged the links between "free land," republican institutions, and popular participation on which Turner's thesis was premised. Turner also embraced his predecessors' master assumption that the nation's identity would be—or had already been—fulfilled in the new West.

Our intention is not to devise empirical "tests" for Turner's propositions, and so determine whether he was "right" or "wrong." We do not think the Turner thesis is likely to inspire further interesting or important contributions to historical writing. But we do think that Turner and his thesis are important subjects of inquiry, not only for historiographers but also for students of American cultural history.[3] Specifically, when seen as the culmination of a century of public discourse on the role of the West, and particularly of the Old Northwest, in national history, Turner's argument sheds new light on the emergence of *regional* consciousness. Thus we turn Turner on his head.

Although Turnerians, neo-Turnerians, and anti-Turnerians frequently appear in the following chapters—and often dominate the proceedings— we reserve our explicit commentary on the significance of the frontier thesis for midwestern history to our concluding pages. Even so, our readers will find that the bold outlines of Turner's interpretation are never far from view. After all, the new states of the Old Northwest *did* achieve remarkable prosperity, and eventually came to exercise a decisive role in the affairs of the union. The temptation to tell this story in triumphalist, whiggish terms is hard to resist, even for skeptical professional historians. But resist it we do. The result may be described as a deconstruction of Turner's narrative. In this deconstructive spirit, we do not set out to demolish his arguments. Instead, we are more interested in revealing what the frontier thesis *conceals*, so bringing to light the shadowy conflicts and struggles that made midwestern history. This does not mean that we are advancing an alternative, "people's" history of the region. We simply suggest that the triumph of commercial capitalism and the rise of a midwestern bourgeoisie were not foreordained. Our intention is to show how a vigorous, enterprising middle class achieved a dominant, hegemonic position in the Midwest. Middle-class midwesterners were the original authors of the "thesis" that Turner set forth in 1893, and it is their experience he so brilliantly epitomized.

The Midwest and the Nation seeks to identify and explicate the conflicts and tensions that culminated in the triumph of bourgeois culture in the region. Beginning with the original organization of the Northwest Territory, the character of the people who would settle the region was a central issue. The authors of the land ordinance of May 20, 1785, and the territorial government ordinance of July 13, 1787, envisioned a dramatic transformation of the Ohio country through the rapid spread of commercial agriculture and the ultimate creation of new, republican states. But their success depended on the kinds of settlers they could attract to the new settlements. Congress needed to find enterprising, market-oriented farmers to purchase its lands and so provide a desperately needed source of revenue. Orderly and industrious settlers would uphold national authority until they were sufficiently numerous to govern themselves. In the meantime, Congress had to keep the region clear of speculators, squatters, and other lawless, lazy, and improvident "white savages."

The Northwest Territory thus was founded in struggles over access to and control over its vast resources. Policymakers of the founding era understood these conflicts in terms of citizenship and character: would the new westerners be virtuous enough to support republican institutions and preserve the American union? A half-century later, when the prosperous states of Ohio, Indiana, Illinois, and Michigan had already joined the union, such concerns were no longer paramount. But middle-class midwesterners confronted a new set of problems that also revolved around private character and public behavior. In order to sustain the region's growth and development, spokesmen for the emergent bourgeoisie launched a variety of related campaigns to educate the ignorant and discipline the disorderly. As a result, political controversies often centered on cultural issues. Exponents of bourgeois values articulated their hopes for continuing prosperity in terms of an ongoing struggle against localists, foreigners, and other "alien" elements in the region. As the crisis of the union deepened, middle-class midwesterners also began to define their free states against the slaveholding societies across the Ohio River. This sectional consciousness converged with a middle-class vision of economic progress and cultural transformation as the new Republican party swept across the region in the 1850s.

Writing in the decades before the Civil War, the first historians of the Midwest described the almost miraculous development of dynamic, interdependent, free societies. For regional patriots, this great success story demonstrated the progressive influence of free enterprise and free institutions. The states carved out of the Old Northwest Territory were bulwarks of national union: indeed, the fundamental principles of "union" itself were best exemplified in the democratic, egalitarian relationships of enterprising midwesterners.

This vision of regional and national history and destiny was broadly appealing in the 1850s, and it remained compelling long after the union had been destroyed and reconstructed—and long after the midwestern middle class had achieved a dominant position. But the story was always more complicated and problematic than its tellers were willing to concede, or able to recognize. Increasingly aware of these contradictions, students of the region's history have picked it apart so completely that no story at all remains. As a result, American historians have looked to other regions for grand interpretative schemes. Our agenda in *The Midwest and the Nation* is to illuminate the connections between regional and national history. To do this, we must do more than reconstruct the story of the Midwest; we must demonstrate that there *is* such a story, and that it is just as important as Turner himself said it was.

In the first chapter, we argue that the Northwest Ordinance of 1787 functioned as a "charter" document for the area; it outlined the basic structures of government and established the principles that would guide the evolution of society. Chapters two through four deal with the impact of the transportation revolution on the Old Northwest. As citizens of the region found their lives defined by the importance of production for the market, they engaged in vigorous debate over the implications of commercial capitalism.

In chapter five, we discuss how, in the crucial decades of the mid-nineteenth century, a trans-local community of like-minded, middle-class people successfully linked the Midwest to a flourishing national economy. Spokespersons for this emergent class insisted that their region was quintessentially American. The South and New England were different from the rest of the country, but the Midwest was distinctive because it *was* the United States. Similarly, the formation of a middle class, midwestern identity depended on the denial of the legitimacy of alternative communities within the region. Midwestern culture, in short, was born in a simultaneous celebration of the glories of capitalism and a rejection of divergent interpretations of the social and political implications of the growth of the market. Chapter six examines the fate of this culture in the wake of dramatic changes in the economic and political structures of the Midwest in the late nineteenth century.

Finally, in an epilogue, we attempt to place Turner and his followers within the context of midwestern culture, contending that they completed the process of regional definition both by interpreting its history as a middle class, capitalist success story and by asserting that the history of the Midwest was nothing less than the history of the United States. Turner's view of American historical development, in short, was the ultimate expression of midwestern culture.[4]

THE MIDWEST
AND THE NATION

I

THE SIGNIFICANCE OF THE NORTHWEST ORDINANCE

The first historians of the Old Northwest were lavish in their praise of the Northwest Ordinance of July 13, 1787. Writing in a period of rising sectional tension, men such as Caleb Atwater, Jacob Burnet, and Salmon P. Chase were eager to show the superiority of northwestern civilization, particularly in comparison with the slaveholding South. Thus they emphasized the significance of the Ordinance in setting their region on a course that led to a society of free, enterprising individuals. The document's antislavery clause, as well as its provisions for public education, religious freedom, and orderly government, had proved decisive in shaping the region's political and social orders. The Northwest Ordinance had, to a significant degree, defined the Old Northwest.[1]

But in the century that followed the Civil War, historians became much more ambivalent about the Ordinance of 1787. To be sure, scholars influenced by Frederick Jackson Turner acknowledged that the antislavery and education clauses and the establishment of procedures for achieving statehood were of lasting importance. Nonetheless, historians such as John D. Barnhart, Beverley W. Bond, Jr., and R. Carlyle Buley were convinced that the key to the origins of northwestern civilization lay far more in the actions of individual settlers than in the pronouncements of the federal government. In arguing that the pioneers of the Old Northwest had defined their own political and social orders, these writers emphasized the liberalizing effects of frontier conditions and posited a fundamental opposition between progressive local settlers and reactionary national officials. Their most significant point was that the people of the Old Northwest were able to enjoy the benefits of self-government only when nationally appointed officials gave way to men elected under their own state constitutions.[2]

According to the Turnerian view, although the Ordinance promised the ultimate attainment of statehood, it also established an arbitrary, colonial government that stood in the way of self-government. When democratic frontiersmen finally overthrew the last vestiges of national control

and achieved independent statehood, they had eliminated the Ordinance
as a practical fact in their lives. Because frontier Americans sought to
govern themselves and claimed free institutions as their right, the Ordinance's promises seemed vague and redundant: territorial settlers made
their own states by vanquishing an appointed "aristocracy" imposed by
Congress under the provisions of the Ordinance.

Clearly, the Turnerian argument is a powerful one; indeed, it has dominated our understanding of the origins of the Old Northwest for over a
century. Even as historians of other American regions have rejected or
absorbed Turner's contentions about the significance of the frontier, students of the history of the Ohio and upper Mississippi valleys have continued to work within his shadow. And with good reason. There were ongoing tensions in the Northwest Territory between national authority
and local autonomy. Just as settlers and territorial officials struggled for
political power, they were divided by conflicting material interests. Congressional land policy proved to be particularly controversial. Many enterprising settlers saw the high price of federal lands—set at a dollar per
acre in Congress's May 20, 1785, land ordinance—as the leading obstacle
to the region's rapid growth, as well as to their own prosperity. Of course
the national government, with its desperate need for a reliable source of
revenue, was intent on keeping land prices as high as possible.[3]

It is hardly surprising that settlers should have invoked America's revolutionary legacy when they opposed the national government's supposedly "colonial" government. But the Turnerians proceeded to translate
this "democratic" rhetoric into a comprehensive interpretative framework, thus oversimplifying a much more complex situation. The Ordinance's provisions may have been controversial in the Northwest because of localist, democratic opposition to central authority and to the
vision of cosmopolitan commercial society implicit in national western
policy. But northwesterners were hardly united in detesting national authority or in rejecting national commercial development, nor were they
uniformly contemptuous of the rights supposedly accorded them in the
Ordinance's compact articles. The Ordinance, like the Constitution, was
a dynamic document—a statement of general principles and procedures
whose ultimate meanings were defined in the process of implementation.
Ordinance provisions could be invoked in various contexts, to various
ends, resulting in a dizzying array of local alignments. In short, the Ordinance was a "living" constitutional text and the history of debate over
its meanings offers valuable clues to the course of regional development.

In conjunction with the 1785 land ordinance, the Northwest Ordinance
set the course for the region's political and economic development—even
when it evoked opposition. As the charter document for the settlement
of the Northwest Territory, the Ordinance established a broad framework
for public debate and controversy. For its congressional authors, the Ordi-

nance represented a heroic effort to guarantee the nation's future prosperity and power by defining the rules of everyday conduct on both the private and public levels. The results, particularly in the early years, were mixed at best. But as the people of the territory moved beyond the conflicts and uncertainties of frontier life and created the stable structures of highly organized, prosperous communities, the legacy of the Ordinance survived. Northwesterners laid claim to their own destiny—and to their own history—as they struggled to interpret its specific provisions and define its general principles.

1. The Origins of a National Western Policy

The Confederation Congress completed its organization of the first national domain when it passed the Northwest Ordinance on July 13, 1787. While Congress established a scheme for the temporary government and eventual statehood of its territory north and west of the Ohio River, delegates at the Philadelphia Convention drafted a new constitution for the entire union. Together, the Ordinance and the federal Constitution set the course for the future growth and expansion of the United States. An "energetic" new national government promised to transform the weak confederacy of American states into a powerful, prosperous and dynamic union capable of extending its authority far to the west.

Most commentators agreed that the Confederation Congress was radically incompetent to deal with conflicts among the states and between sections over foreign policy, trade regulation, and boundaries. Such conflicts were particularly conspicuous in the vast western region guaranteed to the new nation by the Peace of Paris, which formally concluded the American War for Independence in 1783. The rapid spread of white settlement and the growing restiveness of the native tribes threatened to embroil the frontiers in warfare. But no effective, coordinated regulation of frontier settlement, land speculation, and Indian diplomacy was possible until the states relinquished their own territorial pretensions in the region and Congress gained direct control. The western lands controversy thus constituted a crucial test for the American union: would the states be able to reconcile their conflicting claims? Would they be able to recognize and secure common, national interests?

Jurisdictional confusion in the West revealed the dangerous, centrifugal tendencies of state particularism and unregulated private initiatives. The virtual vacuum of effective authority encouraged squatting and land speculation, new state movements, unauthorized purchases of Indian lands, and treasonous negotiations with emissaries of foreign powers. To anxious congressmen, reports from the West conjured up images of disorder and disunion, a mockery of everything they hoped to achieve in the

Revolution. Driven by such concerns, Congress moved with surprising dispatch and effectiveness to formulate a national western policy.[4]

The central premise of congressional policy was set forth in September and October 1780, when the large, "landed" states were called on to relinquish their extensive western claims to make possible the creation of a national domain. Congress then promised, and the promise was repeated in subsequent state land cessions, that land sales revenue would be used for the "common benefit" of the United States and that western settlements eventually would be formed into new, equal states and be admitted into the union. The new nation, therefore, would be neither a confederation of fully sovereign states dedicated to the preservation and extension of their territorial pretensions nor a consolidated, continental republic. The expansion of the United States was made synonymous with the creation of new states.

The first land cession, from New York, was completed in October 1782. But the 1784 cession of Virginia's extensive claims, hitherto the chief obstacle to cooperation between the landed and landless state blocs in Congress, was most crucial for establishing a national title in the Northwest. The state cessions "eliminated a major source of friction among the American states and an impediment to the institution of a stronger central government."[5] Over the next three years, Congress proceeded to draft ordinances to govern settlement and to regulate land sales in the national domain.

The formulation of western policy, climaxing with passage of the Northwest Ordinance, has been celebrated as one of the old Congress's few significant achievements. How, in light of its abysmal record on other controversial issues, was Congress able to act so decisively in this one area? The first answer is that the costs of delay and inaction were so obvious: if Congress did not formulate and implement an effective land policy, a potentially vast revenue source would be squandered; if Congress did not enforce its laws and preserve order, the region would break away from the union. These policy imperatives were felt equally by delegates from all of the states, however divided they were during the protracted controversy over state cessions and despite continuing disagreement over other economic and diplomatic issues.

Vital interests had been at stake in the western lands controversy. The large, landed states hoped to retain extensive territories in order to maximize their prospects for economic growth and political power; the small, landless states sought to equalize the states and share equally in the benefits of western development.[6] But once the land cessions were completed, the states' boundaries—and their relative size—no longer appeared negotiable. With the Northwest under national control, former antagonists discovered common interests. Thus, enterprising Marylanders and Virginians combined forces to link the Ohio country to the Chesapeake by extending the navigability of the Potomac River.[7]

All of the eastern states would benefit from the orderly development of the national West. Improved transportation would facilitate commercial connections between western farmers and eastern merchants, thereby strengthening the union and guaranteeing its future prosperity. Clustered in contiguous settlements, purchasers of federal lands would be easily governed in the brief transitional period before they became capable of governing themselves. Expensive wars with the Indians might be avoided; meanwhile, the sale of increasingly valuable federal lands would provide an apparently inexhaustible source of revenue.[8]

Washington, Jefferson, and other advocates of internal improvements grasped the political as well as economic implications of opening up the western trade. Without an "easy communication," wrote Washington, the westerners "will become a distinct people from us."[9] Recognizing that mutually beneficial trade was the only durable bond of union, congressmen hoped to encourage westerners to cultivate strong ties to the East; for their part, easterners could look for prosperous returns from new western markets. A new conception of the union, premised less on political affinities than on free exchange and complementary interest, was implicit in western policy. Cathy Matson and Peter Onuf suggest that Federalists invoked this same idea of union in making their case for a stronger central government.[10]

Because most congressmen shared this vision of western and national development, the formulation of land and territorial policy proceeded swiftly. But congressional consensus was predicated on widely divergent assessments of how western expansion would affect the balance of eastern interests. As Staughton Lynd writes, "the [Northwest] Ordinance made available a West just sufficiently specific that each section could read in it the fulfillment of its political dreams."[11] Projected settlement by New Englanders under the aegis of the Ohio Company of Associates suggested that the first new state to be formed in the territory would be aligned with the "eastern"—that is, northern—bloc in Congress. At the same time, however, southerners were convinced that the inexorable tendency of population and power was toward the south and west: the addition of new western states would give the South a decisive advantage. Drew R. McCoy shows that southern Federalists invoked such predictions in pushing for adoption of the federal Constitution.[12]

Proponents of western development and of a stronger national union did not necessarily transcend their sectional biases. Members of the Continental Congress and the Constitutional Convention did assume, however, that national and sectional interests could be made to coincide. Given intersectional hostility over commercial and diplomatic policy during the "critical period," it was easier to imagine such a convergence taking place in the undeveloped West. As Peter Onuf writes, "promoters of western expansion" promised "that the commercial development of the frontier would increase the population and wealth of the entire union"; it would also "produce a harmony of interlocking interests without which union itself was inconceivable."[13] Yet, as intense competition over establishing trade routes to the West suggested, western development would most enrich the best situated easterners. The prospect of national economic development, from a broadly speculative perspective, could mitigate sectional differences; in practice, however, the benefits of development were always unequally distributed. Sectional differences thus did not disappear during the process of western development, nor were the "political dreams" of either northerners or southerners fulfilled. Instead, the West emerged as a distinctive region with peculiar interests of its own.

2. The Critical Period in the West

To many concerned observers the American union appeared on the verge of collapse in the 1780s. As Frederick W. Marks III has shown, the new nation's international situation was precarious, particularly on the western frontier.[14] Reformers argued that this was the critical moment to redeem the promise of the Revolution. A "bountiful providence" had favored the new nation with rich natural endowments promising boundless prosperity and power, but rapid, unregulated settlement jeopardized this promise by provoking Indian wars while depriving Congress of desperately needed revenue from land sales. The exodus of productive citizens (and taxpayers) also threatened the old states with depopulation and poverty. Meanwhile, unauthorized settlers defied state and national authority in hopes of holding onto these lands; they set up illegal new states and warned easterners that if their pretensions were not duly recognized, they would break away from the union and even seek alliances with neighboring imperial powers. Commentators feared that disunion—the failure to connect new settlements to old—would lead inexorably to the renewal of war and the loss of American independence.

Gordon S. Wood shows in his *Creation of the American Republic* that during the 1780s nationalist leaders became increasingly concerned about the dangers of democratic excesses on the local and state level.[15] These concerns were exaggerated—to the point of caricature—when conservative easterners looked westward: the frontiers were infested with "banditti," semi-savage squatters and land speculators who supposedly sought to escape the restraints of taxation, law, and civilized society. Robert F. Berkhofer, Jr., and Thomas P. Slaughter emphasize the importance of these negative images of westerners' character and virtue for the formulation of national policy.[16] Many conservative easterners doubted that these licentious "white savages" could ever be transformed into good citizens. How, then, could congressmen contemplate adding new western states to the union? As practical politicians seeking "republican remedies" to the crisis of the union, constitutional reformers and western policymakers arrived at complementary solutions. In order to restrain popular excesses, the framers of the Constitution sought to establish federal supremacy and place curbs on state sovereignty. Western policymakers achieved the same ends by delaying the onset of self-government and statehood during a period of political apprenticeship under appointed territorial officials.

Because congressmen assumed the worst about westerners, they designed a framework for territorial development that would gradually prepare them for political responsibility.[17] The land ordinance therefore provided material support for local education and Article III of the Northwest Ordinance proclaimed that "schools and the means of education shall forever be encouraged." But Congress's western policy was also "educational" in a much broader sense.[18] Controlled settlement (or what Washington called "progressive seating") under the land ordinance would prevent the reversion to savagery that scattered settlement supposedly encouraged. The relatively high price of lands would screen out impecunious, antisocial, subsistence-oriented squatters. Instead, sober, industrious, commercial farmers would be attracted by the promise of orderly conditions, secure titles, and ready access to markets. The grid pattern of land surveys would eliminate the divisive title conflicts that elsewhere retarded settlement and subverted communal harmony. Clustered settlements would be more easily defended against external enemies and internal disorder, and the rapid development of churches, schools, courts, and other local institutions would facilitate the passage to self-government. Assuming this process of social development, the authors of the Northwest Ordinance provided for the gradual substitution of home rule for government by appointed officials.[19]

The new "colonial" policy set forth in the Northwest Ordinance was premised on the analogy of political development to individual growth from childhood to maturity. Congressmen thus were able to reconcile their "realistic" assessment of the capacity, or incapacity, of settlers for self-government with an ultimate commitment to republican principles. Setting the population threshold for independent statehood at 60,000 also allayed anxieties of the original states about being outvoted in Congress by smaller, poorer, and less developed new states. The new states would become more or less equal in fact—at least compared to the smaller old states—before they could claim an equal standing in the union. Congressional western policy further countered the centrifugal effects of expansion by establishing territorial governments that could guarantee federal property interests during the crucial first years of settlement.

The basic structure of territorial development laid down in the Ordinance consisted of a succession of three stages culminating in statehood. Scholars traditionally interpreted this structure in terms of a Turnerian struggle between autocratic territorial officials and democratic forces struggling for self-government. Their premise is that the Ordinance, notwithstanding its compact promises, constituted an obstacle to political progress on the frontier. The standard account of the Ordinance's origins supports this view: it is seen as a retreat from Jefferson's more "liberal" 1784 government ordinance. Jefferson would have let settlers govern themselves before statehood, but conservative eastern land speculators like Manasseh Cutler and his Ohio Company of Associates insisted on a repressive "colonial" regime in order to protect and promote their claims.

In the last generation, historians have begun to abandon the classic story of conflict between frontier democracy and the "interests." Jack Ericson Eblen and Robert Berkhofer have interpreted the development of western policy within a much broader administrative and ideological context. Although their conclusions sometimes differ, these authors all suggest that congressional intentions need to be reexamined. Eblen says that our understanding of territorial policy must be liberated from the "narrow ideological confines of the debate over the Turner thesis." Emphasizing the "continuity and consensus of thought" among Congressmen in the 1780s, Eblen discounts the conventional distinction between the 1784 and 1787 ordinances and concludes that the Ordinance was "nothing more or less than an ordinary piece of noncontroversial legislation."[20] But this does not mean that the Ordinance was inconsequential. As his title, *The First and Second United States Empires*, indicates, Eblen sees a larger "imperialist" consensus on westward—and later worldwide—expansion.

Berkhofer agrees that the western ordinances reflect a policy consensus but is more influenced by the emerging "republican synthesis" in early American historiography in his reconstruction of their premises. Berkhofer's seminal essay on Jefferson and the 1784 ordinance delineates the western problem in now-familiar republican terms, showing that concerns about sustaining public virtue and creating republican institutions over an extended territory shaped the evolution of policy.[21] He points out that republican civic humanist thought taught Revolutionary Americans to fear the rampant individualism and selfishness normally associated with the frontier: privatism was the antithesis of the public-spiritedness so necessary to the maintenance of a stable republic.[22] The size of the United States as well as its heterogeneity, moreover, portended anarchy and civil war. Well-educated eighteenth-century men simply did not believe a nation as diverse and spread out as the United States could long endure. Berkhofer makes the sensible suggestion that western policy— even Jefferson's liberal plan of 1784—was designed to mitigate these dangers by manipulating the size of the new states and determining the conditions of their admission to the union.

Berkhofer's insights deserve elaboration. There has certainly been a revival of interest in the general problem of size, notably in the vast commentary on Madison's *Federalist* number 10;[23] recently Rosemarie Zagarri has offered a broad framework for thinking about *The Politics of Size*.[24] Drew R. McCoy's incisive analysis of Jeffersonian political economy in *The Elusive Republic* connects westward expansion with the central concerns of republican thought; in a recent essay he explores the implications of regional development for constitutional reform.[25]

Peter Onuf has argued that the land policy evolved in Congress in the 1780s helped resolve the tension between republican fears of privatism and the fact that western settlement required men to pursue individual interests: policymakers hoped to transform "the private pursuit of profit" into a "source of national wealth and welfare."[26] Congressmen sought to foster western economic development through a series of well-defined stages. Indeed, to many development-minded Americans in the 1780s, properly regulated commercial exchange was the best means for cementing the union and thus of guaranteeing the survival of an extended republic. But if the United States was to reach its full potential economically and socially, the western hinterland would have to be settled deliberately. This reconstruction of the goals of western policymakers thus explodes the conventional disjunction between economic and political motives in explanations of the drafting of the Ordinance: the establishment of a stable political order was inseparable from plans for economic growth.

3. The Text

The Ordinance was a blueprint or charter document for economic, social, and political development, not simply a republican version of British colonial policy or an effort to put the West under an eastern yoke. It provided for the orderly, regular progression to statehood as the region reached economic and social maturity; it established or encouraged the establishment of courts, schools, and churches to promote public morality and good citizenship; it called for the rule of law in dealing with Indians; and it (apparently) prevented the spread of an institution that many saw as a blot on the American character—slavery. In short, the Northwest Ordinance reflected the determination of Revolutionary statesmen to lead the United States into a new republican order of prosperity, peace, and decorum. Men of national perspective, convinced that commerce and

civilization marched hand in hand, thus sought to fashion a highly organized, interdependent society in the West.

The Northwest Ordinance was an integral part of America's new constitutional order: provisions for western expansion gave substance to the
national idea, offering a plausible model for continental economic development and intersectional harmony. In the context of the 1780s, it is
clear that the Ordinance and the Constitution depended on—and even
completed—each other. But after 1787 the reputation of the Ordinance
declined. Its defects became more and more conspicuous as debate over
the constitutionality of specific provisions came to center on the document's relation to the federal Constitution. By 1850 Chief Justice Roger
Taney could assert that the Ordinance was merely legislation and could
not control Congress's unlimited power over the territories under Article
IV, section III of the federal Constitution.[27] Although state courts treated
the Ordinance more respectfully, Taney's view prevailed among historians as well as jurists.[28] The constitutional authority of the Ordinance diminished as the federal Constitution gained broad popular acceptance.

The key difference in the genesis of the Ordinance and the Constitution
was that the authors of the Ordinance did not feel compelled to justify
themselves: they did not doubt their own authority to organize the new
national domain, guarantee settlers' rights, and provide for the ultimate
formation of new states. Ironically, what later seemed glaring defects in
the Ordinance's drafting reflected the *lack* of controversy about the scope
of Congress's power: no extraordinary procedures were necessary to
counter widespread misgivings. Congress's authority was not controversial because the United States supposedly exercised unlimited, sovereign
power over the national domain: it could relinquish its property—and its
authority—as it saw fit. In contrast, the framers of the Constitution knew
that they were exceeding their authority under the Articles; to justify this
radical assumption of power they invoked the primal authority of the
people, embodied in the state ratifying conventions.

The text of the Northwest Ordinance was shaped by congressional responses to the western problem over a period of several years. Historians
have commented on the ungainly organization and infelicitous prose of
the document.[29] In the 1820s Nathan Dane of Massachusetts, the member of the territorial government committee who had drafted the final
text, claimed to be the author of the Ordinance and thus has been held
responsible for its many defects. But the Ordinance's legislative history
suggests that Dane exaggerated his role and that "authorship" is in this
case a meaningless concept. Paul Finkelman's meticulous textual analysis shows that the Ordinance's language was cobbled together from a succession of earlier drafts. When Article VI, the ban on slavery in the territory, was adopted—at the last minute and to Dane's surprise—Congress

failed to revise the rest of the document accordingly. The resulting internal inconsistencies, Finkelman concludes, left a legacy of ambiguity that undercut Article VI's apparently straightforward prohibition of slavery.[30]

Yet the character of the Ordinance's text is not simply the result of sloppy legislative craftsmanship. With Manasseh Cutler and the Ohio Company waiting in the wings, Congress may have hurried its deliberations in July 1787, but it is not clear that a more leisurely pace would have produced more sterling prose. The contrast with the federal Constitution is instructive: the Constitution, drafted over the course of one summer, is a model of elegant, economical prose and structure. Most important, the framers were self-conscious about their role as authors. In a brilliant essay on the rhetoric of the Constitution, Robert Ferguson suggests that the success of their project depended both on close attention to detail—subsequent generations would scrutinize every word—and on producing a coherent document that mirrored the "more perfect union" it promised to create.[31] Nathan Dane was not an "author" in this sense: he and his colleagues did not pretend to be writing a text that would itself—like the Constitution—function as a source of legitimacy and law. Their policy concerns were much more immediate and prosaic; and, unlike the framers, they could dash off a final draft with minimal attention to style and form because they did not anticipate any questioning of their authority to set the course of western development or of their right to interpret or revise their own acts.

The authority of the Constitution has been progressively extended through amendments and judicial interpretations. In contrast, because much of the Ordinance was designed to become obsolete, its authority diminished over time: as a "living" constitutional text it contracted rather than expanded. The first section of the Ordinance, establishing a system of temporary territorial administration, became inoperative with the attainment of statehood. Congress always considered these provisions subject to change, beginning in 1789 when it reenacted the Ordinance in slightly altered form to make the territorial system compatible with the new federal regime. By the time Congress passed the organic law for Wisconsin Territory in 1836 the Ordinance's government provisions were almost entirely superseded.

Even the supposedly permanent compact articles that completed the Ordinance tended to become obsolete. Guarantees of civil liberties and property rights (Article II) were applicable in the territorial period; they could—and did—take on different form when northwesterners drafted their own constitutions. Other broad injunctions were either unexceptionable (namely the provision for freedom of worship in Article I) or unenforceable (the promise of "justice and humanity" toward the Indians in Article III). The articles governing state constitution-writing, defining boundaries, and providing for admission to the union (IV and V) did have permanent effects, but they also ceased to operate once the statehood process was complete.

Only two provisions of the Ordinance continued to be relevant to the constitutional history of the northwestern states after they were admitted to the union. The stipulation in Article IV that the "waters leading into the Mississippi and Saint Lawrence" remain "common highways" was invoked as a constitutional bar to various obstructions to free navigation. Article VI, prohibiting the introduction of slavery, was much more controversial. Although free soil northwesterners rebuffed attempts to legalize slavery, debate on the relative advantages and disadvantages of the institution tended to undercut the binding authority of Article VI. The Northwest remained free because that was the will of its people, not because of Congress's decree. Taney's decision in *Strader* that the Ordinance was a constitutional nullity marked the culmination of the "deconstitutionalizing" process. The compact articles "were said to be perpetual," but they had *not* been incorporated in the federal Constitution: "they certainly are not superior and paramount to the Constitution." In Taney's estimation, at least, the text of the Ordinance no longer had any authority at all: it had virtually disappeared.[32]

The history of the Northwest Ordinance raises important questions about changing constitutional standards. When drafting the Ordinance, Congressmen betrayed no anxiety about exceeding their authority: although they provided for the "temporary" government of the Ohio region, they did not usurp the people's right to draft their own constitutions when they were ready for statehood. Instead, like a colonial charter, the Ordinance specified the terms on which the national domain would be settled; like a treaty, it stipulated the terms on which the new states would be welcomed into the union. Congress's promises, commentators suggested, became binding when settlers moved into the territory, thus becoming parties to the Ordinance compacts. From the contemporary perspective, therefore, the Ordinance's authority did not require any special grant of authority to Congress or any explicit ratification by the people of the territory. Yet the charter idea became increasingly unpalatable to subsequent generations: on one hand, proponents of territorial rights challenged federal sovereignty and denied that northwesterners had ever consented to the Ordinance's provisions, tacitly or not; on the other, advocates of federal supremacy dismissed any limitations on Congress's authority over the territories. Changing interpretations of the Ordinance thus reveal not only new, more democratic definitions of what was "constitutional" but the continuing tension between state and territorial rights and national authority in antebellum America.

4. Statehood and Boundaries

The people of the Northwest Territory began to scrutinize the Ordinance's provisions more carefully as they sought independent statehood and membership in the union. Compact Article V apparently bound Congress to extend statehood privileges to each of the prospective "states" in the territory when its population reached "sixty thousand free Inhabitants." In practice, however, the ambiguous definition of new state boundaries in the same article compromised this promise. Because Congress could create "not less than three nor more than five States" in the territory, it necessarily retained discretion over their boundaries. The limits of the three southern states seemed clearly defined in relation to each other but would not be fixed to the north until Congress decided whether or not to establish "one or two States" beyond a line "drawn through the southerly bend or extreme of lake Michigan." Even then, the precise location of new state boundaries remained subject to congressional discretion. Peter Onuf concludes that "the resulting uncertainty jeopardized territorial rights. . . . If boundaries were not fixed in advance, the other compact promises would be meaningless: Congress could change a territory's boundaries whenever it threatened to grow large enough to claim membership in the union."[33]

Confusion about state boundaries in the Northwest reflected the geographical ignorance of the Ordinance's authors. To later congresses—and to many settlers in the region—the lines set forth in Article V seemed arbitrary and unnatural. If, for instance, the east-west line through the bottom of Lake Michigan should become the northern boundary of the future states of Ohio, Indiana, and Illinois, none of them would have access to the Great Lakes. Of course, such concerns remained moot as long as native Americans occupied most of the territory and the British controlled the lakes. By the time the southern states were ready for statehood, however, the importance of the lakes to the regional and national economies was clear. Ohio therefore claimed the Erie lakefront, including the future site of Toledo, in Article VII, section 6 of its 1802 constitution. Although the status of the Toledo area remained unsettled—Congress did not explicitly recognize the new state's self-proclaimed boundary— Ohio's jurisdiction over the rest of the lakefront was never challenged. The cases of Indiana and Illinois proved considerably less controversial: Congress exercised its discretionary authority over boundaries by granting both states extensive frontage on Lake Michigan.

There were few objections to Congress's authority over boundaries and a "loose" interpretation of the Ordinance's language as long as they served the interests of prospective new states. The "one or two States" to be established in the north may have been cheated out of valuable territory by the extension of the three southern states beyond the Ordinance's east-west line, but the damage was largely hypothetical. The northern states could not yet be said to exist, even in the most embryonic form. Michiganders subsequently complained that their territorial rights under the Ordinance had been egregiously violated, a complaint later echoed by Wisconsinites. When Ohio, Indiana, and Illinois joined the union, however, the rights of *future* states depended entirely on Congress's willingness to be governed by the explicit language of the Ordinance.

Michigan's application for admission in 1835 was rejected because the new state claimed the Ordinance line for its southern boundary. Ohio, meanwhile, sought to establish its jurisdiction north of that line in the region around Toledo. The authority of the Ordinance's boundary provisions was exhaustively debated during the resulting "Toledo War," but it was soon clear that the relative merits of the arguments were irrelevant. An unrepresented territory simply was no match for a powerful state in determining congressional policy. Thus, according to Congress's June 1836 enabling act, Michigan would only be admitted if it recognized Ohio's claims; as a sop, the new state's jurisdiction was extended across the Upper Peninsula—at the expense of Wisconsin, the fifth state.[34]

Ohio's victory over Michigan conclusively established Congress's discretionary authority over new state boundaries. This meant that none of the other "rights" prospective new states could claim under the Ordinance were enforceable against Congress. As Jack Eblen shows in the most comprehensive study of the admission process, Congress took the initiative in organizing new states: enabling acts—and not the general provisions of the Ordinance—specified the conditions under which they were to be admitted.[35] Beginning with the admission of Ohio, these acts set boundaries, required various guarantees of federal property rights, and assigned portions of the public domain to the new states. The irresistible conclusion was that Congress exercised complete authority over the state-making process and that the territories could claim no rights at all until Congress acted.

Congress's authority over the territories and new states was well established before Michigan proceeded, without authorization, to organize its own state government and press its boundary claims. Why did the Michiganders rely so heavily on the Ordinance, if that document had already been superseded in practice? The best explanation is that broadened popular participation and partisan activity had democratized territorial politics in Michigan and fostered a sense of collective rights. From the national perspective, the notion that the territories were embryonic states with authoritative claims was progressively undercut as Congress extended its authority over state-making: in other words, the constitutional authority of the Ordinance was superseded by relevant provisions in the federal Constitution (in Article IV, section 3). At the same time, however, Congress exercised its supreme authority *by expanding the scope of local self-rule* in successive territorial government acts. The paradoxical result was that rising political consciousness in Michigan Territory temporarily breathed new life into the Northwest Ordinance, an increasingly moribund constitutional text.

The Michiganders' failure to make good on their claims under the Ordinance was an ominous portent for the future. "It was one of the tragedies of American constitutional history," writes Onuf, "that the statehood promise should be cut loose from an authoritative constitutional document, binding on Congress and prospective new states alike."[36] Of course, Michiganders did not depend entirely on respect for the Ordinance's apparently clear language to vindicate their jurisdictional pretensions. They did not hesitate to march an armed force into the disputed territory, or to bid defiance to the union by proclaiming their independence. But the Michiganders did insist that their claims were based on the Ordinance and that the document should set limits on Congress's discretionary authority. If the Ordinance did not have constitutional force, how could the rights of future new states be guaranteed?

5. Slavery

Article VI of the Ordinance, the provision proclaiming that "there shall be neither Slavery not involuntary Servitude" in the territory, also generated sustained controversy. Despite its clear language, the ban proved to be only partial: the so-called "French slaves," property of residents of Vincennes, Kaskaskia, and other French communities antedating American jurisdiction, remained in bondage; hundreds of new slaves were brought into Indiana and Illinois as "indentured servants." But many American settlers were not satisfied with these exceptions and subterfuges. Beginning in 1796 slavery proponents bombarded Congress with petitions calling for the temporary suspension, modification, or elimination of Article VI. Proslavery petitioners argued that the will of Congress was supreme in the territories and that the present Congress could not be bound by its predecessors. Therefore the Ordinance "compacts" had no constitutional force.[37]

The constitutional question was further complicated when the territories became new states. It was certainly within Congress's power to refuse admission to states that did not incorporate the slavery prohibition in the constitutions submitted for its approval. Illinois thus bowed to Congress's will when it joined the union in 1818, despite strong popular support for legalization. But could Congress interfere if Illinois subsequently chose to revise its constitution and legalize slavery? Could the national Supreme Court find a state's violation of Article VI "unconstitutional" without encroaching on its sovereignty or compromising the principle of state equality?[38]

Efforts to legalize slavery, both before and after the organization of new states, precipitated the most extensive public debate about the constitutionality and policy of an Ordinance provision. Participants first sought to establish the "original intent" of the Ordinance's authors. This was not—and is not—an easy task because, as Paul Finkelman's recent study suggests, most congressmen did not care much one way or the other. Noting that the Ordinance's language was imprecise and that, in any case, Congress failed to provide for its implementation, Finkelman argues that the meaning of the clause "was left to whoever held power in the territory."[39]

Scholars who have studied the subsequent history of Article VI support Finkelman's conclusion. Eugene H. Berwanger and Peter Onuf have reconstructed the heated controversies over the antislavery clause which spread west across the territory. The climax came in 1824 when, by a margin of 6,640 to 4,972, Illinois voters rejected a call for a new constitutional convention that everyone expected would legalize slavery.[40]

Clearly, it was the sovereign will of the people, *not* the binding authority of Article VI, that kept the state more-or-less "free." At the same time, however, the Ordinance shaped the debate. Slavery advocates appealed to the principles of state equality and popular sovereignty in seeking to liberate Illinois from the "dead hand" of the past. Antislavery forces conceded the constitutional point but invoked the Ordinance's moral authority as a kind of "higher law" and called upon voters to uphold the founders' commitment to freedom.

In practical terms, any effort to resist legalization on constitutional grounds depended on the willingness of the national government to intervene in Illinois's "domestic" affairs. Of course, the national political climate was already so deeply polarized on the slavery issue that the possibility of such an intervention was extremely small. But antislavery partisans in Illinois were as jealous of their state's rights and as hostile to outside interference as their opponents. They instead relied on the wisdom and virtue of the good people of the state to preserve freedom. "While each succeeding generation was fully sovereign (and so accountable for its acts)," writes Onuf in summarizing their argument, "it was also entrusted with the hopes and dreams of its predecessors: these enduring ideals constituted a higher law, a transcendent bond between past, present, and future."[41]

But why was it so important to keep the Northwest free? Antislavery polemicists answered confidently that the region's long-term future prosperity depended on attracting immigrants from the free states and promoting the enterprise and development possible only in free societies.

They drew invidious distinctions between Ohio, a dynamic and prosperous free state, and Kentucky, where slavery supposedly blighted the countryside and retarded population growth. The proslavery party promised that the influx of slaveowners would drive up land prices and stimulate a local economy that had been devastated by the depression of 1819. But such "relief," antislavery writers replied, would be short-lived at best. The new wealth would be concentrated in the hands of a slaveholding aristocracy; it would not circulate throughout the community, and so benefit all of the people of Illinois. Labor and enterprise would be degraded and the state's economy would languish.

The vision of a dynamic free economy shaped contemporaneous interpretations of Article VI. Antislavery writers celebrated the foresight of the founders, their ability to conceive the glorious advantages of freedom for future generations. It mattered little whether or not they had the "authority" to impose the slavery prohibition on the Northwest. "The authors of the Northwest Ordinance had looked to the future," Onuf concludes. "By embracing their vision and making it their own, northwesterners of succeeding generations could participate in the continuing founding of their rising new states."[42]

6. Territorial Government

Unlike the compact articles, the Ordinance's provisions for territorial government offered northwesterners no clear definition of their rights to counter Congress's arbitrary, colonial authority. Turnerians focused on the resulting struggles for self-government and home rule as they charted the course of frontier democracy. Their emphasis on statehood movements accounts for the relatively low estate—and neglect—of the Northwest Ordinance in the historical literature.

The traditional view suggests that frontier settlers soon smashed the ambitious designs of national policymakers and their territorial appointees. In his book on the territorial governors, the most recent general account of the pre-statehood period in the Northwest, Eblen stresses the importance of examining the "colonial" system in practice. Any "balanced appraisal" of territorial policy requires "consideration of the nature and significance of government at every level, from the township up."[43] But ultimately, despite his dismissal of the debate over the Turner thesis, Eblen comes to Turnerian conclusions about the effectiveness of territorial government under the Ordinance. He attributes "the rapid emergence of a high degree of local autonomy" to the failure of arrogant, indifferent, and inept territorial officials like Governor Arthur St. Clair to implement congressional plans.[44] To be sure, Eblen emphasizes official incompetence and discounts frontier democracy in explaining the weakness of the territorial system. Indeed, his brief survey of political life on the frontier persuaded him that local oligarchy was more characteristic than democratic individualism. But Eblen does not depart significantly from the broad conclusions of Turnerian historians: territorial settlers in the Old Northwest sooner or later thwarted the plans of Congress and successfully asserted their claims to local sovereignty.

The idea that the government of the Northwest Territory was ineffective remains one of the oldest saws in the history of the region. And why not? The main characters, Governor St. Clair and Secretary Winthrop Sargent, were not the stuff of which popular heroes are made: stiff-necked, obsequious to their superiors, arrogant and self-righteous in their treatment of the citizens of the territory, ambitious and yet not very talented, they have not endeared themselves to historians. Then, of course, there are the matters of St. Clair's humiliating defeat at the hands of the Indians in 1791; the inability of the two most important nationally appointed officials to control their local appointees; and the seemingly overwhelming rejection of St. Clair and territorial government in the achievement of statehood in Ohio in 1803. What more could have gone wrong?[45]

One could hardly argue that the careers of St. Clair and Sargent rank among America's greatest success stories. But we can understand both their behavior and their downfall better if we leave aside the questions of personality and competence and view them instead as representatives of the particular point of view embodied in the Northwest Ordinance. In another work, Andrew Cayton has suggested that territorial officials and their allies in the Ohio Company shared a common perspective with many land developers and members of Congress in the 1780s. Many were middle-aged former army officers from the more economically developed regions of America; they were nationalists, committed to a vision of regulated development. They were also firm believers in the value of patronage for establishing hierarchy and order in unruly frontier communities. In the first decade of territorial rule, St. Clair and his allies were trying to do for the West what Alexander Hamilton was attempting to do for the nation as a whole: establish the authority of the central government in order to regulate national economic and social development. Territorial officials were charged with executing the general policy outlined in the western ordinances. Therefore, it is far more important to assess the role of the territorial regime in implementing these policy goals and directing the course of western development generally, than it is to rate their performance—or nonperformance—of routine responsibilities.[46]

In the early twentieth century, disciples of Frederick Jackson Turner argued that the charges of aristocratic tyranny and executive corruption directed at the territorial government during the Ohio statehood contest (1799-1803) were justified. According to Randolph C. Downes, the people of the Ohio country were rebelling against an arbitrary government ill-suited to frontier society.[47] In *Valley of Democracy,* John D. Barnhart called the statehood campaign "fundamentally . . . a movement of the frontier to govern itself according to individualistic and democratic principles so dear to its heart."[48] The long-term significance of the Ohio experience was clear. The people of Ohio had not just created a state. By overthrowing the colonial territorial government, they had made the Old Northwest safe for democracy.

No one takes the rhetoric of the statehood proponents quite so seriously any more. The work of recent scholars deals with the statehood movement in more sophisticated ways. Elaborating on the work of Downes, Jeffrey P. Brown has developed the political context in which democratic ideas gained currency. Territorial politics, Brown shows, involved personal and regional rivalries as much as, if not more than, democratic rhetoric.[49] Donald J. Ratcliffe has demonstrated the degree to which the political debate in the Northwest Territory drew upon the existing political vocabulary of what he calls the "Age of Revolution." Talk about liberty and tyranny, virtue and corruption, recapitulated the themes of the American Revolution. In other words, the ideas discussed in the Ohio country were far from unique. Men simply explained what was happening in the common political language available to educated Americans.[50]

Finally, Peter Onuf suggests that the "overheated" rhetoric of statehood proponents should not obscure Congress's commitment to create new states according to the provisions of the Ordinance. The use of such extravagant language reflected the *reluctance* of many northwesterners to assume the burdens and responsibilities of statehood.[51]

All of these scholars have made important contributions to our understanding of the origins of politics in the territory, but none has explained why democratic rhetoric had such resonance for so many people. If the intellectual and political historians of the 1790s have shown us anything, it is that there was a broad spectrum of beliefs about republican and democratic government in America at the end of the eighteenth century. The debate over Ohio statehood was not a straightforward recapitulation of the ideological arguments of the American Revolution. It was part of a much larger struggle over the political future of the territory and the nation as a whole.

Indeed, the key bone of contention in the Ohio statehood controversy was the definition of the "republican" government the Ordinance required for admission to the union. Fundamentally, the issue in the Ohio country between 1799 and 1803 was not whether Ohio would become a state. The Ordinance of 1787 had established the fact that it would— eventually. Since the terms of the statehood controversy were set by the Ordinance, it cannot be construed as a referendum on its general principles.[52]

The burning question was whether the white males in the region north of the Ohio River and east of the Great Miami were ready for the responsibilities of American citizenship. What was at issue was how power would be achieved and allocated. The authors of the Ordinance had not intended to place the management of western affairs in the hands of ordinary men—the same people they had called "banditti" and "white savages" in the 1780s—or even the likes of the leading statehood proponent, Thomas Worthington, and his young, untried, but remarkably ambitious and confident cohorts. They had attempted to secure the Northwest Territory for the United States by laying a foundation of "republican" principles and by planning for the regular evolution of politics and society. From this perspective, it is easy to understand why the Ohio statehood movement deeply disturbed St. Clair and his allies. What they feared was not a simple rejection of the Ordinance but a larger repudiation of their insistence that power within a republican society should be administered by an experienced, well-educated, nationally oriented elite.[53]

Although St. Clair may have understood the democratic implications of opposition rhetoric more fully than his critics, the Ohio Jeffersonians did not challenge the existing territorial social structure. They certainly had no intention of involving the masses in the structures of power except in the most limited sense. We should keep in mind that those groups in early northwestern society which stood to lose the most by the implementation of national land and government policy were the least likely to participate in political life, even during a period of rapid change. While St. Clair's enemies proclaimed their solicitude for the common people—presumably including at least some of the victims of the expansion of federal power and market relations—it would be absurd to conclude that the opposition drew significantly on these marginal groups. Indeed, we would argue, the belated inauguration of representative government in 1799 precipitated the emergence of a territory-wide political elite committed to the Ordinance's frameworks of political and economic development, and the statehood contest marked its coming-of-age. It was not so much that marginal groups were disfranchised—after all the Ohio constitution provided for universal white manhood suffrage—as that political activity, narrowly understood, was itself the means of legitimating hegemonic values. Territorial *politics*—even in an oppositionist mode—served to integrate scattered local elites and draw them into national political life.[54]

7. Territorial Politics

A systematic administrative history of the Old Northwest Territory would undoubtedly provide us with a clearer perspective on the region's early political development. A most salutary result of such a study would be a better appreciation of the relationship between local and national politics. Turnerians are certainly mistaken in identifying opposition to territorial government with democracy and local self-determination in every case. Timing was crucial: the further away one moves from the Ohio example, the less true their argument seems to be. After all, the territorial governor and his friends took the lead in pushing for statehood in Indiana and Illinois *before* there was widespread popular support for the change.[55] And in Michigan[56] and Wisconsin,[57] where partisan divisions preceded statehood, both parties forged working links with the national organizations. Of course, local politicians sought to expand the sphere of local control—for instance over the choice of officials and the distribution of patronage—but a strong federal presence was a fact of life, and not necessarily an unwelcome one at that. Federal ownership of the public lands meant that the key issue of territorial politics—the precise articulation of national and local authority—would remain important after the new states were admitted to the union.

The early statehood movements should not be seen simply as democratic rejections of autocratic national authority. But they did reflect serious disagreement among local elites over the way their society should be organized, disagreement that paralleled and overlapped national disputes. Just as important, the statehood movements became what the authors of the Northwest Ordinance intended—a crucial stage in the nationalization of frontier politics. While they did not welcome the emergence of political factions, incipient party formation and the establishment "of structures of government congruent with those in the older states" nonetheless served integrative functions. Rejecting the "Turnerian image of the American West as a realm of natural democracy," Kenneth Owens thus concludes that "territorial government was a successful agency of Anglo-American expansion."[58] Similarly, the rise of a polemical press and the widespread use of ideologically charged language should be seen as another aspect of this nationalization of territorial politics, even as it fostered and justified partisan divisions. The relevance of this rhetoric to actual conditions in the territories may be problematic, but its importance cannot be discounted. By invoking variant versions of republican ideology, northwesterners asserted their membership in the larger political community while constituting a political life of their own.

Looking at the Ohio statehood controversy as a part of the larger process of political formation and definition which dominated the public worlds of educated white men in the quarter century after the adoption of the Constitution helps us to understand the intense rhetoric more fully. Recent historians have argued that the Federalists (who included St. Clair and opponents of immediate statehood for Ohio) and their Jeffersonian Republican opponents (who included St. Clair's critics) were fighting over different visions of the American future. But scholars cannot agree on the precise nature of those visions. To some, the Jeffersonians

are nostalgic agrarians, fearful of centralization and commercial economic development, the faithful descendants of the country tradition of
English politics.[59] Other historians see the Jeffersonians as eager and en-
thusiastic entrepreneurs, the foremost advocates of liberal capitalism.[60]
Similarly, the Federalists are sometimes portrayed as conservative and
sometimes as radical.

To a large degree the confusion of historians accurately reflects contemporary confusion. Politics in the 1790s was inchoate: the American
Revolution had effectively destroyed ancient conceptions of the unity of
politics and society by insuring equal access to the exercise of power for
most white males and by asserting—at least theoretically—that each
part of the government was responsible to, and representative of, the people in general. The authors of the Constitution of 1787 and the Ordinance
of 1787 had intended those documents to create political structures that
would subordinate often conflicting local and state interests to the power
of an overarching national authority within the new republican social
and political orders.[61] But Federalist supporters of the Constitution and
the Ordinance had not succeeded in achieving national supremacy—or
at least not by 1800. To the contrary, they were involved with Jeffersonian
Republicans in a serious struggle over the specific ways in which the
often general provisions of those documents would be defined and implemented.

Donald Ratcliffe correctly notes that most of the men involved in political life in the Northwest Territory were not frontiersmen in the classic
sense.[62] They were easterners who had moved recently and directly to the
Ohio Valley. Like many Puritan migrants to New England in the 1630s,
these men tended to think of their problems as peripheral extensions of
or variations on issues being debated at the metropolitan core. Thus, they
often read more into seemingly trivial contests about county seats, patronage appointments, and boundaries than did most frontiersmen, because they thought in different terms and employed a different political
vocabulary. In the political confusion of the 1790s—in a world where the
rules of power were ill-defined or in dispute—even the simplest issue became emblematic of a deeper conflict.

In this sense, the men involved in the Ohio statehood contest were active and committed participants in an ongoing, national effort to come
to terms with the legacy of the American Revolution.[63] The statehood
contest in Ohio bears the same relationship to the Ordinance of 1787 as
the presidential election of 1800 does to the Constitution of 1787. For
the most part, the Jeffersonian Republican critics of the Federalists operated within the structure established by the Constitution. Jefferson and
Madison had no intention of replacing that document, but they had every
intention of defining what its vague provisions actually meant and how
they should work. To the extent that a weak, although far from impotent,

federal government repudiated the Federalist vision of overarching national authority, they succeeded.

The same was true in the Northwest Territory. The achievement of statehood for Ohio did not destroy national authority (after all, the federal government created the state) or weaken a broad commitment to large-scale economic development. The Ordinance itself guaranteed that self-governing states would eventually emerge from the territory. But to the extent that the proponents of statehood enshrined popular and local sovereignty as *sine qua nons* of politics, they defined the "republican" character of the states that would be carved out of the Northwest Territory far more completely than the authors of the Ordinance. Ohio's constitution specifically defined the meaning of "republican" government—a strong legislature and weak executive and judiciary—as the negative image of the Ordinance's provisions for the administration of the territory. The rhetoric of local sovereignty and government of the people may have been more of a means to an end than an end in itself for the elites who spoke it. Still, the constant references to the will of the people and the growth of political participation sparked by the statehood struggle had a lasting, if unintended, impact.[64] In the Old Northwest, republican government came to mean "democratic" government and a high degree of local control. Thus, the Ohio statehood contest established important precedents for the exercise of power in the nineteenth-century Midwest which sharply diverged from the intentions of congressmen and land developers in the 1780s.[65]

8. Apotheosis

By the middle of the nineteenth century the constitutional and political controversies created by the Northwest Ordinance were largely in the past. Northwesterners were much more concerned with their region's economic prosperity and increasing political power. As they celebrated this happy state of affairs, northwesterners began to rewrite their history. They concluded that it was no accident that their region had become the most prosperous and dynamic in the union: this, they said, was precisely what the founders had foreseen and had been the overriding original intention of congressional western policy. Historians and publicists deemphasized the territorial period, when the Northwest Ordinance authorized Congress to impose colonial rule over the pioneer settlers of the region. They instead portrayed the Ordinance as a charter for political and economic development that prepared the rising new states for a glorious future.

In short, a document that had provoked intense disagreement in the first decades after its promulgation had become a focus of regional pride by the 1830s. Indeed, boosters argued that the states of the Old Northwest had become the freest and most prosperous in the United States because of the benign influence of the Ordinance of 1787. Midwesterners thus celebrated the triumph of free enterprise and commercial capitalism as they redefined their history and their place in the American union. Fusing national patriotism with a growing consciousness of sectional distinctiveness, they embraced "a vision of union through material progress."[66]

The reasons for this transformation in attitudes toward the Ordinance are complex—and form the subject of much of the rest of this book. On a constitutional level, the legislation had largely served its purposes. But the celebration of the Ordinance was also a recognition of the ways in which the Old Northwest had evolved economically, socially, and politically in the half-century that followed its writing. With the single exception of Article VI's ban on slavery, the celebratory rhetoric of the 1850s had little direct connection with the actual language and operation of the Northwest Ordinance. Even the new-found respect for Article VI depended on a radical distortion of the original intentions of the founders. The words had not changed. But by the middle of the nineteenth century, the citizens of the Old Northwest interpreted them in a different context, a context created by the interaction of the vision of developers and boosters with the aspirations and initiatives of the multitude of diverse peoples who settled the region after 1787.

II

THE PEOPLING OF THE OLD NORTHWEST

The authors of the Ordinance of 1787 hoped that the Northwest Territory would be transformed into the commercial garden of an American
empire, but it was the thousands of people who poured into the region
who brought that dream to fruition. The Old Northwest in the 1850s was
a veritable bastion of liberal capitalism. Increasingly integrated into an
expanding national (and international) market economy, it was one of the
most highly commercialized agricultural areas in the world.

The economic development of the region, however, was neither linear
nor inevitable. The people who settled the Old Northwest did not come
as single-minded capitalists with their eyes squarely and solely on the
main chance. Recent scholars suggest that settlers were motivated by a
variety of economic and social considerations. If anything, the dominant
motif for many of them was a deep-seated ambivalence about the role of
the market in their lives. The challenge was to balance the sometimes
contradictory goals of maximizing profits and preserving traditional notions about family and community.

1. Settlement Patterns

Historians working on other areas have emphasized the importance of
cultural origins in the creation of new societies. Peter H. Wood, for example, stresses the importance of the agricultural practices that slaves
carried with them into colonial South Carolina; their skills, he argues,
were crucial to the colony's survival and eventual prosperity.[1] Other
writers have pointed out the African origins of songs, religious practices,
and social relationships in the South.[2] David Grayson Allen, T. H. Breen,
Virginia DeJohn Anderson, and other historians of the Puritan migration
have linked New England settlement patterns, family life, and economic
activities to specific regions of England.[3]

Scholars examining the nineteenth-century migration of Europeans to the Old Northwest have also been sensitive to the importance of their subjects' cultural origins. The dominant assumption in the 1950s and 1960s was that the experience of migration wrenched immigrants from their familiar worlds, but more recently historians have stressed the remarkable persistence of Old World values in New World settings. Among the best of such studies are Kathleen Conzen's works on Germans in Milwaukee and in the township of St. Martin, Minnesota, and Jon Gjerde's book *From Peasants to Farmers: The Migration from Balestrand Norway to the Upper Middle West*.[4] Because Gjerde devotes equal time to examinations of Norway and the United States, he neither romanticizes the peasant past nor exaggerates the impact of American economic and environmental conditions. Migration to America allowed people to "retain the essential social fabric of their community in a rural environment that was much more conducive to economic growth than Balestrand." They eventually adopted "new cultural forms," Gjerde concludes. "But the forms were not incompatible with the core beliefs of the community and actually reflected the immigrants' ability to express their world view in new ways."[5]

These studies all assume that migrants had a history that, at least subconsciously, affected what they did and what they thought in their new environments. But while such an assumption seems readily apparent when dealing with European emigrants in the middle and late nineteenth century (and increasingly so to students of colonial America), historians have been less sensitive to the significance of the cultural origins of American-born migrants to the Old Northwest in the late eighteenth and early nineteenth centuries. To a great extent, this neglect reflects the persistence of the venerable idea that the frontier made settlers of diverse backgrounds into "Americans." Even the most critical anti-Turnerians have tended to accept the premise that the frontier transformed settlers, and that their past therefore was of only marginal importance.[6]

This flattened perspective minimizes settlers' cultural inheritance and emphasizes their economic motives. They migrated from places of declining or stagnant economic opportunities to places where they hoped they had a chance of improving themselves. To a large extent, debate has centered on the success of this quest, *not* on settlers' distinctive definitions of what they hoped to accomplish. Scholars such as Paul W. Gates argue that life on the frontier very often offered little tangible improvement in the quality of life.[7] But almost no one has suggested that white American settlers differed from each other beyond the fact that a few had more money than the rest.

Slowly, this portrait is beginning to dissolve. Susan Gray's examination of three nineteenth-century Michigan townships, for example, is predicated upon the assumption that New England attitudes toward land, family, and religion were critical in the initial formation of settlement.[8] The point is clear: those who would study the history of New Englanders in Michigan must first know the history of the Connecticut River Valley and upstate New York. Stale generalizations about Puritan countenances or Yankee tenacity will no longer suffice.

In fact, the work of recent cultural geographers demonstrates that the nineteenth-century Midwest was a patchwork quilt of transplanted communities. D. W. Meinig's *Atlantic America, 1492–1800* shows that settlement streams became mixed as Americans pushed across the Appalachians in the post-Revolutionary period. Unlike the colonial period, when existing settlements simply grew into the hinterland, expansion in the early republic tended to involve "the convergence of migrations from distinct seaboard societies."[9] The populations of the new states of Ohio, Indiana, and Illinois—and later, Michigan, Wisconsin, Minnesota, and Iowa—consisted of a conglomeration of peoples. These peoples generally migrated in homogeneous groups and settled in particular regions. As a result, the Midwest was more like an ethnic and cultural checkerboard than the proverbial melting pot.

Indiana provides a good example of this settlement pattern. Upland southerners, by far the largest group of settlers, took over the southern half of the state in the first years of the nineteenth century. In the 1830s, mid-Atlantic peoples congregated in the central area, while immigrants from New England in the 1830s and 1840s came to dominate the northern portion of the state.[10] Similar patterns emerged in Ohio and Illinois. The regional societies that had taken shape in Atlantic America in the colonial era thus were recreated in the midwestern states in the first half of the nineteenth century.

Cultural heterogeneity was reflected in all aspects of life. As Richard Lyle Power pointed out over thirty years ago in his classic, but strangely neglected, study *Planting Corn Belt Culture*, the cultural traditions of settlers produced different tastes and styles in food, clothes, and housing as well as distinctive religious and political attitudes.[11] More recent students of landscape and material culture such as Henry Glassie and John R. Stilgoe have emphasized the particular ways in which culturally diverse Americans understood and dealt with their environments.[12] Donald A. Hutslar's study of *The Architecture of Migration* is a promising start in exploiting these avenues of research for the Old Northwest.[13]

The emphasis on the diverse origins of settlers should not, of course, obscure the impact of movement and settlement in new environments. Very quickly, those who moved west diverged from those who had stayed behind as they responded to the demands of their new worlds. Some of these adaptations—to new climates, landforms, and food supplies—generally did not disrupt prior cultural patterns. But the challenges of building communities and negotiating power with other kinds of settlers had a more serious impact. As Meinig notes, the "interweaving

strands of Yankee, Pennsylvanian, Virginian, and other movements
were creating new complexities."[14] "The midwestern character" may
owe "something to this mix" of peoples, as economic historian William
N. Parker claims, but that character only slowly emerged. In the first decades of settlement, the people who settled the region tended to view
the world in ways they had imbibed in the areas of their birth.[15]

The study of midwestern society thus requires far more attention to
the cultural origins and migrations of those people who created it. What
this involves is nothing less than the study of the "repeopling" of an
American region. Bernard Bailyn has written that "peopling" means "re-
cruitment, emigration, and immigration," that it "implies settlement,"
and that it "implies, too, the mingling and clashing of diverse groups and
races, the evolution of social patterns, of community and family organizations, [and] population characteristics."[16] In short, to come to terms
with the nineteenth century Midwest we must treat the Indians, whites,
and blacks who settled it from within the North American continent
with the same care that is now being given to European emigrants to
America. What might we learn if we approached settlers from North Carolina in Indiana with the same assumptions with which we investigate
settlers from Germany in Minnesota?

Scholars have always been aware of the diverse origins of the populations of the states of Ohio, Indiana, Illinois, Michigan, Iowa, Wisconsin,
and Minnesota. But they usually describe this great internal migration
in general and static terms along North-South lines. This perspective
may have seemed appropriate in the nineteenth century, when the slavery issue and the Civil War shaped sectionalist thinking. But recent studies of New England and southern history have illuminated the dangers
of generalizing about these regions. For instance, if a southern culture,
built on the foundation of racial slavery, existed in the nineteenth century, Virginians, Georgians, and Louisianans were nonetheless dissimilar
in many ways. So too, differences between upcountry and tidewater
southerners were tremendously important. Students of the Old Northwest need to take these subregional variations into account and so to
move beyond broad—and misleading—generalizations about "Yankees"
and "Cavaliers" to more exact understandings of what settlers brought
with them from their old homes. They should also keep in mind that
these home regions were experiencing significant changes in the nineteenth century. This was particularly true of New England, where internal population movements, the spread of market capitalism, and the beginnings of industrialization transformed the countryside in the last
decades of the eighteenth and the first decades of the nineteenth century.
The origins of immigrants to the Midwest from within the United States
must be examined from both geographical and chronological perspectives.

The migration experience itself undoubtedly affected the behavior of settlers. Moving to the Old Northwest in the nineteenth century was no small undertaking. People who traveled from Massachusetts to Ohio or from North Carolina to Indiana faced tremendous difficulties. Their trips, moreover, often cost as much in time and money as the more celebrated westward treks of later generations.

The sheer size and speed of the migration are remarkable. Because this great folk movement resulted from a myriad of individual and family decisions, did not begin and end at well-defined places, and did not always follow the same routes, there has been a tendency to overlook its importance. Yet this movement of peoples was the greatest single fact of nineteenth-century American history. Millions of people moved, and then often moved again, and then again—all participants in one of the largest and fastest population shifts in the history of the world.[17]

"Migration," write Richard K. Vedder and Lowell E. Gallaway, "created the Old Northwest. More precisely, nearly all of the substantial population growth in the East North Central states from the time of the founding of the Republic to the Civil War resulted from the direct and secondary effects of that great human migration, the Westward Movement." Vedder and Gallaway's statistics readily confirm their sweeping generalization. From a population of white Americans numbering in the hundreds in 1790, the states of the Old Northwest contained 6,926,884 people by 1860. The center of the population of the United States in that year was located near Chillicothe, Ohio.[18]

Vedder and Gallaway's figures reveal that migration was far more important than fertility in explaining this amazing population growth. The population of the oldest state in the region, Ohio, for example, rose from 45,365 to 230,760 in the first decade of the century. With children of settlers accounting for only 23,698 of that increase, the Buckeye state had a net migration rate of 356.44 percent.[19] Between 1810 and 1830, the population of Ohio more than quadrupled from 230,760 to 937,903, while those of Indiana and Illinois grew from 24,520 and 12,282 to 343,031 and 157,445 respectively. Similarly, Michigan's 1850 population of 397,654 was almost fifty times its 1820 number of 8,896. Finally, Wisconsin rose from 11,683 in 1836 to 305,390 by 1850, and Iowa expanded from 10,531 to 192,214 in the same period.[20]

Again, most of this increase resulted from migration. Vedder and Gallaway calculate Indiana's migration rate at 455.47 percent between 1810 and 1820; in the decade of the 1830s, the rate for Michigan was 537.15 percent. Until 1840, in fact, migration accounted for the majority of population increase in the Old Northwest.[21]

Almost immediately, however, settlers began to move on. Ohio in the 1840s became a net exporter of population, and Indiana achieved that status in the 1850s.[22] Because of the tremendous influx of settlers over the previous half-century, fewer than 30 percent of heads of households in Ohio in 1860 had been born in that state; in that year, the figure for Illinois was less than eight percent. As Vedder and Gallaway remark, "In both Ohio and Illinois, there were more heads of households born in other countries than in the state of residence in 1860."[23]

So rapid and all-encompassing was this huge shift of peoples that historians sometimes fail to recognize its importance. Yet surely nothing could have been more a part of the life of a nineteenth-century midwesterner than the constant comings and goings of neighbors and family. Migration was hardly a new phenomenon: Americans had moved about since the founding of the colonies in the seventeenth century. What was novel in the 1800s, however, was the size and scope of internal migration. Because the settlement and resettlement of the Old Northwest involved the interaction of peoples from so many different areas, it was to a remarkable extent a region of strangers. Yet if the work of demographers and economic historians has demonstrated the fact of migration, we still know far too little about *why* people moved and what they *thought* about the whole process.

2. Families and Markets

Many historians continue to argue from a welter of statistical evidence that the causes of migration were almost exclusively economic. Surely, the pursuit of economic opportunities was crucial in the decisions of people to move. But it is also likely that the *ways* in which they moved and the *places* to which they moved were sometimes shaped by non-economic factors. Almost everyone was in pursuit of a higher standard of living, but not everyone defined or pursued that standard in the same ways. Even Vedder and Gallaway, who argue that "the citizens of the Old Northwest resembled the economist's conceptualization of 'economic man' even more than do Americans in general," concede that there was "no statistically significant relationship between land availability and migration" and that "migrants tended to be neither more wealthy nor less wealthy than non-migrants."[24]

The most satisfying account of why settlers migrated, advanced both by Conzen and by Gjerde, combines economic and cultural factors. In most, if not all, cases the impetus may have come from the desire to preserve traditional ways of doing things in the face of massive economic change. Certainly, such a conservative interpretation of the movements of peoples is consistent with our understanding of the migration of Native Americans as well as James Henretta's contention that eighteenth-century rural Americans migrated "to preserve and to extend" their way of life.[25] In a larger sense, the great migration of peoples in nineteenth-century America may be seen as an effort to mediate the impact of the expansion of an international market economy. In other words, migration may have been an ambiguous response to the growth of capitalism—an attempt to reap benefits by buying land and growing crops for a market while preserving traditional family structures and community mores.[26]

Frontiersmen in the states of the Old Northwest in the late eighteenth and early nineteenth centuries hardly resembled European peasants. They were highly mobile people who rarely missed an opportunity to improve their economic condition. But increasingly, local studies show many of them to have been conservative people committed to the sanctity of the family and community, for whom entrepreneurial activity was often more of a means to an end than an end in itself.

John Mack Faragher makes this argument as well as anyone in his *Sugar Creek: Life on the Illinois Prairie*. Throughout his book, Faragher demolishes Turnerian shibboleths, stressing the continuity and stability of daily life and the general resistance to change. Like Conzen and Gjerde, he demonstrates the tenacity of traditional values of family, community, and land use. The settlers of Sugar Creek, Faragher concludes, "had transported a traditional social order to a new environment and had progressively transformed the landscape in ways compatible with their own priorities. . . . Like the society that bound the households together, cultural sentiments along the creek were essentially traditional and conservative. Family and household remained the essential social building blocks; community continued to be constructed from the relations among kinship, neighborhood, and church."[27] Faragher's Sugar Creek was not dominated by profit-minded speculators and entrepreneurs but was instead a complex society shaped by interaction among many different ways of living, some based on race, others on gender, and others on class.

So, too, Susan Gray's New England–born settlers of Michigan tried to balance the demands of family and community with the exciting possibilities of capital development. Ultimately, they were unsuccessful. By mid-century, the primary function of the family farm was to generate capital; sons labored for their fathers more to make money as individuals than to perpetuate their family's collective holdings. This shift was part of a centuries-long process by which conferral of landed patrimony *in situ* ceased to confer place in the social order and by which the rural community, under the impact of economic expansion and commercialization, ceased to be the fundamental social reality.[28]

Still, if "commercial opportunity" ate away at community and familial ties, it was hardly a process that occurred in one generation or simply because of migration to a frontier. Nor was it a transformation that settlers welcomed with open arms. Taking advantage of markets may have been economically profitable, but the social costs were high. And settlers knew it: purely "economic men" they were not.

Faragher and Gray's works illuminate characteristic interpretative possibilities developed in colonial community studies and in the controversy over the *mentalité* of colonial farmers. Heated debate on the spread of market values and profit motives suggests that early Americans were caught up in—and divided by—a global struggle between tradition and modernity. But it would be a mistake to conclude that frontier settlers were aware of being so ambiguously poised between two worlds. Faragher's conservative, family-centered local community should not be seen standing in opposition to the market economy and liberal, capitalist values.[29] Sugar Creek farmers were not conscious of the cultural contradictions we find them enacting. They did not hesitate to exploit economic opportunities as they emerged. But if their means seem capitalistic, their ends often were not.

Juliet E. K. Walker's account of her ancestor *Free Frank* succeeds admirably in making these connections. In showing how Frank's family forged a viable community on the Illinois prairies in the 1840s, Walker demonstrates how enterprising black settlers could respond effectively to the most narrowly circumscribed opportunities. Yet Frank's entrepreneurial skills served the overriding goal of his family's welfare: in this he was not far different from his white neighbors. But Frank and other black settlers faced formidable obstacles in obtaining and preserving their freedom. Frank's first task was to redeem himself and his wife and children from bondage. His success was a tribute to his skill, to his successful assertion of independence in a racially hostile environment and, most of all, to his commitment to the time-honored values of family and kinship which he carried with him from slavery in South Carolina and Kentucky to Illinois.[30]

In *Sugar Creek*, Faragher shows that early in the life of the community "the communal customs of the borrowing system" provided for "self-sufficiency and the development of democratic rhetoric."[31] Although the Illinois prairie was relatively isolated and commercially underdeveloped, settlers engaged in widespread entrepreneurial activity. There was no question of the importance of private property or individual profit to these people. Nonetheless, family and community concerns combined with the physical difficulty of producing for markets to mediate or qualify frontiersmen's commitments to the values of liberalism and privatism we traditionally associate with the frontier of Frederick Jackson Turner.

In Steven J. Ross's study of *Workers on the Edge: Work, Leisure, and Politics in Industrializing Cincinnati, 1788–1890*, we find similar arguments made about the most dynamic urban area in the region in the first half of the nineteenth century. Ross suggests that republican ideology, economic prosperity, and social mobility made "independence, cooperation, and harmony of interests" the dominant characteristics of early Cincinnati. While Ross tends to idealize Cincinnati's first decades, his in-

really?

sistence on egalitarianism and a mutuality of interests between entrepreneurs and workers is compelling. He finds the same kind of artisan repub- *yes, ok*
licanism in Cincinnati that Sean Wilentz describes in New York City in
the same period.[32]

Faragher and Ross trace the decline of early mutuality in the increasing
complexity of social and economic structures. By mid-century Sugar
Creek was divided into a large group of landless tenants and a smaller
segment of prosperous landowners; incipient class conflict came to Cincinnati in the 1830s and 1840s. To be sure, high rates of geographic and
generational mobility must qualify any assertion of economic inequality
in nineteenth century America.[33] Still, the work of Faragher, Walker, and
Ross in conjunction with the older but still valuable work of scholars
such as Paul Gates make it clear that neither economic democracy nor
the values of liberal capitalism were dominant in the Old Northwest of
the early nineteenth century.

Faragher, Gray, Ross, Conzen, and Gjerde do not set up simplistic di-
chotomies between capitalism and community or elites and peasants/
workers. Rather, they are interested in exploring the complex interaction
of traditional values and methods with the revolutionary implications of
commercial capitalism. What they are describing is a very intricate pro- *ok ok*
cess of economic development which involved the intermingling of a wide *complex*
variety of impulses within individuals as well as in society as a whole. *layered*
etc
Ross argues that artisans and workers in Cincinnati were not hostile
to the growth of the market. They saw "no contradictions between the
producer ideology and entrepreneurial capitalism. The two worked in
tandem to enrich the individual and the community."[34] In other words,
workers often were leading participants in the development of market relationships which eventually subverted their faith in the mutuality of
economic interests. The growth of industrial capitalism in Cincinnati
was a haphazard affair. According to Ross, "industrialization took place
gradually and at an uneven rate, affecting different workers at different
times and in different ways. Despite the explosion of class conflict in the
1800s, Cincinnati was not a city constantly gripped by battles between
employers and employees. Rather, it was marked by both periods of
working-class resistance and acquiescence; of rejection and acceptance of
new forms of production."[35]

In a rural setting, Faragher shows the ways in which change was often
"conservative." Innovation for farmers was sometimes the product of efforts to maintain traditional customs or an effort to reconcile economic
and family demands. Even those who welcomed improvements in transportation and produced for the market generally continued to think in
older ways. In the end, Faragher reaches two major conclusions about economic development in Sugar Creek. First, "progress was characterized by
what economists call 'uneven development,' by the improvement of one

segment of the community and the stagnation or decline of another."
Second, most men continued to hold "to the traditional logic that a man
could never own too much land," that is, they often bought or rented land
when it would have made more economic sense to invest their money
in other enterprises.[36] Just like Ross's Cincinnati artisans, Faragher's
Sugar Creek farmers were divided as much within themselves as they
eventually were from each other. These, in sum, were people in transition, trying to make sense of something new in old terms and not always
succeeding. "Community did not 'break down' with the approach of the
modern world," Faragher concludes; "community, in fact, provided a
means of making a transition to it."[37] With regard to the market, the ope-
rative characteristic seems to have been ambivalence.

3. The Model of Commercial Capitalism

Ambivalent or not, the settlers of the Old Northwest collectively created a showplace of commercial agriculture. Within a few decades, they
transformed the region completely. *Changes in the Land*, William
Cronon's ecological history of colonial New England, suggests ways to
approach this transformation, ways that deepen our understanding of the
complex tensions that underlay the economic development of the states
created from the Northwest Territory.[38] yes Wo s lwt but wrong area

Cronon shows how seventeenth-century English settlers remade New
England into a more familiar environment. They replaced "an earlier village system of shifting agriculture and hunter-gatherer activities" with
"an agriculture which raised crops and domesticated animals in household production units that were contained within fixed property boundaries and linked with commercial markets." In short, they turned the
products of the land and the land itself into "commodities," thus reori-
enting the world of the Indians toward the marketplace.[39] Like Cronon's
settlers, the pioneers of the Old Northwest transformed the region into
a bastion of commercial capitalism with strong ties to national and international markets. Virtually all settlers, from Norwegians to blacks, from
upland southerners to Boston professionals, participated in that transformation, whatever their original intentions.

proof?

But Cronon's Puritans were not forward-looking entrepreneurs. Indeed,
he argues that they transformed the New England landscape in an effort
to recreate the familiar worlds they had left behind. In conjunction with
other studies, *Changes in the Land* suggests that seventeenth-century
settlers were a profoundly localistic people committed to the perpetua-
tion of traditional customs and relationships. In fact, it was their very
efforts to make New England into old England that led to the kind of
transformation Cronon describes. As he notes about deforestation:

Reducing the forest was an essential first step toward reproducing that Old World mosaic in an American environment. For the New England landscape, and for the Indians, what followed was undoubtedly a new ecological order; for the colonists, on the other hand, it was an old and familiar way of life.[40]

Radical rearrangements of the landscape are not always—or usually—the product of deliberate design. We need to keep in mind the drastic difference between intentions and consequences. The simple fact that the Old Northwest became an exemplar of enterprise does not mean, *ipso facto*, that this is what its settlers intended. What ultimately produced a society committed to commercial capitalism was the interaction of thousands of peoples' efforts to work out their ambivalence toward the market. The kind of "progress" that midwesterners would come to celebrate later in the nineteenth century was actually a haphazard process and a source of tension and confusion for many people.

There is no question, however, that by the middle of the nineteenth century, the Old Northwest was one of the most important centers of commercial agriculture in the world. Its primary exports were grains (corn and wheat) and animal products (especially pork). While industry had taken root in several larger cities, principally Cincinnati, the Old Northwest remained dominated by farms. Still, the region had a dynamic economy with "the most rapid rate of per capita growth" in the nineteenth-century United States.[41]

The Old Northwest went through two stages of economic development before the Civil War and was then on the verge of entering a third. The first was a period of local economic activity, marked by limited production for largely inaccessible markets; the second was a dynamic era of rapid growth (both in economic and geographic terms); and the third was a period of consolidation and increasing stagnation as the very success of Americans in developing the Midwest resulted in glutted markets and falling prices.

In the first years of settlement under the Ordinance of 1787, economic conditions were relatively stagnant. A lack of specie and the difficulty of getting products to market, in particular, kept production at subsistence levels. Only towns where the United States Army was quartered experienced any degree of specialization and growth. If settlers were looking to escape the tentacles of a large-scale, capitalistic market, they could have done no better than the Old Northwest in the first years of the nineteenth century. For once they had traveled a few miles beyond the Ohio River, immigrants found themselves almost totally isolated from the economic currents of the Atlantic world.[42]

Still, there was economic activity on the frontier. The idea that settlers were ever fully self-sufficient is now generally discredited. People grew corn, turned it into whiskey, hunted, and traded furs, pelts, and other goods. Whites and Indians conducted significant trade in frontier regions. Increasingly, the Indians were dependent on the products of European technology such as rifles and articles of clothing. Indians, on the other hand, exchanged food, furs, and other goods with the French in the Wabash and Mississippi valleys, with the British in and around Detroit, and with Americans in the fledgling settlements in what is now southern Ohio and Indiana.[43]

These various transactions, however, did not add up to a coherent regional economy. Without relatively easy and cheap access to markets in other parts of the North American continent, the economy of the Old Northwest would have remained locally oriented. In fact, the appearance of stagnation was, according to George Rogers Taylor, a source of serious discontent among residents of the Ohio Valley in the first decades of the nineteenth century.[44]

Obviously, conditions changed; in particular, the rapid growth of the American population, the elimination of the Indians as obstacles to settlement, and improvements in transportation made migration to the Old Northwest more attractive in the second quarter of the nineteenth century. Economic historians agree that the most important agent of economic growth in the Midwest after the War of 1812 was the tremendous increase in population. Hundreds of thousands of people were in nearly constant motion in search of improved economic opportunities. They eagerly took advantage of liberal national laws that allowed the purchase of public lands on credit. Auctions throughout the Midwest saw the transfer of millions of acres to hundreds of thousands of Americans.[45]

Some of this land was coopted by speculators, whom Turnerian historians generally portrayed as rapacious absentees. Land speculators fare considerably better in more recent accounts. Malcolm Rohrbough has demonstrated that the public land system was administered fairly and well.[46] And Allan Bogue has led the way in showing that speculators did not constitute a distinct class: nearly everyone speculated on one level or another. Indeed, speculators did many positive things, including paying a high portion of the tax burden and making credit available to farmers. Mortgages, Allan and Margaret Bogue and Merle Curti suggested, were not symbols of oppression but the means by which cash-poor people bought land and made improvements.[47]

Eagerness to get goods to market made many residents of the Old Northwest staunch advocates of internal improvements. Promoters and developers championed steamboats, canals, and finally railroads. Contemporaries as well as subsequent historians knew that "a viable transportation system was the *sine qua non* for the perfecting of a market for commodities between the West and other regions."[48]

Eventually, two transportation complexes evolved. The first, and the oldest, covered the southern half of the region and centered on the Ohio River. In the beginning, all trade flowed south, following the direction of the Muskingum, Scioto, Miami, Wabash, and Illinois rivers. The great destination was New Orleans. Largely through the impetus of competition and private initiative, improvements in keelboats and steamboats helped the southern system maintain its importance through the Civil War.[49]

The chief advantages of the river system were decentralization and its natural character. While Cincinnati and Louisville became great cities, much trade began with men simply loading crops onto boats and floating them down to New Orleans. Major urban centers were not necessary. Just as important was the fact that people did not need to improve the river system in any major way: it worked well just the way it was.

To the north, of course, the Great Lakes dominated the thinking of developers. But the lakes were essentially landlocked until the opening of the Erie Canal in 1825. Just as crucial was the lack of long, deep rivers to carry goods down to the lakes. Thus the lake system required human improvements to work. First came canals, financed largely by state governments in the 1820s and 1830s. And because access to the interior was the key to growth, the cities at the heads of canals, such as Cleveland and Toledo, mushroomed in importance. No wonder villages fought for the privilege of straddling canals.[50]

Still, the residents of the Old Northwest often approached the construction of canals with apprehension about both their economic and their social costs. As Harry N. Scheiber and others have shown, the evolution of public improvement policies was a complicated process, often involving contradictory means and ends. In his detailed study of Ohio, Scheiber describes alternative conceptions of the role of government in internal improvements. One he labels the "'commonwealth' conception . . . which argued for mobilizing public resources because a distinct public interest required collective action. Similar to mercantilist theory of the eighteenth century, the commonwealth idea proposed that only through definition of collective interests could the state provide the essential prerequisites of growth."[51] Allied to the commonwealth notion, according to Scheiber, was "the theory of planning, which called for the systematic ordering of growth by the state government itself."[52]

But there also remained active in the Old Northwest a strong commitment to the primacy of localism and the individual rights of the citizen. Scheiber calls this belief "the doctrine of equalized benefits." "It decreed that equal distribution of costs and benefits among all members of the polity was a higher goal than rational definition of priorities aimed primarily at stimulating growth."[53] In cruder terms, it appeared in many instances in refusals to vote for or to pay the taxes that would support the construction of canals and roads (and public schools as well). Politically, it found expression in support for Andrew Jackson.

The fight over internal improvements, however, was not a contest between clearly defined groups of supporters and opponents. As with the development of the economic structures of the Old Northwest in general, the construction of canals laid bare a welter of contradictions. Most dramatic, for example, is the way in which defenses of local interests could lead to the development of policies designed to subordinate them to larger concerns. Small towns saw great advantages in having canal routes pass nearby, and state politics often revolved around logrolling to satisfy their demands. The transportation networks that eventually subverted localism were not imposed on people; to the contrary, they generally fought over them in order to protect or advance the interests of their communities.

In any case, the railroads soon made canals obsolete. In the 1840s and 1850s, railroads—largely financed by British capital—pushed deep into the hinterlands of Cleveland, Detroit, Chicago, and Milwaukee. With their speed and cheap rates, the new routes began to challenge the supremacy of the river system to the south. By 1853, only 29 percent of midwestern trade went through New Orleans while more than 60 percent left via the Erie Canal.[54] With the coming of the railroads, the population of the upper Midwest soared.[55] Chicago became the great urban center of the Midwest by penetrating the upper Mississippi Valley and diverting the trade of farmers in Wisconsin and Iowa from St. Louis and New Orleans. With fifteen rail lines converging on the growing metropolis in 1860 and grain storage capacity exceeding the total tonnage of the entire South's cotton crop, Chicago's population passed 112,000.[56]

Again, however, not everyone embraced the railroad with unbridled enthusiasm. The cost of the economic opportunities it provided were, in the words of John Lauritz Larson, "the subjugation of local advantages and prejudices to the national network."[57] In his biography of the Boston-born railway builder John Murray Forbes, Larson captures these ambivalent responses. Men such as Forbes looked toward the rapid development of western production for international markets; meanwhile, more locally oriented people viewed the changes wrought by technological innovation with a mixture of excitement and trepidation. Both national entrepreneurs and local farmers may have operated within a capitalist frame of reference. But their perspectives on railroad development differed radically. Iowans in the 1850s welcomed access to distant markets but worried about "the implications of such structural changes in settlement pattern and regional development as high-energy transportation engendered." In particular, many feared the "concentrations of economic power" in the hands of a few unknown and faraway men which were the price of cheap transportation. At issue were "fundamental assumptions about American equalitarianism, regional diversity, and state and local rights."[58] Even as they celebrated the arrival of railroads, then, many residents of the Old Northwest were reluctant to surrender traditional ways of life to the control of the market.

Such doubts notwithstanding, the combination of a rapidly rising population, relatively cheap lands, and increasingly accessible markets produced a tremendous economic boom. As with the growth in population, the speed with which the Midwest emerged as an economic power was little short of astounding. In 1860, the trans-Appalachian West contained a third of the total rail mileage in the United States. And, according to Carville Earle, few midwestern farmers "lived more than 20 road miles from relatively cheap transportation."[59]

Production figures are just as impressive, particularly in view of the region's economic marginality in 1815. In 1859, the Old Northwest produced 46 percent of the wheat grown in the United States and 33 percent of the corn.[60] Ohio was the biggest wheat producing state in the union, and only Kentucky, Tennessee, and Virginia surpassed Ohio, Indiana, and Illinois in growing corn. The region that had exported barely 12 percent of its crops in 1820 (largely to New Orleans), sold 27 percent in 1840 and 70 percent of its wheat in 1860.[61]

4. Cultural Origins and Economic Behavior

Despite the obvious general commitment to commercial agriculture in the Midwest, the region's citizens did not pursue economic prosperity in the same ways. There was considerable local variation in the types of crops grown and in agricultural practices. The quality of the land was important, but so were the cultural practices and customs settlers brought with them.

Clearly, as Allan Bogue and Carville Earle have pointed out, environmental factors affected regional specialization. Wheat prospered far more easily in the "drier and cooler climate" of the northern regions where it was relatively free from the diseases of wheat rust and wheat blast.[62] And Bogue has shown that the uneven surface of the prairie margin protected wheat from winter killing while the drier climate allowed an easier shift from fall to spring-sown wheat.[63] Corn, on the other hand, thrived in the moderate climate of the Ohio Valley.

In fact, corn had long been king in the river system of the south. Since corn was difficult to market, farmers had learned to transform it into other things—such as beef, pork, and whiskey.[64] Thus some areas of south-

ern Ohio, Indiana, and Illinois specialized in cattle feeding; among them
were the central Scioto Valley, the Miami Valley, the region between Indianapolis and the Wabash River, and the Sangamon Valley.[65] More important was hog production. Pigs were cheaper than cattle: they required little care, ate virtually anything, served farmers as scavengers, and were
relatively easy to slaughter and pack.[66]

In the long run, of course, the nature of crops affected settlement patterns and spatial development. Carville Earle, for example, argues that
what people grew affected the ways in which their families and communities evolved. Wheat, he points out, required only a few days' labor, most
of it concentrated at harvest time. A "labor bottleneck" at that time
worked to keep the size of family farms around 100 to 200 acres. On the
other extreme, cotton cultivation demanded 120 days over eight months.
Obviously, an intensive labor force was necessary in the former case, an
extensive one in the latter. In the middle, corn had to be tended in the
first weeks after spring planting; labor was most intensive between April
and July. And since a man could only cultivate about twenty acres in
sixty days, the size of farms was kept down.[67]

The impact of wheat, then, was to encourage a very "fluid labor force"
and with it, moderate size farms and large urban areas. Earle suggests that
cities such as Chicago grew partly because they marketed and forwarded
agricultural products. But "a more subtle and more decisive factor" was
"the tie between wheat farming and labor supply."[68] Since labor in the
Wheat Belt was underemployed, it flocked to urban areas. And, since rural
labor was seasonal, urban wages were low, resulting in the hiring of many
more workers than otherwise would have been the case.

The nature of corn production made the Corn Belt different. Farmers
needed more labor than their counterparts in the Wheat Belt. And labor
was expensive because demand was high. Corn Belt farmers thus often
found a proslavery argument persuasive. According to Earle, slavery
made economic sense when a free laborer (working for only four months)
cost as much as or more than a prime slave (working for the year).[69]

But if crops and economic considerations influenced the ways in which
a society was organized, the cultural predilections of settlers also influenced the kinds of crops they grew and their agriculture. Here again, the
Old Northwest offers a kaleidoscope of practices, far more complex than
a simple split between northerners who grew wheat and southerners who
grew corn.

Ohio, according to the closest student of its agricultural history, included "five specialized [agricultural] areas" in the first half of the nineteenth century.[70] They were the wheat region of the upper Muskingum
Valley, the hog-dominated Miami Valley, the cattle-feeding Scioto Valley,
the cattle-grazing Madison County area, and the dairying of the Western

Reserve. Without discounting the importance of climate and soil on crop selection, it is important to recognize the inherent predilections of different kinds of people. "When the occupant of an Ohio farm began his agricultural operations," notes Robert Leslie Jones,

> it was not only with livestock and some implements, but also with ideas of how to set about doing things. It might be that he was of Pennsylvania Dutch extraction, and therefore did not feel comfortable without a spring house, a bank barn, and heavy-draft horses. Virginians, New Englanders, 'York Staters,' and British immigrants likewise had distinctive approaches derived from their backgrounds.[71]

Residents of the Old Northwest disagreed about the kind of corn to grow. Southerners preferred the gourdseed while New Englanders leaned toward the flint variety.[72] They also brought different breeds of cattle to the region. New Englanders preferred Devons, the yellow Danish, and the red and white or black and white Dutch. Settlers from New York and Pennsylvania brought Holland, Flemish, and West Indian. Southerners opted for the Spanish or English strains.[73]

Agriculture in the Old Northwest must be seen, then, as the result of the cross-breeding of traditional, sometimes idiosyncratic, local customs with the desire to make money and the demands of particular environments. Take cattle and hogs as an example. Forrest McDonald and Grady McWhiney suggest that many people in the South, generally scorned as indigent and lazy, "raised cattle and hogs as their principal occupation and . . . did so out of both tradition and custom."[74] Southerners who settled in the Old Northwest may also have preferred to raise hogs and cattle in order to preserve a distinctive way of life. The animals could be sold for some profit, or at the very least, provide food; meanwhile, hog raising offered their owners a great deal of leisure time. They did not need much land, for they simply let the animals roam wild. Such property was also highly mobile. In short, raising hogs allowed people to reap a profit without adopting what McDonald and McWhiney call "the compulsive pursuit of wealth that dominated both the northern commercial man and (despite their protests to the contrary) most southern planters as well."[75] In a sense, hogs gave their owners independence, even if more "civilized" types disparaged them. (Just as important may have been their taste for pork.)[76]

New England settlers in the Old Northwest, on the other hand, tended not to keep as many hogs or grow as much corn as southerners. "Hog farming," note Jeremy Atack and Fred Bateman in their analysis of "Yankee Farming and Settlement in the Old Northwest," "was not a Yankee *forte.*" On the contrary, New England-born farmers "produced a crop mix . . . similar" to that of those who remained in the Northeast. "Although the Yankee settlers made some concessions and adjustments to the environmental differences" between New England and the Old Northwest, conclude Atack and Bateman, "some practices and habits died hard."[77]

The Old Northwest was transformed economically in the early nineteenth century through the efforts of thousands of migrating peoples to reap the benefits of market capitalism while maintaining familiar customs and assumptions. The settlers were a remarkably diverse lot whose origins and ambitions intersected with the physical environment in a number of ways. Overall, however, the result was the creation of a congenial world for the promotion of commercial agriculture.

The Old Northwest did not develop in precisely the fashion the developers of the 1780s had imagined. Certainly, its economic structures in the middle of the nineteenth century were not the handiwork of the national government. And, as we shall see in the following chapter, its society was far more bourgeois than republican. But there is no denying that on the eve of the Civil War, the states of Ohio, Indiana, Illinois, Michigan, Wisconsin, and Iowa were members of a regional economy based on the export of corn, pork, and grains to markets throughout the United States. In a very real sense, Turnerian assumptions about the flattening impact of the frontier notwithstanding, the citizens of the Old Northwest had transformed their environment far more than it had transformed them.

III

THE ORIGINS OF COMMUNITY
IN THE OLD NORTHWEST

The diverse origins of immigrants to the Old Northwest in the decades after 1787 had a decisive influence on the kinds of community which emerged in the region. As many observers have noted, the dominant cultural motif north of the Ohio River in the nineteenth century was heterogeneity. Still, notwithstanding significant ethnic, racial, and gender differences, widely dispersed groups shared certain values and behaviors that cut across geographic lines. The foundations of what we will call trans-local communities lay in the economic structures of people's lives. In this chapter, we argue that the degree of involvement in the market economy had a tremendous impact on the ways in which people identified themselves as individuals and as members of communities.

Traditionally, historians have found the seminal moment of midwestern culture in frontier settlement and have seen its evolution in linear terms from origins in isolated barbarism to fruition in a democratic, capitalist civilization. The major scholarly debate has been over the nature of geographically defined communities, with historians arguing about whether economic inequalities or relative egalitarianism and political conflict or consensus predominated in them.[1] Some writers contend that all forms of community were weak, stressing the atomistic quality of life on the frontier.[2]

More recent scholars, including Thomas Bender, have urged historians to concentrate on the coexistence and interaction of different forms of community rather than on the displacement of one set of social relationships by another. In general, human beings construct individual identities through identification with other people with whom they believe they share similar values. A sense of community, defined culturally rather than geographically, is indispensable to a human being's understanding of *how* the world works, *why* it operates as it seems to, and *what* his or her role within that world is.[3]

Before the 1830s, the lives of many citizens of the Old Northwest revolved around the same basic routines: clearing land, planting and harvesting crops, hunting and gathering food, bearing and raising children, and the dozens of other chores that were vital to existence. As we emphasized in chapter two, there were significant variations in the methods people employed in pursuing these activities. But in general frontier residents had a great deal in common, most particularly the centrality of the household in both their economic and social lives, a profound commitment to the sanctity of an extended, multi-generational family, and a deep ambivalence about the increasing importance of the market and such institutions as schools, governments, and established churches. There was a widespread tendency, usually credited to southern or Indian influences by historians, to value emotion over intellect, to emphasize stability over progress, and to regard efforts at moral improvement with suspicion.

Still, despite all that they shared, most settlers before the 1830s thought of community strictly in terms of family or a local network of friends. Economically and socially, there was little need for contact with the larger world.[4] The lack of effective communication and transportation networks beyond rivers and lakes, moreover, made it difficult for large numbers of people to be aware of how much they shared with others beyond their local area. No matter how much they were alike, most were essentially isolated into separate geographic units.

There were two exceptions to this generalization. Territorial and state officials were very aware of the importance of trans-local communities of like-minded men and, as we will show in the next chapter, fostered their formation through the development of networks of patronage and embryonic political parties. Alliance with men beyond a specific geographic community was the key to power in the Northwest Territory and the states created from it. More important for the mass of men and women was religion. Evangelical Protestant denominations brought people together by developing institutions and practices such as camp meetings and itinerant preaching that fostered collective consciousness. Whatever the intrinsic appeal of religious beliefs, in other words, an important part of their social function was to articulate a sense of community among widely dispersed peoples who nonetheless shared common experiences.

Still, there was no powerful trans-local community in the Old Northwest consciously intent upon establishing cultural hegemony, deliberately attempting to set the rules of society—the ways in which people were expected to deal with each other—in the first decades after 1787. The failure of the Federalist territorial hierarchy in the 1790s is testament to the difficulties inherent in this task.

But ultimately a powerful community formed much more by class interests than geography or politics—an urban and village bourgeoisie—did take shape, a community that began to define the nature of midwestern society by linking regional consciousness to the triumph of commercial capitalism. The most important catalyst was the transportation revolution in the second quarter of the nineteenth century. The new middle class defined itself to a significant degree through participation in a wide range of occupational, religious, and reform-minded groups. But just as crucial to the formation of this collective identity was an active rejection of alternative forms of community, most especially those values and behaviors associated with many early white settlers of the Old Northwest.

1. Communities in the Countryside

The trans-local cultures that existed in the Old Northwest before the transportation revolution organized the world for diverse peoples whose economic relationships with each other were far less important than personal ties. Of supreme importance was the family.

Demographic historians have argued that there were few differences between frontier families and those in the East.[5] The frontier was hardly the domain of masses of unattached young men. Still, the thorough work of James E. Davis suggests that, at least initially, frontier areas had "proportionately more young people and males than the settled areas."[6] Within a decade, however, there were usually "fewer very young people, more elderly" and "the male majority [had] largely vanished." Because of the high number of young males, women married at an early age, producing more children. While Davis concludes that "the demographic traits of [white] settlers" were "essentially similar to those of easterners," the frontier years seem to have been demographically distinctive.[7]

Michael Conzen's study of a small town developing in the "shadow" of Madison, Wisconsin, supports this conclusion. The first stage of settlement was marked by high percentages of people in their twenties and thirties, many very young children, and few persons over the age of fifty-five. With growing stability in the community, there were more older citizens and a declining percentage of children and young adults.[8] Kathleen Neils Conzen's work on the Germans in Milwaukee demonstrates an initial preponderance of males in the first decade, followed quickly by an evening out of the sex ratio. Indeed, by 1860 in Milwaukee, women outnumbered men.[9] The same was true of Jacksonville, Illinois.[10] Donald Leet suggests that population growth rates were directly related to the availability of land: in Ohio fertility fell by 40 percent between 1810 and 1860 with the gradual filling up and maturation of settlements. People tended to reproduce more, in short, when there seemed to be surplus land awaiting development.[11]

More than economic factors may have influenced family size on the frontier. In the first years, when labor was in short supply, settlements were organized around extended family ties; the importance of family in helping European immigrants in urban areas is also well-established. John Mack Faragher has suggested that the rural community of Sugar Creek, Illinois, was built by "families in association."[12] For many people, including farmers in Illinois and New England transplants to Michigan, what Mary P. Ryan has called "the corporate family economy" remained at the center of their lives.[13] Almost all frontier economic activity took place within the household. Family members emphasized the survival and prosperity of the family over several generations in interdependent work. Ryan suggests that the frontier family was a patriarchal and hierarchical unit in which there was little room for privacy or individual achievement. If anything, the frontier exaggerated the importance of the family. Before the coming of the canals that transformed the region around Utica, New York, the individual remained subordinate to the larger family structure.

The corporate family economy was also characteristic of early settlements in the Old Northwest. The critical factors in determining the duration of such family-based subsistence agriculture were the cultural heritage of immigrants and the relative inaccessibility of markets until the building of canals and railroads from the 1830s through the 1850s. New Englanders, Germans, and Irish moved in family units, and recent historians have documented the importance of kinship in determining where and how people moved. But family was also a crucial factor in explaining why some people stayed in one place and how they learned to cope with their new environment.[14]

Historians have also identified strong gender-based divisions of labor within white families paralleling those of the Native Americans. As long as northwestern farmers were cut off from markets, hunting remained an essential economic activity. Men supplemented their families' diets with meat and acquired furs and skins to trade for goods. More than this, hunting was a key test of masculinity. Sometimes white males hunted alone, but group parties were also common.[15] Around the campfire, telling tall tales over a jug of ever-available whiskey, hunters—or surveying parties— interacted in a homosocial environment, reinforcing shared values of independence and freedom. Military expeditions accomplished the same cultural ends. From the 1780s through the Civil War, war brought men together in long-term hunting trips where the bonds of manhood were forged even tighter.[16]

Like Indian women, the wives and daughters of frontier farmer-hunters took care of the home and children. They also were responsible for tending the family garden, feeding the chickens, collecting food, milking cows, and butchering animals. But white women were not as heavily involved in agriculture as their native counterparts, largely for technological reasons. In particular, the whites' use of a heavy plow made such labor more difficult for women.[17] As a result, white farm women tended to have less power than Indian women. They did not control the distribution of food and were more isolated from other women because whites settled on individual farms rather than in villages. Above all, white society lacked the Indian ethos of reciprocity. No matter how isolated from markets whites were, their transactions tended to be economic. In this sense, men's work, in the form of selling furs, meat, or crops, was publicly acknowledged while women's was not. "The market could connect men's work to a larger social process and remunerate them in the tokens of commerce," notes Faragher. But "in order to qualify as social labor, work had to have this characteristic: to be able to reach out and connect the family to the larger social world. Woman's work, always cyclical, always looking inward, did not qualify."[18]

The same was true for women in the fledgling villages of the Old Northwest. Few women worked outside of the home. Those who did were invariably young, unmarried, and employed in domestic service, that is, in extensions of the cooking and cleaning they did for their own families.[19] There was, moreover, virtually no recognition or reward for the time-consuming work urban wives and daughters did in and about the home. They took care of their families (a back-breaking task in the nineteenth century) while men labored away from the house.

If the family was the basic social and economic unit in the Old Northwest, the most important component of trans-local communities was religion. Churches and revivals were critical in the formation of group identities that transcended family and local ties. Religious beliefs were at the core of cultural definition: they allowed settlers to differentiate among the many strange people flooding into the Ohio Valley. Common beliefs enabled people to forge bonds with strangers, despite social and cultural differences. At the same time, settlers could identify people who were *different* on the basis of religious affiliations. Religion, in short, became the primary path to an articulation of trans-local communities in the years before the transportation revolution.

The basic problem with writing about religion in the late eighteenth- and early nineteenth-century Ohio Valley is that we know so little about it. While there are several excellent denominational histories, they tend by definition to be narrowly focused.[20] A fertile area for research would be the religious beliefs of settlers before the beginning of the Second Great Awakening. It may well be that religion played a minor role in the lives of many people in the Ohio and Indiana countries. We know that organized religion was weak, but we can do little more than speculate about religious attitudes among the unchurched.

With the Awakening, however, a greater intensity in religious belief became apparent. To contemporaries and subsequent observers, the most striking thing about the revivals that began about 1800 was the sheer en-

thusiasm they engendered.[21] In fact, the wild and emotional behavior of
people at places such as Cane Ridge, Kentucky, in the summer of 1801,
seemed to be a massive rejection of the irreligion or apathy that had supposedly characterized western life in the late eighteenth century.

Historians have had no difficulty in interpreting the significance of
such revivals. For scholars influenced by Frederick Jackson Turner, the
Awakening represented a flourishing of the democratic individualism
they associated with the frontier. Spontaneous camp meetings and the
solitary circuit rider were expressions of an open, emotional frontier culture. Itinerants such as Peter Cartwright and preachers such as Barton
Stone—with their emphasis on the universality of salvation—became in
the Turnerian model the religious counterparts of populist politicians
such as Andrew Jackson. No wonder then that evangelical denominations
such as the Methodists, Baptists, and Christians won far more adherents
in the Old Northwest than Congregationalists or Presbyterians.[22]

Subsequent scholars discounted those "democratic" impulses as they
focused on the revivalists' organizational successes. T. Scott Miyakawa's
*Protestants and Pioneers: Individualism and Conformity on the Ameri-
can Frontier* stressed the discipline and organization of evangelical denominations. He pointed out the voluntary or "joining" quality of religious life and the degree to which such supposedly distinctive American
traits as nationalism, egalitarianism, and democracy were brought to the
Old Northwest by dissenting Protestants.[23] In a seminal article published
in the late 1960s, Donald G. Mathews argued that the Second Great
Awakening's major legacy had been an organizational model. Reinforcing
Miyakawa's conclusions, Mathews noted the ways in which religious revivalism enabled people to work for common goals.[24]

Although recent historians have stressed the popular qualities of evangelical sects in the early republic, they have abandoned the notion that
revivals were peculiarly frontier phenomena. Nathan O. Hatch's analysis
of the origins of the Christian movement and "the demand for a theology
of the people" and Gordon S. Wood's study of early Mormonism place
these groups within the larger context of the democratization of American society in the early nineteenth century.[25] Meanwhile, a major legacy
of the Awakening was the utter fragmentation of Protestantism in the
Old Northwest. After surveying the literature on religion in the region,
Peter Williams was left with "a sense that an unprecedented religious and
cultural pluralism had in fact been, perhaps more out of necessity than
design, achieved."[26]

Despite the differences in emphasis and interpretation, most scholars
agree that religion was fundamental in bringing a sense of belonging to
people on the frontier. Religious beliefs, in other words, were the tendons
of trans-local communities. Revivals and itinerants not only brought en-

tertainment and excitement to people whose lives were hard and often monotonous, they also gave people a sense that others shared their assumptions about earthly society as well as the meaning of life. They were, in short, not alone.

More specifically, evangelical religion reinforced traditional institutions such as the family as well as traditional styles of behavior. In an overwhelmingly oral culture, revivalists could win converts by stressing the importance of face-to-face personal relationships with other human beings and with God. Evangelicalism demanded emotion and public demonstrations of faith: salvation was not something one attained in the quiet practice of reading or examining one's conscience. On the contrary, it required a supremely public act of repentance and profession of faith. One's value as a human being was determined by those who witnessed the demonstration of affection and contrition. Indeed, everything depended upon public confirmation. Evangelicals, writes Donald Mathews, insisted upon "initiating the individual into a permanent, intimate relationship with other people who shared the same experience and views of the meaning of life and who were committed to the goal of converting the rest of society."[27] But evangelicals explicitly rejected any kind of social hierarchy, preferring instead to integrate individuals into "a community which cared about [them]."[28]

In sum, through religion, whether in churches or at camp meetings, many of the first settlers of the Old Northwest gained a clearer sense of who they were *and* who they were not. Calling oneself a Methodist or a Shaker or a Congregationalist—or simply a Christian—was part of a larger process of self-definition and social integration. Even those who did not practice religion undoubtedly defined themselves to a great degree in opposition to those who did. Insistence on adherence to certain theological principles and concomitant social behavior thus formed the foundations of trans-local communities in the first decades of American settlement in the Old Northwest.[29]

Middle-class Americans in later years would insist on their distance from the frontier experience; they were appalled by the nature of work on the frontier, the relationships between husbands and wives, and the emotional zest with which many practiced religion. Still, the kin-dominated, highly mobile communities of the Old Northwest make sense in light of the region's loosely structured economy before the advent of canals and railroads. People who lived in relative isolation from markets and who still depended a great deal on hunting and foraging for existence had little need for the institutions and behavior that the authors of the Northwest Ordinance or the nineteenth-century bourgeoisie praised.

2. Bourgeois Patterns of Community

If the Ordinance set the terms of debate in the Old Northwest, it was
largely because it was an effort to deal with the social and political implications of commercial capitalism. As the market expanded into the region in the late eighteenth and early nineteenth centuries, it gradually
forced a rearrangement of social structures and values along the general
lines suggested in the Ordinance. It also brought people to the region who
were committed to commercial development and who embraced the values that went along with it. They understood the importance of a national political structure; they also believed that individual character was
the building block of a stable social order.

Many of these people were from New England. To them, contemporaries and historians have ascribed the stereotypical attributes of Puritan
piety and Yankee acquisitiveness. But their behavior had less to do with
religious tradition than with the fact that New Englanders were so re-
sponsive to changes in the international market economy.

The most famous transplanted New Englanders in the Old Northwest
in the eighteenth century were the associates of the Ohio Company, a
joint-stock organization of veterans of the American Revolution who purchased land from Congress in 1787 and settled the Muskingum Valley
in 1788. Led by Rufus Putnam, a middle-aged Massachusetts surveyor
and soldier, the associates founded their principal settlement at Marietta.

Unlike many other residents of the Northwest, the New Englanders in
the Ohio Company were committed to a national vision of American society. They fully agreed with those statesmen and developers who intended to integrate the West into the national economy. Although the
Ohio associates remained committed to traditional notions about the
family and the church, they had been wrenched from local New England
moorings by long military service. They were proud to be from Massachusetts, Rhode Island, and Connecticut, but were prouder still of their
connections with George Washington and the government established by
the Constitution of 1787.

Like the authors of the Ordinance of 1787, the associates intended the
Ohio Valley to become a highly developed region. They planned to establish commercial agriculture and to link their settlements with eastern
markets through internal improvements. Along with the crops they
would produce for market, men such as Putnam and Manasseh Cutler
believed they would be able to establish manufactures at an early date.
With their precocious emphasis on trans-local, large-scale economic development, the Ohio Company associates stood apart from most early
settlers of the Old Northwest.[30]

Still, the associates generally shared the deep ambivalence others felt about the market. Several of them had had unsuccessful experiences in trade, and many came west to speculate in lands in order to perpetuate and improve the economic and social standings of their families. They were also men consumed with the importance of honor, hierarchy, and personal relationships. Nothing was more revealing of their characters than their intense devotion to Washington and Alexander Hamilton and their total immersion in the Federalist patronage networks of the 1790s. The associates were very traditional men. Rejecting the judgment of the masses, they believed that a small elite of officers and gentlemen should dominate society and government. Not surprisingly, they had limited success on the frontier.[31]

Many later migrants from New England came to the Midwest in the 1820s and 1830s as full-blown exponents of a culture of bourgeois capitalism. The study of the American middle class has preoccupied social historians of the nineteenth century in recent years. Scholars such as Paul Johnson, Mary Ryan, Stuart Blumin, John S. Gilkeson, Karen Halttunen, and Carroll Smith-Rosenberg have described the rise of a largely urban-based community of shopkeepers, professionals, merchants, and other people of middling rank intimately involved in commerce. Concerned about the disorder they saw in American society, middling elements found strength and justification in a strain of evangelical Protestantism nurtured by the Second Great Awakening which promoted self-discipline more than individual release.[32]

The bourgeoisie sought to bring order to a rapidly changing society of strangers. By the 1830s, voluntary organizations of middle-class Americans crowded the urban landscape, seeking the perfection of individual character through personal commitment to the cause of reform. They required the acceptance of the tenets of hard work, honesty, temperance, and moral probity. They also insisted upon rigid gender-based divisions of labor and leisure. Women were elevated to positions of purity and ensconced in the safety of the home where they nurtured children and provided an asylum from the competitive world of business. Men, on the other hand, worked outside of the home, learned the value of self-discipline and delayed gratification, and enjoyed the pleasures of male camaraderie.[33]

The most sophisticated study of the emergence of the middle class is Mary Ryan's analysis of Oneida County, New York, in the first half of the nineteenth century. Ryan argues that the middle class formed "around domestic values and family practices."[34] The expansion of market opportunities, exemplified by the construction of the Erie Canal, offered individual independence, broke down the power of established institutions such as the family and the church, and led to a reorganization of social structures and values. Through female-dominated revivals, evangelical Protestantism established affection, privacy, guilt, and con-

science as the dominant motifs of the community. In the new world of
commercial capitalism, the family lost many of its economic and social
functions to voluntary associations, and with its decline evaporated a
world of public, face-to-face, personal relationships. "Once the whole
town was knit casually together by face-to-face bonds and alliances,"
notes Ryan, "now new sorts of glue were required." No longer "a compos-
ite of households . . . households could only be seen as a conglomeration
of detached individuals."[35]

The new market-dominated world required people to internalize values, to seek judgments within their consciences rather than their communities. It cast people adrift on a sea of migrating strangers, leaving
them free to associate as they saw fit. Although Ryan acknowledges that
this reconceptualization of social roles was led by professionals, shopkeepers, and merchants, she argues against the kind of social control
model proposed by Paul Johnson in *A Shopkeeper's Millennium*. Instead,
her emphasis is on the ways in which changing economic relationships
forced a realignment of social relationships. The American middle class
emerged in a display of self-control, countering the public chaos they perceived by creating bonds of affection in their private lives; the female-
dominated home became the anchor of the middle-class world. Indeed,
Karen Halttunen has suggested that the parlor became a kind of filter between public and private worlds. There the rituals of etiquette and fashion displayed the signal importance the bourgeoisie attached to character
and sentiment.[36]

Many New Englanders carried such values in embryonic form to the
Ohio Valley in the 1830s. They included the Beecher family and many
of their associates at the Lane Seminary and the Western Literary Insti-
tute in Cincinnati. For generations, historians have either praised New
England emigrants as the carriers of civilized culture to the West or
scorned them as arrogant Puritans. But perhaps a better way to character-
ize the Beechers is as a bourgeois family intent on carrying the new social
order to Ohio.

Noting Catharine Beecher's "passion for cultural dominance," Kathryn
Kish Sklar attributes "much of the effectiveness of the Beecher family"
to "its ability to seize the power of social definition during a time of widespread change." In particular, Catharine was intent upon reconstructing
American society on the basis of sentiment and domesticity:

> Womanhood could be designed to engage all one's creative energies, yet si-
> multaneously to smooth the edges of one's regional, lineage, or class identi-
> ties, and to articulate the similarities one shared with other women. The
> same could be said for American manhood . . . gender roles were an effec-
> tive way to channel the explosive potential of nineteenth-century social
> change and bring it at least partially under the control of a national elite.

Catharine Beecher thus came to Cincinnati in 1832 with the intention of spreading a homogenizing moral education through a "corps of women teachers." Her ideology was a clear response to her perception of the capricious world being created by the market. Like her father, she saw her mission as an effort to release Americans "from old agencies of social control" and to form new ties of "social obligation and economic interdependence."[37]

Before the Civil War, the Old Northwest was still an overwhelmingly rural area. But by the 1820s, as we saw in chapter two, economic development had resulted in the growth of local commercial centers. As these villages and cities grew in the 1830s and 1840s—linked with each other and to the rest of the world by new modes of transportation—they attracted thousands of rural young men and women interested in improved economic opportunities. The kinds of jobs available required skills other than brute strength or physical agility. Ambitious young men became clerks, store managers, newspaper writers, salesmen, skilled craftsmen, and professionals such as lawyers, teachers, and doctors. With their wives, the men who filled these jobs constituted a middle class eager to build the kind of society Ryan describes in Utica, New York, and which Catharine Beecher called for in Cincinnati.

The motivations that led some people to champion middle class values were complex. But one of the most important was simply the desire to define oneself through participation in a larger cultural community. As Lawrence Friedman suggests in *Gregarious Saints*, middle-class abolitionists in the 1830s and 1840s

> sometimes struggled tenaciously for the Lord because they were apprehensive; if they relaxed their activities, they could conceivably fall back into the slothful, immoral lower class life from which [many] had risen. By converting sinners, these missionaries therefore proved to themselves that they were part of the genteel evangelical middle class.[38]

The most important reason for some Americans to take up the banner of bourgeois culture was their burning need to establish their social identity through righteous association with like-minded colleagues.

In no city in the Old Northwest did bourgeois values take hold as early or as fully as in Cincinnati. The Queen City in the 1830s was in the process of transition from a regional market center to a manufacturing city.[39] In *Workers on the Edge*, Steven J. Ross suggests that laborers were better off as a class before 1825 when society was "more egalitarian and less stratified."[40] Most people shared a producer mentality and believed in the importance of cooperation among groups. The growth of markets changed this attitude by undermining mutualism and replacing it with "conflict, divisions of interest, and acquisitive individualism." In short, "while the transportation revolution may well have reduced the distance between the cities, it also seemed to widen the distances between and within the classes."[41]

The face-to-face ties that characterized society in early Cincinnati were increasingly supplanted by impersonal relationships based on economic considerations. "The bonds which had united men and women of an earlier era," concludes Ross, "seemed to have disintegrated under the impact of market capitalism."[42] What was happening in western New York was also happening in Cincinnati. The growth of the market transformed social as well as economic relationships: it broke down traditional household-dominated production and shifted economic activities to more public and impersonal forums such as banks and factories. It also wore away at the supremacy of local, geographically determined communities. As towns became linked more closely to cities in the East, their leading citizens became more interested in trans-local news, fashions, and prices. The center of their world shifted from the familiar to the distant: they sought to promote economic progress and guarantee social stability by inculcating values such as punctuality, industriousness, and self-discipline.

Bourgeois values were not embraced with equal enthusiasm everywhere in the Midwest. Most affected were those people whose economic interests gave them a cosmopolitan perspective that transcended local areas, including the many merchants and lawyers tied to developing regional and national trade networks. "More than anyone else merchants began to connect the frontier with the more settled regions of the nation," writes Hoosier historian James H. Madison. "They traveled personally to East Coast markets, and returned with letters, newspapers, and new ideas as well as goods."[43] Less involved were rural people, urban laborers, and traditional local gentries.

Northwestern urban areas had always been dominated by local notables, men, who like the founders of Marietta, believed in government by gentlemen. But in the 1820s and 1830s, a commercially based middle class began to challenge these traditional leaders.[44] Often imbued with the perfectionist spirit of evangelical religion and firm believers in the righteousness of capitalism, professionals and tradesmen in towns and cities throughout the Old Northwest began to emphasize the importance of individual character, conscience, and self-discipline. By mid-century, almost every town possessed a stable power elite committed to the simultaneous growth of the market and bourgeois values.[45] Walter Glazer says of Cincinnati: "a relatively small and atypical group of men [mostly merchants and professionals] ... through involvement and influence within the associational network, ran local affairs." They were, he concludes, an "'interlocking directorate.'"[46]

Middle-class cores dominated society in villages and small towns as well as in major urban areas. As Lewis Atherton noted long ago in *Main*

Street on the Middle Border, "every country town had an inner circle whose personal interests were . . . tightly interwoven with those of the community at large." A "middle-class code" set the tone for village life. The bourgeoisie could not silence other groups—the old landowning elite, immigrants, blacks, and transients—but they did succeed in establishing their values as cultural norms.[47]

In *The Politics of Community: Migration and Politics in Antebellum Ohio*, Kenneth Winkle has shown how the power of local officials in establishing who could vote reinforced the positions of local elites. Despite a gradual liberalization of suffrage laws regarding migrants in the antebellum period, judges and other voting officials could use techniques of "public interrogation" to disenfranchise many newcomers.[48] "A core community of economically successful persisters . . . had the right to define the legal boundaries of the local electorate." Thus, while a local electorate was often "dominated numerically by newcomers and transients," it was usually dominated "politically by a small core of economic leaders. Members of the core community," in sum, "used their persistence to win exaggerated influence both at the ballot box and in political office."[49]

An excellent study of the formation of a geographically defined community in the Old Northwest is Don Harrison Doyle's history of Jacksonville, Illinois, between 1825 and 1870, *The Social Order of a Frontier Community*. "The really pressing problems of this new society had to do not with egalitarian democracy or individual opportunity per se," argues Doyle, "but with how to fashion communities compatible with these ideals in a nascent capitalistic society. . . . The problem of building new communities involved . . . the constant influx of uprooted newcomers, the clash of unfamiliar cultures, and the early difficulty of defining status and leadership in an unformed social structure." In tracing the evolution of Jacksonville, Doyle emphasizes the tension between the often contradictory goals of "mobility and stability, voluntarism and collective discipline."[50]

As was the case with other northwestern towns, "most" of Jacksonville's "population at any given time were transient strangers." Thus "only a small core" of people "had an ongoing interest in the town's future."[51] Imbued with a booster ethos that encouraged material progress and an image of social unity, this core consisted of people in "white-collar" jobs such as "businessmen, professionals, and artisan-proprietors." They tended to be wealthier than average, more upwardly mobile, and more likely to be married.[52] Interested in the economic development of their town, they were also concerned with the triumph of bourgeois culture.

The key to their efforts to reform the population of Jacksonville was the voluntary association. Long-time residents joined dozens of organizations that gave them a place in a larger society of strangers. They estab-

lished their social identity, in other words, by cultivating horizontal social ties. Voluntary associations also became vehicles of social order,
providing miniature models of "order, deference to rules, and self-
control."[53]

Perhaps the most important of these associations was the church. Crucial to our understanding of nineteenth-century midwestern society are
the ways in which evangelical Christianity helped forge new social
bonds, particularly within the urban middle class. The first revivals in
the region had helped foster incipient trans-local communities. But the
new middle class that began to emerge in the 1830s found in evangelical
Protestantism both the justification and the model for a reorganization
of society.[54]

Revivals tended to appeal most to women and children. With the disintegration of the family as a unit of production among professionals and
people involved in trade, females found sources of mutual support and
public power in churches. Women became the guardians of private virtue
and individual character, as evangelical religion promoted an increasingly
feminized definition of private character and public culture.[55]

Excluded from partisan politics, women were particularly active in efforts to spread temperance and public education. Through what Nancy
Cott has called "the bonds of womanhood," female associations and networks designed to advance the cause of Christian morality, bourgeois
women were able to exercise influence in the public sphere without challenging the limits set by domesticity.[56] Involvement in antislavery and
temperance movements allowed women to participate fully in the debate
over the social and political implications of the transportation and commercial revolutions.[57]

But women in nineteenth-century America did not constitute a monolithic group. As Nancy Hewitt has noted in her examination of women's
organizations in Rochester, New York, "women did not follow a straight
or singular path from benevolent work through evangelicalism and abolition to women's rights."[58] Hewitt identifies three separate paths for
white, middle-class, Protestant women: members of female benevolent
societies worked for the gradual "amelioration" of perceived social ills
such as drinking; "perfectionists" sought the total eradication of evil
with evangelical fervor; and "ultraists," who identified themselves as socially marginal victims of patriarchy, promoted radical change in American society as a whole. While Hewitt's divisions may reflect more of a
chronological evolution than she allows, she nonetheless demonstrates
the importance of remembering that "the direction of material and moral
progress would be decided not by a battle between the sexes over these
roles but by a struggle among various segments of the new urban middle
classes for economic and political domination."[59]

Still, a reorganization of gender roles was at the heart of bourgeois culture. One of the principal features of middle-class life was its increasingly rigid homosociality. Men and women lived separate lives. The former worked in offices or stores and spent leisure time interacting with other men in clubs, business associations, and sports. Females remained within the private world of affection and domesticity. Both belonged to networks of people that transcended their local community. Women's religious circles were mirror images of the commercial contacts of their husbands.[60]

Just as important were trans-local networks of female kin, which, according to Marilyn Ferris Motz in *True Sisterhood: Michigan Women and Their Kin*, 1820–1920, "provided a sense of community, a community transcending even geographic isolation."[61] In a society in which females had very little legal power, women relied on sisters, mothers, daughters, and cousins to support each other economically and psychologically; kinship networks offered help to women seeking divorces, women who were ill or without husbands. In short, Motz suggests that such networks filled two functions: they "lessened a woman's dependence on her husband" by offering other means of support, and they protected women from violations of social norms within marriage. "A network of female kin thus provided a woman with a lifelong source of support which she could use to balance her dependence on her husband as well as to provide assistance for the nuclear family."[62]

As with the eastern bourgeoisie, the middle class in the Old Northwest emphasized self-control as the key to survival and prosperity in the world of commercial capitalism. While they advocated moral reform for all people, they were particularly hard on themselves: certainly no family spent more energy wrestling with personal guilt than the Beechers. Most revealing, however, are the ways in which middle-class northwesterners tried to improve themselves. One of the most successful efforts was the lyceum movement of the 1830s, which brought familiar public lecturers to cities and towns throughout the region to preach the advantages of self-improvement.[63] By the 1850s lyceums had given way to literary societies and clubs for young, upwardly mobile single men, wholesome alternatives to taverns and brothels for those cut off from the affectionate ties of maternal home. Encouraged by merchants and other businessmen, these societies became central to what Mary Kupiec Cayton has termed "the self-culture movement." According to Cayton,

> the apostles of the self-culture movement began to advocate the cultivation of an internalized system of morality especially fitted to the newly commercialized portions of the country, particularly urban areas. Introspective self-examination of conduct would provide highly mobile young men of the urban centers, isolated from traditional institutional bolsters of morality, the means for maintaining character in a disordered environment.[64]

So thoroughly committed to the inculcation of bourgeois values were Ralph Waldo Emerson's midwestern audiences that they had no trouble in translating his "misty" transcendentalism into "a set of already familiar, pragmatic, common sense rules for attaining individual financial and social success."[65] By the 1850s, the middle class was well on the way to elevating "culture" into an industry. Attendance at shows, concerts, and lectures by persons of national or international reputation became a distinguishing mark of bourgeois character. The peculiar midwestern contribution to this phenomenon was a defensive prickliness about the quality of local society. The midwestern bourgeoisie sat through many a tedious lecture and endured many a boring singer in order to demonstrate worldly sophistication. But then, by their own logic, they had to: a person of character contributed to the social order by being "cultured" as well as virtuous. Even the leisure of the middle class had begun to transcend local boundaries.

Although much of the effort of midwestern commercial elites was directed at self-improvement, they also increasingly devoted attention in the 1840s and 1850s to the improvement of other kinds of people. Among their targets were the Irish Catholics and Germans who flooded into the region and stood out because of their distinctive religious practices. But it would be wrong to suppose that bourgeois reform was directed only at immigrants. There were home-grown deviants as well. Despite the power of urban elites and the growing importance of the market, many midwesterners remained committed to older, local ways of life. Rural peoples generally did not experience the effects of economic and social transformations to the same degree as urbanites. In rural areas, the more personal world described by Faragher still remained very powerful. So too, in the cities, many laborers and traditional elites were suspicious of bourgeois reform.[66]

Middle-class midwesterners were not engaged in a calculated grab for "social control." Mainly, they were people whose lives had been transformed by the market; many, if not most, were migrants from rural to urban areas. What they found in a culture of self-discipline was a sense of personal identity in a rapidly changing world. Quite naturally, they wanted other people to share in their discovery. And they became zealous in advocating their positions, no matter the opposition.

And opposition there most certainly was, as a brief survey of three causes near and dear to the bourgeois heart—public education, temperance, and antislavery—will show. Serious conflict over these issues developed between defenders of locally oriented communities who insisted upon the supremacy of personal relationships, and bourgeois reformers eager to order a society of strangers connected primarily by the impersonal ties of commerce. The issue was not whether commercial capitalism would prevail in the Old Northwest; by the 1830s and 1840s that was a given. Rather, the question was what kind of behavior and values were appropriate in the new world being created by the interplay of thousands of acquisitive individuals with improved transportation and economic networks.

3. Conflicting Visions of Community

The Land Ordinance of 1785 had provided for public support of education. Article III of the Northwest Ordinance stressed that "Religion, Morality and knowledge being necessary to good government and the happiness of mankind, Schools and the means of education shall forever be encouraged."[67] But in the decades that followed, pitifully little was done to accomplish that goal. Land sales produced only meager income, and community commitment to public education varied widely. "For most settlers," observes Carl F. Kaestle, "the impulse to promote common schools did not have much urgency. . . . Indeed, it was widely resisted by settlers who had very little hard currency even in good times."[68]

But there was more than money behind the resistance of many people to public education. While bourgeois spokespersons emphasized the importance of education in building the character and acquiring the skills necessary to prosper in a commercial society, other residents of the Old Northwest saw education as a threat to local control and to more traditional, family-centered values. Schools run by professionally trained teachers from outside the community threatened to supplant parents and relatives as the primary guardians of children.[69] This, of course, was exactly what reformers sought. "They advocated the school as a vital instrument of social discipline for youth," writes Doyle of Jacksonville in the 1850s, "an essential supplement to what they saw as the eroding authority of traditional institutions in the family and the church."[70]

More than that, education geared to the demands of urban commercial life was simply inappropriate in rural and ethnic communities. Many busy farmers, notes Wayne Edison Fuller in *The Old Country School*, "seemed instinctively to fear that education, at least too much education, went hand in hand with wealth, luxury, and leisure and ended in corruption and decadence."[71] What they valued was "common sense," a vague concept to bourgeois reformers but meaningful to rural people interested more in seeing their children learn how to interpret a local world than to acquire reading and writing skills.[72]

Despite the efforts of reformers such as Ephraim Cutler in Ohio, public education movements in the Old Northwest did not succeed until the 1850s.[73] Only then, when the economic transformation initiated by the transportation revolution drew vast numbers of people into market-related activities, did states begin to pass laws providing for free public education.[74] Wisconsin led in 1848, followed by Indiana in 1852, Ohio in 1854, and Illinois in 1855.[75] But even these laws accepted compromise with opponents by maintaining a high degree of local control in districts.

The leaders of the fight for free public schools tended to be New England-born and imbued with the spirit of evangelical Protestantism. Caleb Mills of Indiana was typical. A minister from New England who became head of the normal school at Wabash College in Crawfordsville in 1833, Mills spearheaded a campaign in the 1840s to get the Hoosier legislature to hold a referendum on public education. Although 56 percent of the voters approved the idea, it took until 1852 to get a law and until 1867 to achieve legal sanction for property taxes in support of public education.[76]

The Bible of the public education movement was the series of readers developed by William Holmes McGuffey. Tremendously popular throughout the Midwest in the nineteenth century, the readers inculcated the specific values education reformers hoped students would imbibe. As Lewis Atherton has written, "The dominant, middle-class code of McGuffey and his followers held that life was a serious business." The readers praised perseverance, truth, honesty, and hard work while denouncing laziness, gambling, purposeless frivolity, and drinking. Students learned to revere the family and the church and to believe in the desirability of material progress and self-improvement: character was the key to success.[77]

Just as important as the male public education advocates were the females who did most of the teaching. Men such as Mills and Calvin Stowe of Cincinnati considered women to be the finest teachers because of their moral purity and their distance from the male-dominated public world.[78] Many New England women poured into the West to teach; their initial migration followed paths established by networks of friends and institutional sponsors. Eventually, according to Polly Welts Kaufman, about 70 percent of them married and settled in the West.[79] By the 1850s, the midwestern middle class had begun to found seminaries to train their daughters to teach close to home.[80]

These early teachers were persistent and confident in their mission. They had to be. Among the problems they encountered on a regular basis were loneliness, uncooperative parents, poor equipment, irregular attendance, and difficult students. Sometimes they overcame these obstacles; other times, they gave up.[81] Teachers encountered the same suspicion or apathy as advocates of public education. They, in turn, denounced popular reluctance to support schools and teachers as stingy, backward, and ignorant. But those labels only ring true given the assumptions that literacy and bourgeois morality were crucial prerequisites of life in America. Surely they were for those who aspired to "success" in the urban and commercial world. But the case is not so clear for the vast numbers of people in the Old Northwest in the first half of the nineteenth century whose ties to urban areas and markets were more remote and tenuous. "It took generations," writes Kaestle, "to overcome the pervasive resistance to state-sponsored schooling. . . . [and] Anyone who believes that opposition . . . was found only among southerners and Catholics misunderstands the origins of public education. The controversy also involved fights between localists and centralists, between Democrats and Whigs, between egalitarians and pluralists."[82] What lay at the bottom of these disagreements was the degree to which people were oriented toward the market.

The temperance movement revealed similar tensions. No other issue was more crucial to the definition of the American middle class than the effort to get people to drink less or not at all. Temperance mattered because it was directly equated with self-discipline. No person of character could risk the loss of control inherent in heavy drinking. The reasons for bourgeois enthusiasm for temperance are clear: stability and predictability were crucial to the maintenance of their public and private worlds. Among merchants and professionals, drinking was detrimental to both business and reputation. As Jed Dannenbaum puts it in his study of temperance in nineteenth-century Cincinnati, "heavy drinking no longer seemed appropriate in a changed American society."[83]

True enough, in the case of the Cincinnati bourgeoisie. But for many other people, less interested in market practices or values, drinking remained a central part of their culture. As Elliott Gorn argues in *The Manly Art*, many working-class males lived in a tough, competitive, masculine world; drinking with friends at taverns after work was a significant part of their lives. To demand that working-class men surrender alcohol was tantamount to asking them to surrender their manhood, or at least one of the most important ways in which they defined it.[84]

Not only working-class men were offended by temperance. Heavy drinking had been an important feature of life in the Old Northwest in the early period. As W. J. Rorabaugh shows in *The Alcoholic Republic*, the normal annual per capita consumption of alcohol by people over the age of fifteen in the first third of the nineteenth century was 7.0 gallons. Americans have never imbibed more than they did in this period. The average male drank perhaps four times what the average man drinks in a year today. Whiskey was crucial to the frontier economy because it made the long-distance transportation of corn easier and cheaper. But it was also a constant companion for many men working on farms and canals.[85]

When the American middle class attacked drinking, then, they were attacking a way of life that had become foreign and threatening to them. In Cincinnati, as Dannenbaum shows, the middle ranks of society—those who were geographically stable, upwardly mobile, church-going, and

"While a sig. portion of the middle class would tor Longworth's vineyards; likely not so agreeable pw would drink his wine."

married—led the temperance movement in the 1830s and 1840s.[86] Although the movement initially relied heavily on moral suasion, by the 1850s it had become intimately involved in politics. But it was already having an impact; in 1845, the average per capita consumption was down to 1.8 gallons.[87]

consumpt down

A similar lesson can be drawn from the slavery controversy. Increasingly in the 1830s, growing numbers of the urban middle classes in the Old Northwest viewed slavery as a moral wrong, a base infringement on the right of individuals, and a dark stain on the American nation. Much of the support for antislavery centered on religious institutions such as Lane Seminary in Cincinnati and Oberlin College; once again, many of the supporters of the movement had New England backgrounds and connections. And once again, their activities stirred up considerable opposition in both rural and urban areas.

Abolitionists were not all middle class, and middle class northwesterners were hardly unanimous in denouncing slavery. Still, antislavery became a crucial issue in defining bourgeois culture. On the issue of slavery's morality—as opposed to its economic viability or practicality—men and women found self-definition and fellowship. Abolitionists were, as Lawrence Friedman has suggested, missionaries. Confident that God was on their side, many tried to live the exemplary life of "a Christian self-made man."[88] The war on slavery brought together the perfectionist impulse of evangelical religion and the bourgeois obsession with self-improvement. Slavery was morally wrong not only because it unjustly tyrannized blacks, but because it also made whites lazy and immoral. Antislavery, on the other hand, allowed men and women to discipline themselves by crusading for a righteous cause.

Nothing better illustrates the ways in which bourgeois reform served both personal and larger social ends than the lives of such antislavery leaders as Gamaliel Bailey, Salmon P. Chase, Joshua R. Giddings, Owen Lovejoy, and Benjamin Wade.[89] As Peter F. Walker has suggested about Chase, these "enterprising young men, obliged to live in this 'amazing' world [of Jacksonian America], helped reconcile themselves to it by taking up the cause of abolitionism."[90] Antislavery provided an avenue of self-identification through membership in a trans-local community dedicated to supposedly universal principles rather than to local idiosyncrasies. Deeply imbued with evangelicalism, this first generation of bourgeois reformers was not sheltered from "alternative" styles in the fashion of their Victorian children. Rather, according to Bertram Wyatt-Brown, they "were quite conscious of . . . the hyper-masculine and patriarchal order against which they could pose themselves as a means of self-identification. They had had to deal with fistfights, barroom temptation, and peer-group pressures as youngsters in New England."[91] No wonder then that antislavery advocates such as Salmon P. Chase acquired reputa-

key descriptor until ≈ 1850

tions as selfish, ambitious, and driven, for they were engaged in a personal quest for fame which took the form of a struggle to revise American society as a whole. Abolitionists, writes Walker,

> were less men and women desperately drumming up a coterie of true believers than they were the nineteenth-century American middle class writ in bold relief. . . . they were less tories sourly displaced from social niches of deference and respectability than they were secular paracletes offering a means for achieving self-esteem and social respectability in a marketplace society.

They were, in short, "expositors of certain 'truths' peculiar to their own circumstances and the origin of *their* time."[92]

Members of the old "gentry," on the other hand, perceived the middle-class crusade against slavery as a threat to their world. The leaders of the movement were generally newcomers or outsiders tied into business and cultural networks that transcended local areas, and thus they seemed to endanger long-standing forms of personal relationships among members of geographically defined communities. In the words of Leonard Richards, the citizens of many cities "deeply feared the invasion and development of mass media techniques, systematic agitation, and centralized organization and control."[93] People in rural and ethnic communities, where family-based cultures were still very much alive, may have felt the same way. Right or wrong, many people in the Old Northwest perceived abolitionism as a threat to local control and time-honored traditions.

The controversies surrounding public education, temperance, and abolitionism demonstrate the increasing power of middle-class ideals. More important, they reveal the degree to which the bourgeois community took shape by defining itself in opposition to existing cultural assumptions and practices. By the 1850s, the bourgeoisie in villages and cities throughout the Old Northwest had formed the most important translocal community in the region. Indeed, they were increasingly making the two synonymous: midwestern culture and bourgeois culture were one and the same. While a great many people celebrated this merging of community and geography, it is important to remember that others did not. The culture of the Midwest was the product of the interaction of several different communities and not the result of a single line of development from "backwardness" to "civilization."

Still, with the completion of transportation networks and the Old Northwest's rise to economic prominence as one of the leading agricultural regions in the world, more and more people found the social reorganization implicit in bourgeois culture appealing. A new social order, in other words, consolidated the new economic order created by the acquisitiveness of thousands of individuals. If developers and congressmen in the 1780s had attempted to integrate the Old Northwest into the emerging economic and political networks of the new republic by transforming it into a showplace of commercial agriculture, the midwestern middle class in the 1850s was attempting to make sense of that transformation by reorganizing the complex processes through which individuals simultaneously define themselves as individuals and join with others to form coherent communities.

IV

THE ORIGINS OF POLITICS IN THE OLD NORTHWEST

Recently historians have begun to restore issues and ideas to a central place in the story of the political evolution of the Old Northwest. But taking the rhetoric of political leaders seriously has not led scholars to return to the simplistic Turnerian dichotomy of democratic farmers struggling against aristocratic speculators. Rather, they argue that political conflicts reflected the interplay of economic interests and ideological beliefs.[1]

The emerging story is one of white males disagreeing over the distribution of power and the course of economic development *within* the general context of a commitment to representative government and commercial capitalism established by the Ordinance of 1787. The fundamental political struggle was not over whether the market should or would come to the Old Northwest but the degree to which traditional relationships and values would be transformed by that development. Politics became intensely important in the first half of the nineteenth century precisely because it provided the best arena in which men could discuss and make sense of changing economic and social landscapes.

1. Politics before the Transportation Revolution

By establishing the procedures by which territories could become states, the Northwest Ordinance made representative government the basis of all political structures in the Midwest. After 1787, almost no one would question the assumption that popularly chosen officials would eventually administer power in the region. The triumph of the Ordinance assured that the ultimate nature of government in the Old Northwest would be "republican" in character, meaning it would be based upon principles of popular sovereignty and balanced government.[2]

The authors of the Ordinance did not anticipate, or at least did not wish to see, the development of factionalism in the territory. As many scholars in the past several decades have pointed out, few people in the 1780s or 1790s had any notion that political parties could be useful or permanent fixtures in the American republic. To the contrary, parties were seen as signs of decay and disarray, of impending anarchy and serious stress in the social order. Men as diverse as Washington and Jefferson, moreover, tended to ascribe the origins of factionalism to the selfish actions of a few interested individuals. Parties, in other words, were the products of corruption.[3] One of the great legacies of the American Revolution was thus an intense distrust of political parties and divisions that manifested itself in efforts to reform or to destroy parties well into the nineteenth century.[4]

Despite the sincere and long-standing fear of parties, factionalism almost inevitably developed in the Northwest Territory and the territorial units subsequently created from it. By denying citizens a significant voice in the first stages of territorial development, the Ordinance actually encouraged political divisions.[5] Certainly, factionalism had long been part of the political scene in colonial America. In New York and Pennsylvania in particular, groups had formed around individuals in pursuit of a common objective. And since the territorial governments to a great degree replicated the relationship between royal governors and legislatures, it is not surprising that the actions of governors St. Clair, Harrison, and others provoked opposition.[6]

What made politics in the territories of the Old Northwest different from factionalism in the English colonies, however, was the diverse social origins of its settlers and the role of the national government. Both sparked disagreements and both also tended to draw people into alliances that transcended the boundaries of local communities.

The fact that many settlers of the region were strangers to each other made them inherently distrustful. The largely Virginia-born settlers of the Scioto Valley in Ohio, for example, simply found it difficult to get along with the New Englanders who resided in the Muskingum Valley and the Western Reserve. In the late 1790s, the Virginians sought to counter the New Englanders' influence with Governor St. Clair by forging ties with politically marginal groups. Similarly, the fact that the national government, in writing and implementing the Ordinance, took the lead in attempting to develop the Northwest angered a great many people who felt excluded from the sources of power around the territorial government. In the cases of Ohio and Indiana, governors St. Clair and Harrison both found themselves opposed by quasi-popular movements, and they countered by organizing groups loyal to them. The divisions that took shape during the territorial period, moreover, carried over into the statehood periods.[7]

As Andrew Cayton has suggested elsewhere, the rival groups were often divided by serious disagreements over the nature of government and society in the Old Northwest. In Ohio, a division developed between those committed to a proto-liberal society in which local communities and individuals were free to determine their own affairs and those who believed in the necessity of institutional restraints and orderly development. Such an ideological difference characterized the struggle between St. Clair and his opponents and carried over into arguments about the proper roles of courts, parties, and legislatures in the new state.[8]

Indeed, the most important issues separating men in the new state of Ohio before the 1820s were largely related to the working out of questions about government left unresolved by the Ordinance. Thus, the Ohioans found themselves at odds with each other over the relationship between legislatures and judges, over the capacity of individual citizens for self-government, and over the power of the national government in state affairs. The language of both Jeffersonian Republicans and Federalists in Ohio thus remained very much tied to the republican world of the American Revolution.

Yet, as Donald Ratcliffe's analyses of voting behavior in early Ohio demonstrate, politics was no longer the preserve of gentlemen. Ratcliffe argues that "the political system was . . . becoming dominated by the need to win popular support, and the wishes of constituents increasingly governed the behavior of elected representatives."[9] Ohio's political leaders, caught in fundamental disagreements about the contours of power and the social order in the new state, sought to mobilize popular support in order to win elections. Given the structures created by the Ordinance and the populist rhetoric on which Ohio had been established, they had very little choice.

In other words, whatever doubts they may have had about popular democracy, Jeffersonian Republican leaders such as Thomas Worthington embraced and perfected techniques designed to organize and rally potential supporters to victory in elections. Especially in closely contested areas, county conventions became the primary means of choosing candidates, and newspapers became the organs of particular points of view.[10] By the end of the War of 1812, in Ratcliffe's judgment, "Ohio Republicans were on the point of fully realizing the party institutions of the Jacksonian era."[11] Increasingly, Ohioans interested in achieving a common agenda found it useful to subordinate their personal goals to the discipline of party politics. As was the case in other states, then, Ohio saw the origins of parties in the efforts of elites to marshal a reliable following in order to carry their point of view.[12]

These efforts were extremely successful. Ratcliffe's close study of voting turnout in early Ohio shows a "democratic revolution" in participation with the achievement of statehood.[13] He notes a "drastic increase" in voting for the 1802 constitutional convention and even higher turnouts once the new constitution insured virtually universal white manhood suffrage.[14] The resolution of the statehood issue did not result in a return to low turnouts. If levels were lower than those in seaboard states, they almost always exceeded 40 percent in local elections, were even higher in congressional elections, and continued to grow to "undreamt of" heights in the 1820s.[15] While in their first elections Ohioans did not vote as frequently as residents of the older states, voting increased steadily, with 60 to 70 percent participating in gubernatorial elections in the 1820s and 80 to 90 percent in the 1840s.[16]

Ratcliffe ascribes this steady growth in popular political participation to the high level of political conflict. In closely contested elections, men organized and agitated with increased enthusiasm. Such had been the case almost from the beginning in Ohio. The "Federalist revival" of 1807 to 1815 failed to save that group's political fortunes, but the resulting partisan conflict served an important role in political development by "alarming Republicans and enforcing their unity."[17]

While there is ample evidence, then, to argue that white males in the Old Northwest increasingly turned to partisan politics as the best means of acquiring and maintaining power, it is important to remember that the emergence of parties was far from complete. Conventions and high voter turnout demonstrate that partisan feelings were often intense, but they do not demonstrate the acceptance of partisanship as a permanent feature of life in the Old Northwest.

Many early party leaders felt decidedly ambivalent about partisanship. Clearly, Ohio Federalists were reluctant to politicize the masses of white men and so open up the political game to more than a small elite group. But Republicans very often felt the same. Men such as Worthington and Edward Tiffin were never quite certain what to make of their organization; it was a useful tool, yes, but rarely did they think of it as anything more than a means to an end.[18]

Through the early 1820s, political leaders in Ohio and Indiana remained committed to older conceptions of politics. They usually thought and acted in local terms; their organizations were more highly developed at the county than at the state level. Men continued to think of politics as colonial elites had, as the duty or business of gentlemen. Ohio's Jeffersonian Republican leader Thomas Worthington had little more trust in the people than did his Federalist opponents. What distinguished him and his colleagues was their belief that the people, properly educated and guided, could decide who was best qualified to lead them. But governing would be left to gentlemen. Indeed, it was Worthington's basic distrust of the people, intensified by his perception of vague popular support for the Burr Conspiracy and the continuing appeal of Federalist candidates in Ohio, that made him a strong advocate of political organization and discipline. He and his allies even established wigwams of the secret Tammany Society in Ohio in 1810. Their goal was to restrict true decision making to small groups of men who knew and trusted each other.[19]

Politics, in short, remained very much a *personal* affair. Loyalties often reflected patronage ties to local or national leaders, based on what in the eighteenth century was called "friendship." Men were personally loyal to someone they admired in a position of power; they deferred to him, served him, and expected to be appropriately rewarded. The classic pattern of this behavior in the Old Northwest was set by territorial officials and supporters who cultivated George Washington in the 1790s. Powerful men such as Arthur St. Clair and Winthrop Sargent dutifully wrote what we would now consider obsequious letters to the president (and Alexander Hamilton) proclaiming their fealty to the man and his measures. They received many favors in return, most notably in the form of lucrative new appointments.[20]

Such behavior was hardly limited to Federalists. The Republican organization in Ohio grew out of Thomas Worthington's personal friendships with men throughout the state; Worthington's power in turn depended on his powerful friends in Washington, D.C. As much as political organization and popular politicization took place—and they are central to understanding the origins of politics in the region—personal loyalties remained more important than impersonal party ties.[21]

The local nature of politics reinforced its personal character. In the early nineteenth century, Ohio politics revolved around struggles among the diverse regional cultures in the state. New Englanders in the Muskingum Valley and the Western Reserve tended to vote for Federalists or "conservative" Republicans hostile to Worthington, while the Virginians in the Scioto Valley remained strongly committed to more "radical" Republicans. In this sense, personal and regional loyalties fused as partisanship involved contests of local communities led or represented by prominent local figures.[22]

Finally, Ohio's political leaders in the early nineteenth century by and large tended to see organization as a means of destroying their opponents. St. Clair and Worthington did not expect to exchange power in a civilized game of "ins" and "outs." They frightened each other; they saw their opponents as enemies who threatened social stability and republican government. Political organization, then, was not an end itself. Few Ohioans praised parties or called for their institutionalization; on the contrary, they attacked and scorned them.[23]

Unfortunately, there are fewer recent studies of the origins of politics in Indiana and Illinois than there are for Ohio. Yet our sketchy information suggests similar patterns. Indiana politics before the 1830s, according to James Madison, was based upon personal and sectional rivalries. The most conspicuous leaders—Jonathan Jennings, William Hendricks, and James Noble—were popular men from different parts of the state. Politics, as a result, was marked by little campaigning, little organization, and a strong aversion to parties. Indeed, it was not until the late 1820s that "rising party loyalty began to challenge personal loyalty as a prime engine in political contests."[24]

2. Politics Out-of-Doors

The political leaders of the Old Northwest in the early nineteenth century remained wrapped in the mantle of republicanism, arguing about questions of individual character and social order that were not particularly compelling to many people in their states. White males in the communities of the Old Northwest, meanwhile, continued to practice more tried and true ways of exercising power. Before 1819, when the market had only marginally penetrated the region, many men simply took matters into their own hands, either individually or collectively. They remained committed to far more personal and direct means of protecting their interests and defending their reputation.

Good examples of this kind of behavior would be the rough-and-tumble fighting described by Elliott Gorn. While writing primarily about the southern frontier in the early nineteenth century, Gorn's observations about the importance of physical fighting to lower-class white males can be extended north of the Ohio River. Settlers from the South brought the oral, personal, kin-based culture of their home region to the new states of Ohio, Indiana, and Illinois. We know that a great many brought a strong interest in extending slavery into the Old Northwest. It is also possible that they brought "a taste for violence and personal vengeance" with them as well.[25] They would fight to protect their own reputation or that of their kin—and do so by deliberately challenging the genteel style of gentlemen. "A rough-and-tumble was more than a poor man's duel, a botched version of genteel combat," argues Gorn. "While the gentleman's code of honor insisted on cool restraint, eye gougers gloried in unvarnished brutality."[26]

We have few serious studies of such behavior in the Old Northwest, although brawlers and sharpshooters are stock figures in old accounts. The appearance of these lower-class men is usually associated with disorderly conditions on the frontier or along rivers.[27] Yet it seems likely that such behavior represented a distinctive cultural perspective, not simply a lack of "civilization."

For men who settled disputes in duels or fights, the foremost issues were not republican government or the nature of the social order, but their own position in a local, largely oral society. What concerned them was the protection of their good names from insults. They proved their value—their power—through fights, wrestling matches, shooting contests, and a variety of other tests of skills. They entertained themselves by telling stories and teasing each other, and by competing with each other for prizes and respect. But these activities were not for pleasure alone. Rather, they enabled men whose concerns were limited to a fixed time and place to demonstrate power and acquire respect in direct, often physical, ways.[28]

We can only speculate on the meaning of such encounters to participants. But condemnations of lower-class rowdiness by custodians of bourgeois culture in the mid-nineteenth century suggest a powerful revulsion from an alien and threatening way of life. Middle-class reformers sought to redeem the characters of the farmers, hunters, boatmen, and immigrants who spent far more time drinking, talking, and wrestling than engaging in "honest" labor.[29]

We might explore this issue further in the area of white-Indian relations. In many cases, violent individual or small group encounters between Indians and American frontiersmen fit the pattern Gorn describes. To be sure, conflict over land and other economic resources was crucial. But the ways in which "backwoodsmen" dealt with the Indians suggest that conceptions of honor may have played a role as well. Much to the chagrin of territorial officials and military officers, frontiersmen subverted any possibility of peace with the Indians by engaging in a never-ending cycle of aggressions and reprisals.[30]

Throughout the 1780s and 1790s, supporters of national authority in and out of the territory denounced the "barbaric" and "anarchic" behavior of Kentuckians and Scots-Irish settlers toward the Indians. They frowned upon locally organized expeditions and expressed outrage when whites practiced "uncivilized" brutality against the Indians. The most famous example was the 1782 massacre of Christian Delawares at Gnadenhutten.[31] Regular army officers such as Josiah Harmar and Anthony Wayne were appalled by the refusal of Kentucky militiamen to submit to discipline and to follow orders during the campaigns of the 1790s. Repeatedly, frontier residents were dismissed as little more than "white Indians."[32]

Because the authors of the Ordinance were most concerned with the intertwined social and economic development of the West, they worried that the "irregular" behavior of frontiersmen threatened the future of the region. And they were right to do so. But it is important to remember that frontiersmen often acted out of different cultural contexts. If they were uncivilized by the standards of congressmen, they were not so by the standards of the frontier. Both Indians and whites in the Ohio Valley lived in a world that was centered on kin and local community. They did not eagerly embrace the means for resolving disputes devised and sanctioned by territorial officials. On the frontier, law was neither the written word of a distant Congress nor the edict of an appointed judge. Rather, it was the often implicitly shared assumptions of peoples living in small communities that put a premium on the defense of individual reputation and family honor. In such a world, the philosophy of an "eye for an eye" made far more sense than negotiations, written agreements, and military discipline.[33]

If residents of the Old Northwest exercised power against the Indians in direct and personal ways, they often responded in similar fashion to whites whose behavior or values seemed to threaten the sanctity of local communities. Mobs were far from uncommon in the nineteenth-century Midwest; at various times and places, citizens rioted against public officials, bank officers, reformers, and religious sects. In 1800, for example, a group of men in Chillicothe tried to attack Governor St. Clair, who was staying in a tavern; cooler heads eventually prevailed but not before a knife was drawn and heated words exchanged.[34] Later in the decade, at Union Village near Lebanon, Ohio, there were serious riots against Shakers, who were feared because their practice of celibacy and separation of the sexes seemed a direct threat to the sanctity of the family.[35]

Even into the 1830s and 1840s mobs continued to act against abolitionists, Mormons, Catholics, and others. Hostility to Mormons was particularly intense. In the 1830s, people around the Saints' settlement at Kirtland, Ohio, verbally and physically harassed them until they moved to Missouri. There the Mormons encountered even more violence, climaxing in the deaths of eighteen people at the hands of an 1838 mob at Haun's Mill. The Mormons moved on to Illinois where they established a large and prosperous community at Nauvoo. But peace did not last long. Suspicious of the Mormons' intentions and rumors of polygamy (another clear threat to the family), a mob in Carthage, Illinois, murdered the imprisoned leaders Joseph and Hyrum Smith in June 1844. Other groups attacked and destroyed the property of Mormons in the area. The result for the Mormons was the long trek to the Salt Lake in 1847.[36]

Traditionally, historians have ascribed such behavior to the rawness and looseness of "frontier" society. But other forces may have been at work. While we know far too little about the character of these mobs, the works of Pauline Maier, Paul Gilje, and Leonard Richards suggest that the mobs were probably not simply disorganized rabble. Crowd activity in the urban East, at least, was generally purposeful: riots—whatever the specific issues that sparked them—often involved diverse segments of a community in a violent but not disorganized defense of traditional customs or local rights. Certainly, Richards's study of anti-abolitionist mobs in Cincinnati and Alton, Illinois, in the 1830s supports this generalization.[37]

In other words, mob activity, like "unauthorized" Indian raids, may have been less the product of frontier barbarism than the continuing commitment of many residents of the region to traditional means of defending family and community. The larger point is that the practice of personal, direct justice, whether it took the form of the individual fights described by Gorn or of group actions against threatening people, represented an alternative organization and expression of power to that implicit in the Ordinance of 1787. Despite the phenomenal growth of political parties in the early nineteenth century as well as the increasing power of courts in resolving routine disputes, many residents of the Old Northwest continued to adhere to more direct and violent ways of exercising power.[38]

3. The Jacksonian Party System

Still, there is no question about the increasing importance of the party as the major means of exercising power in the nineteenth-century Midwest. The period between 1820 and 1860 was in many ways the heyday of partisan political parties. Huge percentages of white males voted, elections were often very close, and voters were intensely committed to their party. Harry Watson, in his study of the "Second American Party System" in one North Carolina county, argues that the emergence of mass parties was "the largest social movement of its day, far more widely appealing than any romantic reform movement and even more pervasive than religious revivalism."[39]

Much of the credit for the triumph of parties lies in the groundwork laid by early political leaders, who, in their efforts to eliminate each other, unwittingly developed institutions and mechanisms that made factions permanent. More important, however, was the transformation wrought by the increasing power of the market. As we noted in chapter two, it was only in the 1820s and 1830s that the transportation revolution tied the Old Northwest directly into the national economy. With that revolution came a rise in the importance of trans-local contacts and networks and the emergence of a bourgeois core in many communities committed to the region's economic and social development. Not surprisingly, the pursuit of economic interest carried some people into new kinds of relationships that transcended local community and family.

Historians from Frederick Jackson Turner to Donald Ratcliffe have pointed to the Panic of 1819 as a turning point in the political history of the West. Traditionally, scholars have noted that the collapse of the Bank of the United States and subsequent bank failures and foreclosures politicized large numbers of men, who saw partisan activity, particularly in support of the presidential candidacy of Andrew Jackson in 1824 and 1828, as the best means of redressing their personal economic grievances. In the process, they democratized politics, attacking the vestiges of aristocratic corruption and privilege and demanding full participation for all white males. In reaction to this spurt of populism, local notables and sober middle-class entrepreneurs slowly and belatedly organized what became the Whig party in the 1830s.[40]

The impetus behind this politicization came from a growing realization of the importance of the market. The Panic of 1819 and the following depression did not merely frighten people; it demonstrated the degree to which economic and political decisions made far beyond the local community had an impact on everyone's lives. In many ways, the major question that faced the people of the Old Northwest in the three decades following the panic was how to deal with the changes brought by the market revolution. Not surprisingly, the emphasis in politics shifted in the 1820s from issues of republican government and social character to economic ones, especially internal improvements, banks, and land policies. The question was no longer whether the West would be developed economically or whether its residents could perform as republican citizens. Rather, it was precisely how the commercial development of the region should take place. Watson put his finger on the fundamental question of Jacksonian politics when he concluded that "voters had to decide how they wanted their community to fit into the rapidly developing world of international capitalism."[41]

Watson's framework allows us to synthesize the two most powerful interpretations of politics in this era in the Old Northwest. For the past three decades, historians have argued about the primacy of ethno-cultural and economic factors in determining voter behavior. Ronald Formisano's study of parties in Michigan from 1827 to the Civil War and Stephen Fox's work on Ohio represent the best statements of the ethno-cultural thesis, while Donald Ratcliffe and James R. Sharp's analyses of voting patterns in Ohio epitomize the economic interpretation.[42]

Proponents of both views have sought to buttress their arguments with hard, quantifiable data. The results of their work are evident in the growing sophistication of our understanding of Jacksonian politics in the Midwest and elsewhere; indeed most of what we will say about parties builds on their evidence and conclusions. Still, the motivations of voters remain elusive: any successful interpretation of Jacksonian politics must recognize the fluidity and ambiguity of party loyalties.[43]

This conclusion is amply supported by Kenneth J. Winkle's The Politics of Community, an imaginative study of the relationship between migration and politics in antebellum Ohio. Successfully blending social and political history, Winkle's analysis of one community suggests that "most eligible voters . . . moved at least once in the decade before the Civil War, and they moved long distances." The result of this "sometimes startling mobility" was to keep "local electorates in constant motion."[44] Most significant in the long run were the ways in which massive migration forced a redefinition of suffrage. In early nineteenth-century Ohio, the right to vote was determined by residence in a township; since elections were like "meetings," migrants often were at a disadvantage. "Newcomers . . . cast ballots," writes Winkle, "subject only to the approval of all the other voters present."[45] Physical residence was not enough. But ultimately, widespread migration forced revision of this rule. According to Winkle, suffrage was transformed from a "consensual" to a "volitional" process. "By 1859 the transition . . . was complete: Intention now meant everything, and physical presence had virtually no meaning at all. The individual belonged simply because he *wanted* to belong."[46] Suffrage was redefined to accommodate a world of highly mobile citizens. Winkle's work clearly demonstrates the inherent difficulties in attempting to analyze voting patterns in a constantly fluctuating environment.

Still, by focusing on political developments in the Jacksonian era as responses to the expansion of the market brought about by the transportation revolution, we can develop an interpretative framework that accounts for ambiguity and complexity in political behavior. The major political issues in politics in Ohio, Indiana, and Illinois between 1819 and the late 1840s centered on economic concerns. There was a high degree of interest in national questions such as the role of the Second Bank of the United States and the need for a protective tariff. On the state level, politics focused on internal improvements, bank charters, and paper money. The debates over all of these issues reflected conflicting visions of how the development of the nation and the region should take place. In some cases, "symbolic issues" with no immediate impact on voters' economic interests galvanized far-reaching debate about the growth of the market and its implications for society. Watson suggests that party battles were not between "exploiters" and "victims" but between "rival communities" struggling for "predominance." Thus politics in Jacksonian America continued the debate initiated by the authors of the Northwest Ordinance over the development of the region. Given the diversity of settlers and the spectrum of attitudes toward commercial capitalism we have discussed in previous chapters, it is not surprising that the debate was intense.[47]

Banks raised the greatest controversy in the Old Northwest in the 1820s, 1830s, and 1840s. Nothing was more critical for the economic development of the region than banks: they provided a medium of exchange that facilitated trade and were sources of credit for the purchase of land and other entrepreneurial activity. Banks had appeared in Ohio shortly after statehood and were integral to the growth of the state's economy.[48] But the Panic of 1819 and the resulting depression focused hostile attention on banking institutions, especially the branch of the Second Bank of the United States in Cincinnati. The Bank's contraction of the money supply and energetic pursuit of debtors gave it the reputation of a "monster" unresponsive to popular wishes. Partly because directors of its local branches were often prominent citizens, moreover, the Bank became known to some as an "aristocratical" institution, a bulwark of privilege and injustice. State-chartered banks in Ohio and other states acquired similar reputations.[49]

Anti-bank sentiment in the Old Northwest during this period reflected a pervasive ambivalence about the market in general. Northwesterners wanted to take advantage of bank credit, but resisted the resulting loss of control over their own economic lives. Banks were the most visible symbols of the increasing power of commercial capitalism in the region. In the 1820s, many men were simultaneously repelled by and attracted to them; by the 1830s, with President Andrew Jackson's "war" on the Bank and the devastating impact of the Panic of 1837, divergent positions on banks emerged. The Jacksonian, or Democratic, party, was increasingly antagonistic to banks and paper money, seeing them as tools of corrupt aristocrats. Among the Democrats, however, there was a developing division between soft and hard money men, with the former taking a more moderate position. Meanwhile, the Whigs, a political coalition that took shape in the mid-1830s in direct opposition to Jackson's veto of the recharter of the Bank, favored banks and paper money as necessary to the development of the Old Northwest.[50]

In the 1840s, positions hardened. In all the states in the region, "hard" Democrats moved to complete distrust of banks. According to William G. Shade, they acted "out of a faith that the 'natural laws of trade' would easily assure honesty if corporate privileges were removed and small notes eliminated." On the other hand, Whigs stressed "economic development. Banks and bank credit could serve a dynamic function in the developmental process."[51] Both, in short, were "necessary to the process of civilization."[52]

What Jacksonians and Democrats were debating was more than the value of banks. They were engaged in a national argument over the completion and refinement of the plans of the men who had written the Northwest Ordinance and tried to implement it in the 1790s. The plans of late eighteenth-century developers and promoters had largely lain dormant until the transportation revolution that began in the 1820s fulfilled their dreams of linking the West to the East and making the region the center of a great commercial empire.

Yet, if the debate over economic development took place within the general framework laid out in the Ordinance, there was ample scope for controversy over its proper direction. For decades, historians saw little to separate Jacksonians and Whigs; they were, in the view of scholars as diverse as Richard Hofstadter and Bray Hammond, all entrepreneurs.[53] From Marvin Meyers, we learned that the political rhetoric of the Jacksonian era expressed deep-seated anxiety about rapid change.[54] Ethno-cultural historians such as Lee Benson acknowledged differences between the parties but attributed them less to substantive policy differences than to the choices of "negative reference groups."[55] Finally, Edward Pessen has devoted much of his career to pointing out the contradictions between rhetoric and reality among party leaders, noting that they were all elitists to one extent or another.[56]

But recent scholars have shown that there were fundamental differences between the two parties, differences rooted in a complex interaction of cultural, personal, and economic factors with the spread of the market. What was at issue was opposing world views or visions of the future as powerful as those held by statesmen in the 1780s and 1790s. Certainly that is the thrust of Watson's study of Cumberland County, North Carolina, J. Mills Thornton's analysis of antebellum Alabama politics, and other recent work.[57]

In his sensitive study of *The Political Culture of the American Whigs*, Daniel Walker Howe assesses the importance of culture and class in antebellum political ideology. Whigs were concerned with more than economic development; they were also interested in achieving cultural uniformity by transforming heterogeneous, localistic Americans into suitable members of a bourgeois society. In their concern with the promotion of social as well as economic development, the Whigs were the heirs of the developers of the 1780s; they differed only in seeking to foster bourgeois rather than republican character. Howe notes the defining characteristics of Whigs as "their moral absolutism, their paternalism, and their concern with imposing discipline. . . . To put things very broadly, the Whigs proposed a society that would be economically diverse but culturally uniform." The Democrats, on the other hand, "preferred the economic uniformity of a society of small farmers and artisans but were more tolerant of cultural and moral diversity."[58] Howe and Watson agree that the Whigs were the innovators, the spokesmen for the new economic order, while the Democrats remained committed to laissez-faire principles that allowed for local sovereignty and differences. Put in class terms, Whigs tended to be representatives of the new bourgeois order, while Democrats tended to be more traditional and local in their values.

What evidence we have suggests that this general framework held true in the Old Northwest. Whigs were committed to development and Democrats to democracy for white males. The social bases of support for their positions indicate a welding of cultural and economic influences. James R. Sharp has shown that support for Whigs and soft Democrats in Ohio was strongest in areas of "highly commercialized or incipient industrial constituencies" (with the exception of Cincinnati where hostility to banks remained strong); regions "outside or peripherally in the market economy" remained loyal to the Democracy.[59]

William Shade's study of Illinois voting suggests that southern-born farmers living in the older, southern sections of the state "formed the core of opposition to banks."[60] Shade found similar patterns in Indiana and Ohio.[61] Throughout the region "well-off businessmen," especially merchants, were "probably" Whigs, as were, "to a lesser extent," manufacturers and "other entrepreneurs."[62] While Shade rejects any class-based interpretation of support for parties, he notes the clear influence of the market and social origins. Whigs were generally "commercial-minded" Yankee Protestants, while Democrats were generally "agrarian-minded" southerners.[63]

Among historians working on the political history of the Old Northwest in recent decades, Ronald Formisano is the most persuasive in rejecting socioeconomic differences as the basis of party disputes in the 1830s and 1840s. Indeed, Formisano believes that the parties in Michigan agreed "on the basics of political economy."[64] Formisano attributes party affiliation to differences in ethnic background and religious beliefs of ordinary voters, not in the rhetoric and policies of party elites. Politics in antebellum Michigan thus revolved around "antagonistic relations between political subcultures."[65] Formisano stresses the importance of "negative reference groups" in explaining the voting patterns in Michigan. The Whigs attracted the support of New England-born evangelicals, while the Democrats appealed to other, generally hostile groups. In Formisano's view, questions of "alien suffrage" counted for more than economic issues in determining party lines.[66]

Formisano's findings, however, are not incompatible with those of Sharp and Shade. In fact, there is reason to believe that ethnic and religious views reinforced economic positions. Given our understanding of middle-class culture, it is not surprising that Whigs would be the proponents of both economic development and social homogeneity. Whigs, as Shade has argued, saw government "as a tool the people could use to create the necessary conditions for commercial as well as moral progress."[67]

Formisano is undoubtedly right that cultural questions lay at the heart of popular political allegiances. But he is wrong to insist on the incompatibility of economic issues and cultural concerns. The banking question was not as explosive an issue in Michigan as elsewhere in the 1830s and 1840s, because the new state was not as economically developed as its southern neighbors. Surrounded by the lakes, Michigan did not embark on a plan of internal improvements. As Formisano notes, "the canal-building bonanza that affected some Western states left Michigan almost untouched." The "transportation revolution," in short, "came to Michigan only piecemeal."[68] Farmers continued to take products to markets in 1860 much as they had in 1837. Interestingly, Michigan had only negligible bank capital in the late 1840s and just one million dollars worth by the mid-1850s. In contrast, Ohio had eight million in 1854, Indiana, over seven million in 1855, and Illinois almost six million in 1857.[69]

If "Michigan society in 1860 resembled that of 1837 in all essentials," it is hardly surprising that the debate over the implications of the market revolution raging in Ohio, Indiana, and Illinois was muted in the Wolverine state.[70] Because economic issues were not as pressing, the cultural differences that underlay much of the political and social life of the Old Northwest came to the fore more easily. It seems clear that the social origins of residents of the region, most particularly their economic practices and their religious preferences, had a vast impact on the way they voted. In many states, economic issues simply served to spark and organize those feelings into clear positions on issues such as banking. But in Michigan they stood out on their own.

Thus it might be better to think of the division between Whig and Jacksonian less in North-South terms and more as a split between people who embraced the economic and social implications of the market revolution and those who persisted in adhering to traditional customs and notions of family and community life. Oddly enough, this conflict of values and goals shows up most decisively in their respective attitudes toward the institution of parties themselves. The leaders of political organization in the Midwest as elsewhere in the nation, by and large, were the Jacksonians. The same men who were committed to local sovereignty and laissez-faire led in the development of techniques that united men in trans-local ties for the achievement of a common agenda. Conversely, the Whigs, as Ronald Formisano and Stephen Fox have shown, were much more ambivalent about the party as an institution and much less likely to engage in strict party discipline.[71] Why did the same men who were apparently far more involved in the trans-local networks of business and voluntary associations than their opponents drag their heels when it came to party organization? Why, in the area of mass political parties, were the localists the innovators?

The answer lies in the very nature of the two groups. The Whigs were far more homogeneous culturally than their opponents. While not all men who voted for Whig candidates were members of the emerging bourgeoisie, significant numbers were. Heavily influenced by evangelical Protestantism, Whigs tended to be committed more to moral reform than to political victory. Their campaigns, in the words of Daniel Walker Howe, had "something of the flavor of religious revivals." In fact, argues Howe, Whigs were "disciplinarians" whose "electoral campaigns formed part of a cultural struggle to impose on the United States the standards of morality we usually term Victorian. They were the standards of self-control and restraint, which dovetailed with the economic program of the party, for they emphasized thrift, sobriety, and public responsibility."[72]

In other words, the most likely Whig voters in the Midwest were middle-class citizens in small towns and cities. James R. Sharp found in Ohio in the 1840s "a high correlation between wealth and Whiggery and lack of wealth and support for the Democrats." In a study of ninety-seven members of the Wayne County, Michigan, elite in 1844, Alexandra McCoy identified 62 percent of them as Whigs, 29 percent Democrats, 5 percent Liberty party, and 4 percent unknown.[73] In *Sugar Creek*, John Mack Faragher concluded that "the foundation of Whig support in the community . . . remained the 'better sort.'" Still, Whigs attracted the support of the rural poor with cultural appeals and strong organization centering on local churches.[74] In Jacksonville, Illinois, "'solvent merchants,' who opposed Jackson's attack on banks . . . joined New Englanders . . . to form the core of a large Whig majority in the town."[75] Finally, Kenneth Winkle's study of local political culture in Ohio reveals that in the constitutional convention of 1850, Whigs supported "election rules that disfranchised newcomers, while Democrats proposed rules that favored migrants."[76] In other words, Whigs knew that their support was strongest among the persistent middle-class cores of local communities.

The Whigs' overt moralism and their commitment to the spread of a homogeneous culture in America complemented their concern with the economic and social implications of the market revolution. The same people who celebrated enterprise and changes in family structure were also committed to the achievement of social transformation through politics. Support for banks, for the leadership of an educated elite of character, and for the cluster of bourgeois values centering on self-control were cut from the same cloth. What they all involved was acceptance of the changes wrought by the transportation revolution. This world was not precisely the one envisioned by the authors of the Northwest Ordinance—they had not fully recognized the social implications of the economic development they were calling for—but it was close enough.

Because the Whigs were more homogeneous, because they were people involved in all kinds of trans-local networks based on business and religion, they felt profound ambivalence about parties. As a group they detested the corruption and compromise that they associated with the political process. Self-righteous and deeply committed to specific causes, Whigs were less likely to accept electoral defeat and more likely to desert the party over specific issues than their opponents. Anti-masons and anti-slavery men found only temporary havens in Whiggery.

If many Whigs harbored what Ronald Formisano has termed anti-party feelings, it was not necessarily because they were old-fashioned elitists unwilling to accept change. On the contrary, the middle-class voters who made up the bulk of Whig support in the 1830s and 1840s were part of a dynamic social movement. They were the people with a specific agenda, with a positive program for the economic, social, and cultural development of America. They looked upon the political party as an occasionally useful means to the achievement of the new order. But, by and large, they were more comfortable with moral crusades. That their deep sense of righteous commitment often made it impossible to remain within the confines of a party does not make them anachronistic or idiosyncratic. It simply identifies them with a conception of the uses of power which diverged from the still relatively novel notion that partisan political activity was itself a positive good.

But if the Whigs were the men most willing to embrace change, why was the political party a lasting innovation of the Jacksonians? The answer is that the Jacksonians were a coalition united by little more than the determination to defeat the institutions and values of the Whigs. From its beginning in the 1790s, the Democratic party was the home of many different kinds of people, or what a historian of antebellum Ohio politics has called "near-permanent sub-groups."[77] From the beginning the Democracy therefore required stricter organization than its more homogeneous opposition, whether Federalist or Whig. The social base of the Jacksonians, moreover, was among people whose commitment to the market and to trans-local networks was weak. Where the typical Whig might have been a merchant in a small town involved in business and religious relationships far beyond the borders of his community, the typical Jacksonian was a farmer or laborer whose world was pretty much locally defined. The party became the means by which diverse, local men combined to fight against the Whigs' agenda.

The Jacksonians, moreover, seemed to thrive in the competitive, partisan world of politics that seemed little removed from traditional, masculine culture of personal fights and personal honor. They admired Andrew Jackson as much for his physical defenses of his reputation as for his supposed championing of the common man. Jacksonian political organization, in other words, not only united diverse, locally oriented men whose ties to the market may have been marginal; it provided a means for channeling and extending a rough and tough masculine culture. In partisan contests, men found a new, ritualized, stylized version of the duel or gouging contest.

These themes are fully revealed in the life of the most successful Democratic leader in the antebellum Midwest, Stephen Douglas of Illinois. As his biographer Robert W. Johannsen has shown, Douglas in the 1830s and 1840s made his political career by stressing the importance of party discipline and organization. Running campaigns to attract votes from both southern farmers and Irish Catholic canal workers, Douglas stressed popular (or local) sovereignty and a laissez-faire approach to values and practices. In other words, he formed a coalition by insisting that government (and by extension, the Whigs) should leave people alone.

But his appeal was not all negative. Douglas believed that the political party was a useful institution for people who otherwise felt excluded from the key economic and social networks in their society. In style as well as rhetoric he appealed to people whose values diverged from the bourgeois self-control model. Often compared to "a prizefighter," Douglas thrived in a rough-and-tumble political world in which oratory was considered as much a test of strength, endurance, and manhood as a demonstration of ideas.[78] The "Little Giant" rose to power by displaying his manliness in ways that aped even as they restrained the violent tendencies of less prominent men.

Douglas was completely committed to party discipline. Only through organization could the disparate Democratic coalition stand a chance against the Whigs. According to Johannsen, he "had only one objective, the triumph of his party." Throughout his life, he possessed an "almost obsessive insistence on party regularity." Like other Jacksonian leaders, Douglas made politics his career. For him, it "was a trade, and he pursued it with a single-minded devotion."[79]

Without pressing the analogy too far, it is possible to suggest that the Jacksonian Democrats appealed—both in style and substance—to men who wanted to resist the social implications of the market revolution. That is not to say that they were opposed to capitalism. Simply put, they did not want the economic revolution to become a cultural one as well. Whigs, on the other hand, tended to embrace both revolutions. Within the general context of the coming of commercial capitalism to the Old Northwest, the Democrats were the champions of localism, personal honor, and freedom from a trans-local aristocracy of bankers, merchants, and reformers, while the Whigs stood for the remaking of character as well as the economy according to the dictates of a national, bourgeois culture.

In sum, then, politics in the Old Northwest originated in conflicts over the meaning of the economic and physical changes sweeping the region in the first half of the nineteenth century. From the beginning, political campaigns revolved around serious issues. The question was never the classic Turnerian one of democracy versus aristocracy; nor were the parties, as the Turnerians' critics would have it, virtually indistinguishable. Within the general commitment established by the authors of the Ordinance of 1787 to economic development and representative government, residents of the states created from the Northwest Territory debated the merits of contrary visions of the region's future. Two dominant perspectives eventually emerged. The first, identified most strongly with the Whigs, embraced the ways in which the transportation revolution was transforming community and family as well as economic activity. The second, associated with the Jacksonians, attempted to reap the benefits of commercial capitalism while resisting the social implications of its triumph.

For most white males in the 1840s, the party had become the perfect voluntary society: it organized groups of highly mobile strangers into powerful coalitions dedicated to the achievement of certain general goals. It united men who were rarely personally acquainted with each other in ties that transcended local communities. But from a longer perspective the political party had become a vehicle of cultural definition. For what formed the basis of political organization was a sense of sharing assumptions about the ways in which the world worked. Through politics men made sense of social and economic developments and attempted to secure first the legitimacy and then the hegemony of their interpretation of them.

V

THE POLITICS OF CULTURAL DEFINITION

By the 1850s, the intertwined economic and social structures of commercial capitalism clearly dominated the Old Northwest. To a variable but significant degree, nearly everyone was involved in production for the market. Interlocking networks of small town and urban merchants, professionals, shopkeepers, clerks, skilled workmen, and their wives and daughters had emerged as the primary proponents and interpreters of the new social order. Imbued with the pietistic spirit of evangelical Christianity and deeply committed to an ideology of self-improvement as the cornerstone of the larger social order, they had located the keys to their culture—the ways in which individuals identified themselves in relation to others—in hundreds of voluntary societies, in an increasingly rigid separation of the public male-dominated world of business and the private female-dominated world of the home, and in a vision of the good society as one which respected personal independence, hard work, and equality of opportunity. This middle-class culture found its fullest political expression in the Republican party, which originated and came to national power in the 1850s.[1]

On one level, what we are describing is nothing more than the articulation of a class-based ideology prevalent throughout much of the northern United States and western Europe in what Eric Hobsbawm has called "the Age of Capital."[2] But bourgeois values had particular resonance in the Old Northwest. The region was born and took shape with the ascendancy of commercial capitalism in the United States. By the 1850s, the vision of the authors of the Ordinance of 1787 had reached fruition: the Old Northwest was the very model of a highly developed commercial society fully integrated into national economic and political structures.

As Peter S. Onuf has argued elsewhere, many prominent northwesterners were aware of their region's success story. They celebrated the population and prosperity of the Ordinance states as the fulfillment of the American founders' design for an expanding empire of liberty. They believed that the Midwest embodied American culture; it *was* the United

States, the truest and fullest expression of a liberal, capitalistic society. The apotheoses of middle-class values and the Midwest were one and inseparable. If the Old Northwest had become a distinctive region, it was only because other areas of the nation had not kept pace with it. The creation of a national territory in the 1780s had led to a society that eighty years later considered itself the national norm.[3]

To suggest that the white urban, Protestant middle class of small towns and cities dominated the nineteenth-century Midwest is *not* to suggest that the region was homogeneous or consensual, however. Perhaps the most striking fact about the history of the Midwest in the second half of the nineteenth century is the constant struggle among all its peoples over the ways in which they should live their lives. Ironically, the existence of such serious debate was critical to the definition and preservation of the larger liberal, capitalistic economic and social order. If the values of the white middle class dominated the region, it was because conflict took place largely within the parameters of its ideology and because the persistence of conflict confirmed the legitimacy of that ideology. The most important source of disagreement was divergent interpretations of the social and political implications of a liberal, capitalistic society, not the viability of capitalism itself.[4] In short, the greatest measure of the hegemony of bourgeois values was the degree to which relatively powerless communities—farmers, laborers, women, blacks—laid claim to them in the late nineteenth century.[5]

1. The Origins of the Republican Party

The 1850s witnessed one of the most significant political realignments in American history. Out of the collapse of the Jacksonian-Whig party system eventually emerged a new political entity—the Republican party —strongly associated with the Midwest. No other region of the United States identified itself so thoroughly with the Republican party in the last half of the nineteenth century. The source of the party's appeal was that it was the political embodiment of the values and aspirations of the American middle class. Republicans defined themselves in the 1850s largely through attacks on negative reference groups, immigrants and southerners in particular. But in so doing they celebrated the virtues of free labor and bourgeois domesticity. And not surprisingly the party attracted hundreds of thousands of adherents throughout the Old Northwest almost overnight. Through the politics of cultural definition, the region and the party came of age together.

The late 1840s and 1850s was a period of tremendous growth in the immigrant population of the United States. Between 1846 and 1854, al-

most three million foreigners came to America; together they constituted
14.5 percent of the country's population in 1845.[6] The number of immigrants to the United States in 1847 alone amounted to one-third of the
total number of people who had emigrated between 1819 and 1840.[7]
Seventy-eight percent of the new arrivals were German or Irish. Overwhelmingly Catholic, they were also often poor and unskilled. In search
of prosperous farmlands or jobs in construction and industry, thousands
of Germans and Irish surged into cities such as Cincinnati, Milwaukee,
Chicago, and Cleveland as well as the countryside. In 1850, 44 percent
of Cincinnati's population was foreign-born; 26 percent were Germans
and 12 percent Irish.[8]

In many respects, immigrant communities strongly resembled those of
native white Americans; foreign-born citizens were just as geographically
mobile and as occupationally stratified.[9] Germans tended to live in distinct geographic areas, while the Irish and native-born increasingly congregated more along class rather than ethnic lines. Although the Germans of Milwaukee did not constitute an insular ghetto, Kathleen Neils
Conzen shows that they "managed to create a community on the basis
of a similar language, residential propinquity, and common attitudes toward the enjoyment of life."[10] The German community had its own voluntary societies, associations formed around church ties (whether Protestant or Catholic), sporting events, and cultural activities. But German
groups seemed less committed to the moral reform of individual members of society than to the construction of a sense of community that
would benefit and protect its members. Despite differences, they "evolved
a satisfying alternative society of their own."[11]

Nowhere did the German community reveal its power more than in
the political arena. While they did not constitute a monolithic group or
machine, Germans were able to marshal the political power to defend and
assert their ethnicity, which Conzen calls "a language, a neighborhood,
a set of associations within which friends were found, a way of enjoying
life."[12] Ironically, the very strengths of the German community led to its
own dissolution; together, its members were able to accommodate themselves to a new environment.

Conzen describes the process of immigration from the immigrants'
perspective. Her conclusion—that the Germans of Milwaukee were neither completely assimilated nor excluded from native culture(s) but built
their own community—is also true of other ethnic communities in the
mid to late nineteenth-century Midwest. These included Germans, Italians, Scandinavians, and Poles in villages and rural areas as well as in the
more fully studied major metropolitan areas. In most respects, the experiences of these immigrants replicated those of earlier, native-born migrants to the Old Northwest.[13]

But in several crucial ways they were fundamentally different. Many native-born Americans felt threatened by the large number of immigrants at mid-century. Some poorer people worried about the economic consequences of increased competition for jobs and land, but others—especially the stable middle-class core of cities and villages—were disturbed by the kinds of alternative communities created by people such as the Germans of Milwaukee. And their primary objections were rooted in questions of culture.[14]

To native-born Americans fully committed to a bourgeois ideology of hard work and self-restraint, the immigrant epitomized everything they did not want the Old Northwest, let alone the United States, to become. Historians have shown that there was a virtual nativist frenzy in the 1850s in response to the sudden huge influx of Catholic immigrants and economic dislocations caused by the construction of railroads.[15] The most specific manifestation of nativism was the short-lived but very popular Know-Nothing party, the political arm of the Order of the Star Spangled Banner. Between 1853 and 1856 the Know-Nothings' denunciations of Catholic immigrants and "the Papal Power" attracted thousands of voters. Michael F. Holt suggests in *The Political Crisis of the 1850s* that many nativists were worried about the preservation of republican government in America; the Know-Nothings presented themselves as populists, as a reform-minded people's party dedicated to rooting out all forms of corruption and aristocratic power.[16]

While the upheavals of the 1850s were unusually intense, the kinds of complaints lodged against immigrants were not new. Indeed, according to nativist critics, the undesirable traits of German and Irish immigrants in the 1850s were the same ones long associated with Indians and many white Americans. They were lazy and improvident, and they drank too much. They practiced their religion ritually and publicly, conveying little sense of the internal conviction the middle class deemed the *sine qua non* of faith. They were not interested in progress, as the bourgeoisie defined it, but wasted money and time in frivolous leisure activities. They indulged their desires rather than practicing moral improvement. Often, they preferred to educate their children in their own cultural traditions. The problem of the immigrants, in short, was acute for many residents of the Old Northwest in the 1850s less because they were Catholic or poor than because they seemed to threaten those values and practices that made the United States free and prosperous.

Many members of the solid bourgeoisie worried about the institutionalization of intemperate and undisciplined behavior in slums and rising crime rates.[17] Such fears led to a shift by temperance advocates from moral suasion to prohibition in the 1840s. No longer did they seek to reform individuals; now they went to battle against "the Rum Power" which kept people enthralled.[18] In Cincinnati, the early 1850s saw a strong campaign for the passage of the Maine law, which would have forbidden the manufacture and sale of all intoxicating liquors within the state of Ohio. The battle pitted Protestant, middle-class native-born Americans against members of the city's upper class and the German and Irish communities. But the prohibition movement, what Jed Dannenbaum calls "the unifying spearhead of a new, socially-oriented political movement," was unsuccessful.[19] In fact, its major achievement was to unite warring factions of the local Democratic party in opposition to the Maine law.

It is important to remember that prohibition was not a naked assertion of class power. Many workers and artisans adopted the temperance cause, just as they accepted middle-class values as the road to success in American life. Similarly, many middle-class midwesterners continued to drink.[20] The importance of the prohibition campaign, rather, lies in the symbolic realm. More was at issue than the right to drink. For many immigrants and for quite a few native Americans, imbibing beer or whiskey was perfectly normal, a necessary accessory to the enjoyment of life and all celebrations of freedom and leisure. But for middle-class cores in the Midwest, drinking was a symbol of more than social disorder; it represented a lack of self-control, a wasting of the individual time and resources so necessary to social progress and economic development.

The larger significance of the immigrants' alternative communities for the origins of midwestern culture lies in the ways in which they forced the bourgeoisie to define acceptable behavior. To nativist Protestants, immigrants showed what would happen if they failed to exercise cultural hegemony. In other words, they forced a fuller definition of the rules that were supposed to govern human relationships. The Old Northwest was always a place of diversity, of alternative communities; the Midwest became a place in which people did things differently but in which one set of official rules dominated. In this sense, the success of the middle class in making drinking unacceptable if not illegal typified the nature of midwestern culture: it denied the heterogeneity that had characterized the region from the time of its first settlement.

In such ways, the original goals of the developers and congressmen of the 1780s were kept alive. Most of them could never have imagined the prohibition of alcohol. But later generations of middle-class midwesterners believed that drinking and other alien cultural behaviors jeopardized regional economic development. In order for the Midwest to sustain its leading position in the expansion of commercial agriculture, its citizens had to behave as models of industry and self-discipline. The rhetoric of the middle class had changed from that of the 1780s; the emphasis now was on self-improvement rather than republican citizenship. But the larger goal remained much the same.

If the Protestant middle class identified foreign immigrants as the greatest internal threat to the social order in the 1850s, they clearly saw the South as the most important external challenge. American politicians managed to keep the issue of slavery largely out of national politics in the years between the Missouri Compromise of 1820 and the Mexican War. But the seizure of extensive territories from Mexico, the rapid expansion of settlement, and the resolution of the issues of banking and internal improvements that had divided Jacksonians and Whigs forced the question to the forefront of political debates in the late 1840s. What concerned many northerners in the 1850s was what they considered the disproportionate influence of the South in the federal government and the potential expansion of slavery into western territories.[21]

Historians disagree strongly about whether the South and the North were really very different in the decades preceding the Civil War. But reality in this case may be beside the point. Clearly vast numbers of southerners and northerners *perceived* the two regions as being different and acted accordingly. To many in the Old Northwest, the South represented a backward area, hamstrung by slavery; it was hostile to free labor and therefore to the highest stages of economic development. More than a political threat, southerners, like Indians, immigrants, and white Americans ambivalent about capitalism, appeared to advocate an alternative conception of community. Theirs was a world in which people lived off the labor of a degraded race and personal honor meant more than private conscience. The issue of the "Slave Power," in other words, was cultural as well as political.[22]

Political historians are now engaged in a great war of statistics, arguing about the relative importance of nativism, antislavery, and sectionalism in the disintegration of the Jacksonian political system and the origins of the Republican party. The states of the Old Northwest have been prime areas of discussion because the Republicans did so well in the region. Although some works argue that one issue was more important than others, the most successful are those that suggest a fusion of issues in the momentous events of the 1850s.[23]

According to William E. Gienapp and Michael F. Holt, the issues of slavery and nativism merged in the mid-1850s to produce the Republican party. The new organization was forged around the fears many people felt about the supposed influence of both the Slave Power and the Papal Power in America. The Democratic party, on the other hand, remained committed to principles of laissez-faire in both economics and culture. Democrats, argues Bruce W. Collins, continued to fear the Money Power, that is, bankers and merchants, as the greatest threat to the prosperity and peace of the United States.[24]

All of these interpretations make sense. But from the longer perspective of regional development, the political realignment of the 1850s marked the end of an era of cultural confusion and the beginning of a period of cultural consolidation. To a great extent, the economic issues that had divided Jacksonians and Whigs had been resolved by the early 1850s. The question was no longer whether the transportation revolution would transform the region. It had. Banks were there to stay. And the ambivalence many midwesterners had once felt about commercial capitalism was no longer a crucial factor in the region's political life. Growing popular dissatisfaction with the two great parties in the early 1850s reflected this underlying sense that they had served their purpose. Many people increasingly perceived both the Democratic and Whig parties as corrupt, bloated organizations run by professional politicians whose primary interest was advancing their own careers.[25]

In this context, the meteoric success of the Know-Nothings and the rise of the Republicans infused politics in America with new meaning and vitality. The new parties shifted the debate away from economic concerns to those of culture. The questions that divided them were no longer related to the ways in which the market revolution would take place but centered on who would define the values and create the institutions of the new world to which it had given birth. Slavery, temperance, nativism, and religion became vitally important in the 1850s because they forced men to confront on a symbolic level the problem of defining American society.

The ascendancy of the Republican party, Eric Foner argues, represented the general acceptance of market capitalism in America.[26] Republicans celebrated a world of individual entrepreneurs, a country in which ordinary men could rise to the top through hard work and self-discipline. In short, Republicans embraced the bourgeois culture brought into being by the transportation revolution.[27] Their party in the 1850s and 1860s engaged in an effort to preserve and protect the bourgeois ethic and to defeat all its presumed enemies, be they slaveholders or priests. As Ronald P. Formisano has suggested, the Republicans were successful because they combined elements of the old Whig program with a new egalitarian appeal to native white Americans.[28] Through the Republican party, the bourgeoisie made middle-class and American values synonymous.[29]

The Democrats continued to attract a great many voters, battling the Republicans on nearly equal footing throughout the Midwest. They successfully appealed to those whom the Republicans defined out of the American equation: Catholic and southern immigrants. Following Foner's suggestion, the Democratic party can be seen "as the representative of the great pre-modern cultures within American society—the white South and the Irish immigrants."[30] Democrats also continued to offer an alternative vision within the general capitalistic context. Unlike the Republicans, who, writes Bruce Collins, felt "foreboding about the future of free enterprise" to such an extent that they felt compelled to defend it against everyone who seemed different, the Democrats were "optimistic about the future of Northwestern free society within a culturally pluralistic Union."[31]

While the Republicans attracted some German votes, their greatest strength lay among native-born Americans. Within that group, however, there were important differences. The Republican party was far more heterogeneous than the Whigs, but it clearly constituted the political vehicle of the Protestant middle class in its efforts to establish bourgeois culture in the Old Northwest.

Foremost among the characteristics of Republican voters was their strong antipathy to the South and what they saw as its lazy, unproductive way of life. They confirmed their strong sense of moral superiority by contrasting their region with the South. Anti-southern feeling was an intra-regional phenomenon as well. Gienapp describes a "sectional pattern" to voting within the Old Northwest in the 1850s. Southern-born migrants tended to vote for Democratic candidates, while New Englanders supported Republicans. Gienapp believes that this split was the result of generations of cultural conflict, which, he contends, "the emergence of the Republican party greatly intensified." In fact, it "sharpened lines of division, and stimulated mutual antagonism" between Yankees and southerners.[32]

Arguing that "the slavery issue, variously understood, dominated mid-century Ohio politics," Stephen E. Maizlish suggests that the political reorganization of the 1850s involved "the triumph of sectionalism."[33] In their growing antipathy to slavery and the national power of the South, many citizens of the Buckeye state increasingly thought in regional terms. Ohio Republicans distanced themselves from the South by denying the legitimacy of the white southerners' way of life.[34]

But the battle between the South and New England in the Old Northwest involved more than a struggle between migrants from two regions. Republicans, Onuf has written elsewhere, developed a definition of union "that excluded the slaveholding South." They celebrated their "free institutions and . . . the fruits of unprecedented economic growth" by denouncing southern backwardness.[35] For many, in fact, their vision of America as a nation of entrepreneurs "was best exemplified *within* Ohio and the other free states of the Old Northwest."[36]

At the same time, Democrats, whether they were southern-born or Irish, employed New England as a simple negative reference point. For them, the Northeast represented what they did not want to see in the Midwest. New England was the home of a Puritan oligarchy, an intolerant aristocracy bent upon controlling the economic and moral development of the West. The Ohio Democrat Clement Vallandigham proclaimed that he was "inexorably hostile to Puritan domination in religion or morals or literature or politics."[37] If Republicans thought the South was a wasteland of laziness and underdevelopment, Democrats viewed New England as epitomizing excessive religious and political influence in the lives of ordinary people.

Republicans also tended to be more pietistic or evangelical than Democrats. In Michigan, Ronald Formisano has shown that Catholics largely voted for the Democrats, while the core of the Republican party consisted of "evangelical Protestants. . . . Indeed, the Republican party, though perhaps less explicitly, was far more the *Protestant party* than the Whig had ever been."[38] Religion was perhaps more important in Michigan than elsewhere because of the small number of southern immigrants. But throughout the Midwest, Republicans tended to be strongly committed to a Protestant nation. Whether evangelicals or not, Republicans were by and large supporters of prohibition and foes of Catholicism. The party possessed what Gienapp calls "a sense of moral urgency."[39]

Economically and geographically, the Republicans were strongest in "rural areas and small towns."[40] Not surprisingly, they were weakest in big cities with large ethnic populations. In terms of wealth, judging from a study of Cincinnati, the Republicans did poorly "among the poorest segment of society . . . and they won their strongest support proportionally from the middle ranks of the city's population." Ethnic and religious differences aside, the Republican party was, above all, a middle-class party. According to Gienapp, "Republicanism" in the mid-1850s

> was centered in the rural and small-town middle class, among farmers, skilled workers, and other small independent entrepreneurs who dreamed of rising socially and economically and subscribed to the free labor vision of northern society as one of widespread opportunity and fundamental class harmony.[41]

The appeal of Republicanism, as Gienapp suggests, transcended anxieties about the Slave and Papal powers. As much as many people defined the official culture of the Midwest in opposition to what they perceived to be the shared cultural characteristics of Catholics and southerners, they were also committed to the positive fulfillment of a vision of commercial and social development that had originated in the Ordinance of 1787. Through the Republican party, they intended to complete the transformation of the Old Northwest.[42]

2. Reconstruction in the Midwest

Once in power, Republicans had to be more precise about the specific ways in which they intended to implement their vision of the proper society. On one level they succeeded in identifying themselves with the nation in the early 1860s; they made loyalty to the party an act of patriotism. But as they won their great battle with the South for political power within the nation, it became increasingly clear that the Republican creed of the 1850s meant different things to different communities of people.

From the beginning, the Republican party stood for far more than opposition to immigrants and the extension of slavery. By and large, its leaders sought to use the power of government in both economic and social spheres. In most states, Republicans were strong advocates of continued economic and social development. They were for railroads and internal improvements, banks and credit, and temperance and public education. The Republican party, in other words, intended to carry the Old Northwest into ever higher stages of material and moral progress.

The Civil War at once embodied and revised this effort. Begun less to free the slaves than to free the United States from slavery, the war was the most all-encompassing of nineteenth-century reform movements. Slowly but surely, Abraham Lincoln committed the national government to emancipation, thereby setting in motion a massive reorganization of southern society. But some people also hoped the war would create strong national economic and political institutions that would bring order and efficiency to American life. The Civil War, in other words, would lead to the triumph of the principles that had guided the authors of the Northwest Ordinance. The rhetoric now was bourgeois rather than republican. But the ultimate goals—the consolidation of power in the hands of interlocking national networks of the best men, the creation of an homogeneous culture, and the breakdown of local autonomy—were the same. The firing on Fort Sumter, John Lauritz Larson writes, inaugurated a "centralization of power in the nation" that would benefit "progressive entrepreneurs."[43]

In the event, the Civil War had a tremendous impact on the Midwest. Economically, the war boosted industrial development in major urban areas. The Midwest had long had rudimentary manufactures. The war did not create industrial capitalism by any means, but it did accelerate industrial growth on a grand scale. Increased demand for clothing, weapons, and food proved to be an enormous stimulus to the infant industries of the Midwest. The newly important federal government played a strong role in this growth. In Cincinnati, for example, "the intense competition for lucrative government contracts to produce thousands of sundry garments for Union soldiers," notes Steven J. Ross, "helped to revolutionize the city's ready-to-wear clothing industry by prompting manufacturers to adopt increasingly uniform standards and measurements for the rapid production of vast amounts of clothing."[44] In Wisconsin, the war stimulated demand for the manufacture of farm machinery, as Badger State farmers sought to produce larger and more diverse crops.[45] The meat packing, tanning, and clothing industries in and near Milwaukee also received boosts.[46] What Foner calls "the war-inspired boom in industrial profits and investments" and "the relentless upward course" of manufacturing output were remaking the Old Northwest.[47] "The Civil War," notes John H. Keiser, "focused attention upon industrial growth . . . as both a military necessity and an unparalleled economic opportunity for individuals. . . . The end of the war left [Illinois] tooled up and ready for phenomenal growth."[48]

The Civil War and Reconstruction were, for the most part, heady times for entrepreneurs of all kinds. There were huge profits to be made in building railroads and developing new industries. They also found in the war effort lessons and models for the management of big businesses. The war was fought on an unprecedented scale, and the coordination and administration of vast armies demanded innovations in organization and regulation.[49] Men learned how to move large quantities of men and/or materials cheaply and efficiently. The war confirmed the beliefs of enterprising individuals such as John Murray Forbes in the value of national organization and the inefficiency of local autonomy.[50]

The most dramatic political impact of these developments was a splintering of the Republican consensus forged in the 1850s. Republicanism, like most successful political agendas, had been remarkably vague; it committed the party and its supporters to what Foner terms a vision of "a social order, founded on the dignity and opportunities of free labor, and to social mobility, enterprise, and 'progress.' It gloried in the same qualities of northern life—materialism, social fluidity, and the dominance of the self-made man—which twenty years earlier had been the source of widespread anxiety in Jacksonian America."[51] While a great many different kinds of people could accept these precepts in theory, putting them into practice in a national industrial order divided factory owners and laborers, railroadmen and farmers. Industrialists, for example, tended to emphasize those aspects of Republicanism which upheld both a laissez-faire approach to economic development and the sanctity of property, while workers stressed the importance of equality of opportunity and the inherent dignity of productive labor.

Intraparty disputes reflected the internal ideological crisis of the Republicans. Committed to the continued economic and moral development of the Midwest and the nation, Republicans found themselves at odds with each other over how and to what extent they should proceed. Clearly, on the state as well as the national level, the war legitimated the idea that government ought to exercise a positive role in the lives of its citizens. In the words of Illinois Governor Richard Yates in 1865, "The war now being waged has tended, more than any other event in the history of the country, to militate against the Jeffersonian idea, that 'the best government is that which governs least.'"[52] Some Republicans seized upon the opportunity presented by northern victory in the Civil War to press for changes that would fulfill bourgeois ideas of the proper economic and social order. But they were frustrated by intraparty differences over the direction of policy and the proper role of government in its implementation.

Many midwestern Republicans in the 1860s and early 1870s were willing to use the power of state governments to improve social and economic conditions. According to Philip D. Swenson, "Illinois, as much as South Carolina and Mississippi, was reconstructed after 1865" as the state government responded to "increased demands for state regulation of allegedly immoral behavior." The legislature repealed the black laws in February 1865 and removed the word "black" from state suffrage provisions in the new constitution of 1870. Illinois also made preliminary, if ineffectual, efforts to regulate railroads. Meanwhile, the Michigan state government, in the words of George M. Blackburn, moved "from a limited to a far more activist role." The size of the government increased; railroads were subjected to some mildly regulatory statutes; public education was made compulsory in 1871; tax funds were appropriated to support the University of Michigan; improvements were made in the institutions for the deaf, dumb, and blind, for the insane, and for prisoners; black suffrage was barely secured in 1870; and the liquor trade was taxed and regulated in 1875. In Wisconsin, Republicans by and large supported internal improvements, black suffrage, and regulation of the liquor industry but were divided over the question of railroad regulation.[53] Robert R. Dykstra has concluded that the Iowa Republican party in the 1860s and 1870s "was indeed a progressive instrument."[54] It became especially committed to the question of black suffrage, which was approved in 1868, while remaining divided over the liquor issue.[55] To a significant degree, midwestern Republicans in the 1860s and early 1870s were willing to use the power of government to improve social and economic conditions. But their actions were hardly what one would have expected from the dynamic Republicans of the 1850s.

Stephen L. Hansen argues that Illinois Republican leaders used the Civil War as a model for maintaining party unity. "By 1868," he claims, the "Republican party was like an army, demanding strict discipline, unswerving loyalty, and rigid organization. . . . Elections were like battles."[56] The key to success in the 1860s was unswerving voter loyalty maintained by highly developed party structures. Given the factionalism that characterized the Republican party in the 1860s in states such as Ohio, Hansen exaggerates Republican unity.[57] Such rigid organization may have characterized party activity in the 1880s and early 1890s, but it did not do so in the 1860s and early 1870s. While Republicans were rarely out of power in the Midwest, they were clearly in a state of flux.

3. Alternative Interpretations of Republicanism

There were many reasons for their contentiousness. Partly it had to do with the nature of the Republican coalition; diverse ethnic and geographic groups found it more difficult to maintain unity once the war was won and they confronted issues such as black suffrage. But even more it had to do with the continuing effort to sort out the contours of midwestern culture. If in the 1850s Republicans had defined the Midwest as the province of free white individuals committed to a morality of self-discipline by condemning southerners and immigrants, in the 1860s and early 1870s they faced the limits of that world. The major sources of Republican disunity were racism and the changing nature of the regional economy. Tension within the party paled, however, in the face of the growing intensity of debates in midwestern society as a whole about the precise definition of bourgeois values.

Most midwesterners of whatever ethnic origins were simply unwilling to extend their free labor ideology to blacks. Eric Foner argues that "the decade following the Civil War witnessed astonishing advances in the political, civil, and social rights of northern blacks."[58] In Indiana, according to Emma Lou Thornbrough, "the years immediately following the Civil War were marked by substantial legal and political gains."[59] By 1870 in Ohio, writes David A. Gerber, blacks moved from being "pariahs . . . to citizens and members of the political community." Perhaps the most significant change was that whites had to think of blacks in new ways.[60]

Still, Foner concedes, changes "proved in many respects less far-reaching" than in the South, largely because of the persistence of racial prejudice.[61] Even some Republicans were lukewarm about civil rights legislation out of a fear of making their particular state "a haven for blacks."[62] Most northern blacks "remained trapped in urban poverty and confined to inferior housing and menial and unskilled jobs."[63] In Milwaukee, Joe William Trotter, Jr., concludes, "Afro-Americans were almost totally excluded from the city's industrial expansion"; in 1880, 67.9 percent of black workers were porters, waiters, servants, cooks, and common laborers.[64] "By 1915, an unofficial but decided separation of blacks from whites in [Milwaukee's] economic, political, and social life had intensified."[65] Similarly in Detroit, despite the political gains of the 1860s, blacks remained segregated and the victims of discrimination and Negrophobia.[66] The gains of Reconstruction were tremendously important, but the long-term development in the late nineteenth-century Midwest was toward increased social segregation and economic marginalization of blacks.

While their party suffered from its identification with blacks, many Republicans themselves were unwilling to embrace fully the implications of the revolution they had wrought in the South. What made racial exclusion particularly galling was the degree to which the relatively small black communities in the nineteenth-century Midwest adopted middle-class values. Juliet E. K. Walker's *Free Frank*, the founder of an Illinois town, was not the only person of color with an entrepreneurial bent.[67] In the cities of Detroit and Milwaukee, there was a substantial black bourgeoisie fully involved in a world of voluntary organizations and committed to an ideology of progress. Indeed, as William and Jane Pease have pointed out, many northern blacks adhered to "the philosophy of the American middle class. . . . Negro communities were dedicated to training their inhabitants in the virtues of self-reliance, individualism, and independence."[68]

Although racism was important in revealing the limits of Republican radicalism, it was only one of many problems facing the party. Increasingly, party leaders in the late 1860s and early 1870s were accused of corruption and indifference. They seemed less interested in reform than in the preservation of their collective and individual political positions. While local Republicans often remained committed to issues such as temperance and most supported the Reconstruction of the South in general terms, state leaders tended to "wave the bloody shirt" and be done with it. Just as problematic was their association with railroads and other corporations. The growing perception of political corruption was partially responsible for the Liberal Republican movement of 1872, which attempted to replace supposed political hacks with "best" men of character. The Liberal Republicans failed, however, and Republican machinery became even more ossified as the 1870s progressed.[69]

The most important challenge facing the party was the impact of economic change. The Republican defense of free labor and bourgeois culture in the 1850s was geared to a world of commercial capitalism. But with the war and industrial growth, many Republican leaders and some conservative Democrats turned their attention away from the freedom of the individual to the sanctity of the corporation. By the late 1860s, these men were interested in protecting railroads from government regulation. They had shifted from individual to corporate freedom. Increasingly, leading midwestern Republicans were willing to encourage the development of cultural homogeneity but not to regulate industries. If anything, they argued, government should be employed to protect corporate interests.

Advocacy of corporate freedom was the logical extension of the conceptions of economic and social development originally advocated by the authors of the Northwest Ordinance. But the goal was no longer to promote the prosperity of a region of commercial farmers. What these Republicans now envisioned as the highest stage of development was a nation of interlocking economic corporations. To such men, attempts to regulate railroads or to attack monopoly were little more than expressions of a dangerous, inefficient localism.[70]

They also were advocates of a particular interpretation of the Republicanism of the 1850s. Eager to defend the sanctity of private property and the independence of businessmen, they increasingly thought of labor as simply another commodity. Commenting on a strike among iron workers in 1874, one defender of manufacturing interests wrote that "things of this sort" made him "ask whether we are really as free as we pretend to be. . . . If any individual cannot dispose of his labor when and at what price he pleases, he is living under a despotism, no matter what form the government assumes."[71] Whatever we may think of such an attitude today, it was a logical extension of the Republican sanctification of private property to include human labor.

But this was far from the only perspective on the legacy of 1850s' Republicanism. Ohio's Liberal Republicans, for example, were more complex, according to Michael E. McGerr, than our traditional understanding of them as "a displaced upper class" would suggest. The Liberal movement of the early 1870s reflected a splintering of the Republican coalition at the highest level. Buckeye state liberals were members of "the wealthy elite of professionals and businessmen involved in the development of industrial capitalism."[72] Many were former Democrats, still committed to the old Jacksonian opposition to a high tariff and temperance legislation. They promoted civil service reform, sought an end to radical Reconstruction, and opposed protectionist measures they thought would lead to monopoly and inequality. When their movement failed to dislodge former Whigs from positions of power in the party, they returned to the Democracy. In sum, writes McGerr, the Liberal Republican movement in Ohio reflected a "disagreement among the wealthy over the best means of industrializing the nation" within the general context of a celebration of "the virtues of industrial capitalism."[73]

Still, if Republican and Democratic leaders accepted the changes wrought by industrialization, most midwesterners were more ambivalent. Raised in the antebellum world of commercial agriculture, many farmers and small-town businessmen feared the increasing power and national character of industry as a threat to that world. Whether Democrats or Republicans, they believed in the values of competition, individual enterprise, and local control. For such people, the railroad, which they coveted in order to get goods to market, was also an instrument of destruction. Railroads integrated local producers into a larger economy and consolidated the power of national networks of merchants and capitalists; they were the harbingers of a new economic and social order.

High rates, political corruption, and the frequent indifference of railroad operators to local concerns sparked a movement for government regulation. In the upper Mississippi Valley, the Patrons of Husbandry, or the Grange—an organization intended as "an agrarian fraternity dedicated to education, social intercourse, and the improvement of the farmer's life"— became, in Larson's words, "the reluctant vehicle for a massive regional protest against the railroad and industrial power."[74] Grangers pressed for rate reform and achieved some restrictive legislation by 1874 in Illinois, Iowa, Wisconsin, and Minnesota.

The Grange was more than an agrarian protest, however. Although not all Grangers had been Republicans, they in effect offered an alternative reading of the Republican legacy. Larson concludes that the Iowa Grange "reflected exactly those values of political economy that had carried . . . the infant Republican party to power" in the 1850s, particularly the rights of all men to the fruits of their labor and to unbridled access to the marketplace.[75] Fundamentally, George H. Miller contends, Granger laws and legal cases "were rooted in the mercantile order of the antebellum period."[76] While the farmers and local businessmen in the Grange embraced the values and methods of cooperation and combination, they did so in order to achieve their goal of protecting what had become the "traditional" world of commercial agriculture.

Ultimately, with the long period of declining prices and overproduction that confounded the American farmer in the 1870s, 1880s, and 1890s, farmers would turn to more elaborate forms of cooperation and solidarity. They would have to imitate the people they were fighting. But it would be wrong to dismiss them as simply agrarian protesters.[77] They were struggling to sustain the republican vision of a world of independent agricultural capitalists that had defined the Midwest in the 1850s.

A similar situation developed with regard to the labor movement in the Midwest. As Steven Ross notes, after the Civil War the upper and middle classes increasingly tended to honor "the product rather than the producer."[78] As we will show in chapter six, many people no longer saw the skilled artisan as the ideal workingman. Yet Ross demonstrates that working people were slower to abandon this notion than others. They clung "to a vision of work and community rooted in an earlier world dominated by artisans, shopkeepers, and farmers." In the 1860s and 1870s, Cincinnati's industrial workers upheld this vision, sometimes violently, by resisting their degradation to "dependent, slave-like wage earners who could not fully exercise their rights as workers or citizens." They sought to limit the impact of industrialization by calling for an end to "industrial slavery," much as the Republicans had attacked chattel slavery in the 1850s.[79]

The same was true of German workers in Chicago. Many artisans who emigrated to that city in the aftermath of the revolutions in 1848 found a congenial ideology in the Republicanism of the 1850s. As Bruce Carlan

Levine has suggested, they envisioned "a society in which all producers enjoyed political equality, social respect, and economic well-being," in which "inordinate extremes of wealth and poverty would vanish, along with the unequal enjoyment of political privilege."[80] Strong supporters of the Republican assault on chattel slavery, German artisans and radical intellectuals found it easy to transfer their critique to the wage slavery of industrial capitalism in the 1860s and 1870s. Although they were "ultimately spurned" by political and economic leaders, their version of Republicanism "became a bridge to the still more independent and radical labor movements of later years."[81]

The climax of such movements came in the 1880s with the formation of the Knights of Labor, a union which functioned, according to Richard Jules Oestreicher, as "a working-class fraternity, based on the spirit of Christian brotherhood."[82] Ross suggests that the Knights sought to overcome "the evils of industrial capitalism . . . by the creation of a new industrial and moral order based upon the 'nobility of labor' and the cooperation and harmony of all honorable producers." In their vision, "each worker would also be an owner; each man and woman would be an independent producer, not a 'wage slave.'"[83] In essence, the Knights revived the Republican ideology of the 1850s—a world of free labor and independent property owners.[84]

Similarly, Nick Salvatore's biography of Eugene V. Debs demonstrates how the middle-class culture of the Midwest even led some small-town residents to socialism. Debs grew up in Terre Haute, Indiana, where entrepreneurial talent was seen in millennial terms as "destiny's instrument to lift the town closer to the heavens."[85] "Manhood," Salvatore notes in describing the patriarchal aspects of midwestern bourgeois society, "was in large part defined in public fashion, through one's actions as a citizen, a member of a specific community, and as a producer of value for one's family and the community and in one's personal relations with others."[86] Such an ideology made sense as long as there was "hope for individual mobility" and community progress.[87] But by reducing labor to a commodity, factory and railroad work made it difficult for an individual worker to maintain his self-respect as a "citizen producer."[88] Debs eventually came to a stinging critique of industrial capitalism partly because of the impossibility of reconciling the values of his youth with new economic structures.

The working out of bourgeois culture in the second half of the nineteenth century also led to changes in the consciousness of many middle-class women. Because the "cult of domesticity" assumed that women were pious and virtuous, they had been encouraged to be active in temperance and antislavery societies. The female's mastery of the private sphere and her role as guardian of the family made her the perfect social critic. Legally excluded from the political arena, women were nonetheless frequently the staunchest advocates of the social vision associated with the Republicans in the 1850s.

From the beginning, however, women's understanding of their role diverged from that of men; their goals, moreover, rapidly changed as well. Participation in reform legitimized by bourgeois culture, ironically, engendered a proto-feminist critique of that culture. Women found power in banding together to reform the world—power over their husbands' and sons' behavior, power to shape the nature of their society. "Borrowing from antislavery ideology," argues Ellen Carol DuBois, "they articulated a vision of equality and independence for women, and borrowing from antislavery method, they spread their radical ideas widely to challenge other people to imagine a new set of sexual relations."[89] Although Republicans failed to heed the growing calls for female suffrage during Reconstruction, many women nonetheless moved beyond the confines of the roles prescribed for them by the dominant bourgeois culture. Feminism gained momentum through an extended (and sometimes angry) discussion of the ideological implications of bourgeois domesticity.[90]

This subtle transformation in the role of women was especially apparent in temperance activities. In 1874, a group of native-born, married, middle-class women in Hillsboro and Washington Court House, Ohio, founded the most important of these organizations, the Women's Christian Temperance Union (WCTU).[91] Its goal was to eliminate social evils by persuading people, especially men, to stop drinking intoxicating beverages.

The WCTU obviously did not succeed in bringing prohibition to the Midwest. Men (and women) continued to drink. But the temperance movement epitomized the ways in which the bourgeoisie dominated the region. Although temperance organizations did not achieve their goals, their agitation for legal prohibition and public education allowed them to set the terms of the debate. Drinking may not have been abolished, but it surely became something that respectable people frowned upon (at least in polite company). The issue was somewhat different from what it had been in the 1850s, however. Now women directed their activities less at immigrants than at their own husbands and sons.[92] Temperance would defend home and family against the evils of alcohol, thus mitigating abuses of patriarchal authority such as wife beating, neglect, and desertion.[93]

In fact, the WCTU became the means by which women stretched and ultimately transcended bourgeois gender roles. Crusading together for moral reform intensified their sense of their collective power; doing good in ways expected of proper women encouraged them to try to improve their own condition. "The Woman's Crusade," writes Barbara Epstein, "was part of a long-term process by which middle-class women gained the strength to act on behalf of what they perceived as their interests."[94]

By the 1870s, in sum, the bourgeois vision of the world had become intertwined with the growing confidence of midwesterners in themselves and in their region. Although the Republican party and its middle-class supporters were not always victorious politically, they did set the parameters of cultural debate. Indeed, the extent to which the vision of the region's destiny set forth during the Republican ascendancy of the 1850s and 1860s continued to dominate political discourse is apparent in struggles among opposing groups of midwesterners to appropriate its legacy. In a national sense, the Midwest defined itself culturally by emphasizing how different it was from the South and New England (and Europe for that matter). But internally, the strength of the region's culture lay in the ongoing and multifaceted debate of its residents over the nature of economic structures, the configuration of social relationships, and the exercise of political power in the new world of the American Midwest.

VI

THE POLITICS OF
ACCOMMODATION AND THE
SIGNIFICANCE OF THE FRONTIER

In the 1850s and 1860s—decades of political tumult and war—the bourgeois vision of a society of hardworking, independent men and virtuous, domestic women had engendered a sense of collective identity among many residents of the Old Northwest. Regional patriots celebrated the fact that commercial capitalism and their region of the United States had come of age together. No longer settlers of a fringe frontier seeking integration into the larger Union, they were now midwesterners, citizens of what they believed to be—in both a literal and a figurative sense—the American heartland.

Within decades of their moment of triumph, however, a new kind of challenge confronted middle-class midwesterners. In simple terms, it amounted to the question of how to retain moral urgency and ideological dynamism in the face of that most dangerous of enemies—success. Part of the original appeal of bourgeois values lay in the promise of prosperity and salvation to those who could reconcile the demands of individual freedom and social responsibility. Neither static nor fixed, bourgeois ideology drew its energy from the heterogeneity and contentiousness of the social context in which it emerged. Recognizing the power of alternative social constructions, the midwestern bourgeoisie had defined itself through its unrelenting efforts to impose its values on the peoples of the region.

Yet, by the end of the nineteenth century, the very success of these efforts was jeopardizing the cultural hegemony of the middle class. On one level, the exercise of power put the bourgeoisie on the defensive. Largely victorious in their campaigns for political and regional dominance, middle-class midwesterners lost their zeal for reform. Some of the peoples they had attacked were absorbed into the middle-class world. Others who refused to subscribe to the bourgeois agenda were effectively ignored. On a deeper level, however, the triumph of bourgeois values created a new dialectic in which older notions were transformed or revised. In other words, midwesterners had to deal with the consequences— intended and unintended—of what they had fashioned. And that dilemma led to the ultimate challenge: to explain to themselves how and why their world had come into existence—and why it had failed, in so many conspicuous ways, to live up to its original promise.

1. The Impact of Industrialism

The entrenchment of industrial capitalism in the last third of the nineteenth century created a sense of crisis in the midwestern bourgeoisie. To a significant degree, large-scale economic enterprises such as corporations and factories threatened the values of the region's core population.

The mid-nineteenth-century midwesterner had seen himself as an entrepreneur with a large degree of financial independence; the ideal citizen was a merchant or farmer or artisan who sold the products of his labor in the marketplace and simultaneously secured the foundations of his own, his family's, and his community's prosperity and character. The social order of the Midwest had essentially rested on the activities of thousands of individuals in small commercial centers.

In the long run, however, the success of liberal capitalism betrayed its own original promises by contributing to the rise of large-scale manufacturing and the massive expansion of a few urban areas—such as Cincinnati, Cleveland, Detroit, Chicago, and Milwaukee. Indeed, by 1890, only 39 percent of midwesterners were farmers. According to Richard Jensen, 17 percent of the region's population lived in its thirteen largest cities and another 10 percent in urban areas of more than 10,000 people.[1] Much of this urban growth was attributable to immigrants from both the countryside and Europe. Many were attracted by the opportunities for work in rapidly expanding industries. In his study of the nineteenth-century working class in Detroit, Richard Oestreicher notes that the population of that city more than doubled between 1880 and 1900, growing from 116,340 to 285,704; the number of industrial workers tripled from an estimated 14,500 in 1880 to 45,707 in 1900.[2] Similar expansion occurred in Cincinnati, Cleveland, Milwaukee, and a score of smaller urban areas.

Chicago's growth was the most spectacular. The Windy City more than doubled its population in the decade of the 1880s alone, rising from 500,000 to more than a million residents. As the major rail crossroads in the nation, Chicago quickly became the commercial center of the Midwest. It dominated the grain trade, the lumber business, and the meat packing industry. It was also increasingly important in the production of steel, railroad equipment, and agricultural tools. Chicago's regional economic influence, meanwhile, was expanding through the rapid growth of retail and mail-order merchandise companies started by men such as Aaron Montgomery Ward, Marshall Field, and the partnership of Richard Sears and Alvah Roebuck. Chicago had risen from the ashes of the devastating fire of 1871 and rebuilt itself—architecturally as well as economically—into the embodiment of the American commercial spirit. A French visitor called it "the most active, the boldest, the most American, of the cities of the Union." A New Yorker simply said: "America is Great," "and Chicago is her prophet."[3]

The significance of the interrelated industrial and urban growth of the Midwest in the last decades of the nineteenth century was two-fold. On one level, it brought unparalleled technological progress and material plenty to the region. But it also affected the social and emotional lives of midwesterners. Industrialism brought structural and demographic shifts that demanded a thorough-going reevaluation of the nature of the midwestern social order.

Foremost among them were changes in the very nature of work. In centralized, highly mechanized factories, workers had less control over the rhythms and processes of their lives and jobs. Faced with a long-term decline in prices after the depression of the 1870s, American businessmen responded with consolidation and efforts to impose more regularity, or system, in the workplace. There had never been a golden age in which laborers ran factories. But, as David Montgomery and others have shown, the collective strength of workers diminished significantly in the last third of the nineteenth century.[4]

Factory labor in the late nineteenth century was increasingly specialized and routinized. As we suggested in chapter five, the kinds of skills that workers had brought to their jobs in the mid nineteenth century were no longer welcome. According to Steven Ross, Cincinnati laborers lost their "ability to set the pace of production. Rather than the machine following the work rhythm of the laborer, the laborer was often forced to follow the rhythm of the machine."[5] Skilled mechanics who formed the basis of the Cincinnati work force before the 1870s found their positions threatened by mechanization and by increasing competition from young men, women, and children.[6] The same thing happened to people in traditionally middle-class occupations such as clerking and teaching. In many ways, the sheer size of midwestern cities fostered a pervasive sense of alienation and segmentation. Nowhere was this process described more richly than in Theodore Dreiser's novel *Sister Carrie* (1900). Human beings seemed to have become interchangeable parts in a world without coherence or meaning.

In the 1920s, the sociologists Robert and Helen Lynd found the people of Muncie, Indiana, obsessed with making a living. The residents of their "Middletown" were "people intently engaged day after day in some largely routinized, specialized occupation."[7] The Lynds lamented the widening "gap between the things people do to get a living and the actual needs of living."[8] "Inventions and technology," they noted, "continue rapidly to supplant muscle and the cunning hand of the master craftsman by batteries of tireless men doing narrowly specialized things over and over and merely 'operated' or 'tended' in their orderly clangorous repetitive processes by the human worker."[9] The consequences of this shift in the nature of work were to wipe out "many of the satisfactions that formerly accompanied the job."[10]

Industrialism, in short, transformed the Midwest's interrelated social and economic structures. The great men of the region were no longer merchants or bankers but corporate officers. The basic units of production—farms and shops—were joined by factories. Cities that had grown to prominence as regional market and transportation centers became renowned as producers of steel and textiles. This concentration and specialization of economic activities robbed men and women of the sense of some degree of control over their labor. As a result, the incentives for participation in the bourgeois culture of self-discipline and self-improvement were sharply reduced.

Many middle-class midwesterners worried particularly about the degree to which the foreign immigrants could be assimilated into their new culture. "The cities of the Midwest, which became the 'Corliss engines' of industrial growth after 1870," writes David Montgomery, "displayed markedly European characteristics."[11] In Cincinnati in 1890, "foreign-born parents and their children made up sixty-nine percent of the population in 1890."[12] In Detroit, "six out of every ten workers . . . had been born outside the United States."[13] The increasing numbers of "foreigners" led many middle-class midwesterners to question whether working people could ever share a commitment to bourgeois notions of economic success and personal character.

Historians of American labor have devoted much energy to the question of whether there was a distinctive working class in American cities. In general, the answer is no. Because they were divided by language, customs, and religion, immigrants never constituted a distinct class. As Richard Jules Oestreicher has written in Solidarity and Fragmentation: Working People and Class Consciousness in Detroit, 1875–1900, "Detroit's workers lived in separate communities within the city" and "viewed their problems as workers from the perspective of their own cultural system. . . . Each of these communities was a unique cultural system, with a mutually reinforcing set of values, symbols, informal personal associations, and formal institutions." The Irish and the Germans, for example, lived in relatively separate enclaves and clashed as much with each other as with native-born citizens.[14] Exacerbating such natural tensions were differences in job experience and uneven industrial development even within a single city. In sum, working peoples had too little in common with each other to coalesce into a trans-local community as powerful as the middle class.

Recent studies suggest that a similar process took place in the country-side through the formation of settlement clusters. Chain migration and an emphasis on "farming as a joint enterprise involving mutual obliga-tions of family members to one another, to future generations, and to the land" often fostered a symbiotic relationship between ethnic identity and community.[15] Even today there are many places in the Midwest which bear the stamp of a particular ethnic group.

Many historians also believe that European immigrants generally sup-ported middle-class goals and values. Occasional outbursts of violence and rhetoric notwithstanding, most immigrants seemed to have em-braced the acquisitiveness and enthusiasm for economic development that was at the heart of the bourgeois world. Jon Gjerde has shown, for example, that the lives of Norwegian immigrants in Wisconsin and Min-nesota were increasingly a mixture of middle-class values and Old World customs.[16]

Still, as recent historians such as Oestreicher and Ross argue, immi-grants and native-born workers occasionally found common ground in their job experiences and economic circumstances. At times, they were able to subordinate their obvious differences to form what Oestreicher calls "a subculture of opposition: an interlocking network of formal insti-tutions and informal practices based on an ethic of social equality, coop-eration, mutual trust, and mutual assistance."[17] In Detroit, Cincinnati, Chicago, and elsewhere, this subculture flourished most dramatically in the 1880s. Its "organizational cohesion" was the short-lived Knights of Labor.[18]

The 1880s was a crucial decade for working-class protest in the Mid-west, as in America as a whole. In Cincinnati, the popularity of the Knights of Labor reflected the belief of many of the city's working people in the need to counter the ill effects of industrialism. Ross argues that many workers resented the dissociation of work from the rights of citi-zenship. In Detroit, the Knights cut across ethnic and occupational lives to form "a working-class fraternity."[19] In each case, the "objectives" were "to change the terms of employment, alter the relationships between em-ployees and employers, produce political changes, reform society as a whole."[20] While, as Oestreicher suggests, working-class life at times amounted to a culture of opposition to the new industrial order, the most important aspects of the large working-class protests of the 1880s were the sense of community provided by organizations such as the Knights and the very bourgeois nature of their rhetoric and goals. Ross, in fact, contends that angry Cincinnati workers were seeking little more than a restoration of the traditional notions of community, law, and equity, which they perceived as being threatened by industrialism.

Middle-class midwesterners rarely perceived working-class society in such a sympathetic light. Rather, they tended to equate all workers' demands with socialism and to see the working-class world as a hothouse of violent, revolutionary challenges to the bourgeois social order. The most important manifestation of this fear was the execution of the so-called Haymarket conspirators in Chicago in 1888. The frenzied response of political leaders and middle-class citizenry to the mainly German anarchists can only be understood in the light of their concerns about the future of American society.

Chicago's bourgeoisie worried about the abuse of liberty by Europeans. The liberal minister David Swing, for example, argued for "a careful definition of what freedom is."[21] The concern was that immigrants from different cultures could not behave in respectable fashion, that they could not balance freedom and order, that they lacked the character so necessary to the middle-class, midwestern social order. Such people did not come to Chicago, wrote one newspaper after the Haymarket incident, "to secure that freedom of which they are deprived at their homes, but to indulge in that license which, in the places of their breeding, is forbidden them, or if indulged in is swiftly punished with rope, bullet, or axe."[22]

While the growing physical presence and political beliefs of many laborers worried the late nineteenth-century midwestern bourgeoisie, it was the daily behavior of members of the working class that represented the most profound threat to the middle-class world. In his study of workers in Worcester, Massachusetts, in the late nineteenth century, Roy Rosenzweig has suggested that the key to understanding bourgeois antipathy to working people lies in aspects of people's lives that employers and reformers could not control, specifically, how they spent their leisure time. Rosenzweig argues that saloons were the centers of an alternative culture, one that celebrated "an ethic of mutuality and reciprocity" rather than the competitive individualism of the marketplace.[23] Men drank, gambled, "wasted time," in short, behaved in ways that were an affront to middle-class Americans.[24] Rosenzweig is quick to point out that ethnicity, gender, and a host of other issues prevented the formation of a single working-class culture, and he does not believe that the recreational activities of workers challenged the dominant social and economic order. Rather, drinking in saloons and public celebrations of holidays represented what Raymond Williams has defined as an "alternative" culture, that of someone "who simply finds a different way to live and wishes to be left alone with it."[25] In her study of working women and leisure in New York City, Kathy Peiss has shown how this process worked. Far from middle-class domains, "Public halls, picnic grounds, pleasure clubs, and street corners were social spaces in which gender relations were 'played out,' where notions of sexuality, courtship, male power, female dependency, and autonomy were expressed and legitimized."[26]

Joanne J. Meyerowitz's *Women Adrift: Independent Wage Earners in Chicago, 1880–1930*, is a careful analysis of the behavior and values of single, working women in the largest midwestern city. She demonstrates the ways in which such women "formed social and economic relationships" among their peers and with men as substitutes "for the support and companionship of family." Indeed, unmarried, working women's lack of family, frequent mingling with men, and occasional sexual frankness, argues Meyerowitz, "challenged the dominant Victorian sexual ethos" by belying "the tenet that all women, single or married, needed the economic and moral protection of family life."[27] Clearly, their "subcultures" did not correct economic inequalities between men and women; in fact, they tended to promote "female economic dependence and encouraged women to value themselves as sexual objects." But *Women Adrift* vividly reveals the ways in which working-class women nonetheless formed what amounted to an alternative culture by defying "the sexual double standard," exploring "sexual desire," and establishing "independence from supervision, at least in their leisure hours."[28]

While we need further examination of working-class life in the Midwest, it seems clear that when laborers protested or organized, they frequently did so less to reform or exercise influence over the larger society than to protect their particular culture. No wonder then that immigrants so often voted for the Democratic party; no wonder that they were offended by Republican efforts to prohibit drinking or force their children into public schools. Even on the labor issue what they called for was equity and justice, not revolution.

If that is true, then why did not the middle class in the late nineteenth century simply leave immigrants alone? Historians have offered many answers, some having to do with evangelical Protestantism, some with status anxiety, some with the protection of property and social order. But perhaps what made efforts to reform immigrants so necessary was that they provided a means of defining the bourgeois community, of demonstrating its cultural hegemony, of ritually reenacting the nature of correct social relationships. The constant deprecation of working-class, Catholic, and agrarian communities, the recurrent revivals and crusades against alcohol, were less important in controlling others than in developing the character of middle-class citizens.

2. The Transformation of Republicanism

Given this context of industrial change, it is not surprising that political historians such as Paul Kleppner and Richard Jensen have discovered that the Republican moral zeal in the Midwest climaxed in the late 1880s. The key issues were temperance and public education. Campaigns against alcohol and for English as an official language came naturally to middle-class Republicans. Crusades asserting the cultural integrity of the bourgeoisie had been the defining element of class and regional consciousness. But the controversies of the late 1880s revealed both the limits of middle-class authority and its increasingly anachronistic quality.

Partisanship in the Midwest in the 1870s and 1880s was extremely vigorous, with record voter turnouts. Participation was stimulated by the extreme closeness of elections. "About half the midwestern voters in 1888 were, in varying degrees, committed to the principles of Republicanism, and a slightly smaller number to those of the Democrats."[29] Even during the Republican ascendancy of the 1860s, the Democrats remained a powerful party. During the Civil War, the Democratic party became a magnet for people who either sympathized with the South or wished to see the fighting come to end. Democrats garnered votes by denouncing Republicans as lovers of blacks even as they suffered from the taint of Copperheadism and treason to the northern—that is, Republican— cause. In the decades following the war, there were few obvious differences between the two major parties on the national or state level. Often dominated by so-called Bourbons who favored industrial development, the Democratic party apparently offered nothing distinctive.[30] In the 1880s, according to Jensen, Democrats attacked Republican-supported protective tariffs as an unnecessary interference "with the course of economic development"; high tariffs were "a tax on American consumers" and contributed to the growth of monopolies and trusts."[31] Seeking to connect themselves with Jackson and Jefferson, Democratic candidates in the Midwest "claimed to be the party of the common man, the bulwark of the Constitution, defending the little people against the encroachments of paternalistic and corrupt power wielded by greedy monopolists and Eastern moneybags."[32]

By the 1880s, the most powerful Republican leaders were stalwart defenders of the new industrial order. The party that had originated in a rush to reform had become a leading bulwark of the status quo, and its early advocacy of free labor gave way to the defense of free enterprise. In the 1880s, the official party credo insisted that "the future of America . . . lay with the city and the factory." Thus the major Republican issue was a call for a high protective tariff to stimulate American economic growth. Although Republican leaders might agree that "excessive profits" were "socially undesirable," they argued, writes Jensen, that "competitive free enterprise would guarantee that profits were, or eventually would become, only equal to a fair return to the invested capital and entrepreneurial talent that had been stimulated to enter industry."[33]

Important as issues such as the tariff were, however, ethno-cultural differences were at the heart of partisan conflict. Republicans continued to appeal primarily to native-born evangelical Protestants, while Catholics and others whose religious practices revolved more around liturgy than piety tended to vote Democratic.[34] The major rhetorical strategy of Republican candidates was to "wave the bloody shirt," constantly reminding voters that their party had saved the union from the tyranny of the slaveholders.[35] Intense party loyalties were often based on family tradition and community culture. The result of such partisanship was electoral campaigns that resembled wars; parties functioned like armies in organizing, disciplining, and recruiting voters.[36]

On the local level, however, Republicans continued to wage campaigns for prohibition and public education that were fully in keeping with the party's origins. Late nineteenth-century Republicans dominated villages and small towns throughout the region. "The higher in status was a voter's work within his domain," Melvyn Hammarberg concluded from his study of *The Indiana Voter* in the 1870s, "the more likely was his party allegiance to be a Republican one."[37] In Trempeauleau, Wisconsin, Republicans had "overwhelming dominance."[38] The same was true in Jacksonville, Illinois.[39] As Ronald Formisano and others have noted, Republicans persisted in intertwining "party, religion, and national character." Theirs, they deeply believed, was "the moral party."[40] They were the proponents of the middle-class values described by Lewis Atherton in *Main Street on the Middle Border*.[41] As the novelist and politician Brand Whitlock put it in his recollections of growing up in Ohio in the 1870s,

> it was natural to be a Republican; it was more than that; it was inevitable that one should be a Republican; it was not a matter of intellectual choice, it was a process of biological selection. . . . One became . . . a Republican just as the Eskimo dons fur clothes. It was inconceivable that any self-respecting person should be a Democrat.[42]

Local midwestern Republican politics reflected the values of the dominant class. Patrick F. Palermo argues that politics were "entrepreneurial in nature within the socio-economic context of community boosterism." Through the rituals of seeking and winning offices, men "combined self-interest with community service to make them indistinguishable." Loyalty to the local community was paramount. Political patronage functioned as a filtering process, weeding out men who sought office for purely selfish reasons or who aspired to office above their social standing. Thus, local Republican organization served to reinforce the power and values of community leaders. "When local politicians [in the late nineteenth-century Midwest] spoke of business-like government, they did not envision a modern bureaucratic state," concludes Palermo. "They were talking about this exchange of services and benefits between honorable men within the community."[43]

To be sure, Republicans did not win every election or carry every issue. But they did set what Rufus Putnam, the founder of Marietta, Ohio, had called the "tone" of society in the Midwest. They were the guardians of the official culture. They made sobriety, self-restraint, decorum, industriousness, and piety the norms. What the village bourgeoisie offered, in fact, was a watered-down version of the Republican creed of the 1850s. They continued to value personal independence based on the ownership of private property, a goal the party's founders had shared with both artisans and farmers. Independence, they believed, still depended on acquisitiveness, competition, hard work, and freedom from the restraints of government. The whole ideology, moreover, retained an overlay of Christian millennialism. The midwestern bourgeoisie still sought progress—economic and social development—through the exercise of individual character. In the United States, Wisconsin Republican Robert M. LaFollette told his fellow congressmen in a classic statement of the party's creed,

> the limitations upon the intellectual growth and development, the social place, and the financial success and triumph of each person are fixed by his own character and power alone. I care not what his birth or station, though born to an inheritance of poverty and toil and obscurity, if he be capable, if he be honest, if he be industrious, if he have courage and pluck and persistence, he will win wealth and power and honor and fame [because] all around him lies inviting and unlimited opportunity.[44]

The Democrats were not quite so certain of all this. As with the Republicans, the real importance of the Democratic party lay in its symbolic appeal to certain kinds of people. By and large, the Democratic constituencies were communities of people outside the bourgeois strongholds. They included Catholics, non-pietistic Protestants, and some Protestant immigrants; men of southern heritage voted slightly more often for Democrats than Republicans. Jensen has suggested that religion was the most important determinant of voting behavior in the Midwest in the 1880s. He may well be right. Certainly, party support cannot be understood in simple class or occupational terms.[45] But what does seem clear is that the Democratic party attracted voters who, to one degree or another, felt alienated from the pietistic, bourgeois Republicanism that set the tone of life in the American Midwest. Democrats, in short, tended to be people who were outside the most important networks of economic power and social influence.

The Democratic party often led the resistance to Republican-sponsored efforts at local reform, generally opposing prohibition and compulsory public education. On a broader level, Frank L. Klement has demonstrated a continuity between Copperheadism and support for railroad regulation in Illinois in the 1860s.[46] In these ways and others, midwestern Democrats remained faithful to the spirit of their Jacksonian ancestors.

Now to say that Democrats often resisted Republican efforts to enforce a cultural hegemony or to eliminate localism in economic affairs is *not* to say that they were anti-capitalistic. Most Democrats were as entrepreneurially minded as any Republican. But the Democrats' respect for localism and laissez-faire in moral matters attracted members of marginal groups who sought to exercise some power—or to prevent its exercise by others.

The cultural differences between the two parties reached a climax and a turning point in the last dozen years of the century. The most studied case is the controversy over the so-called Bennett Law in Wisconsin in 1889–1890. The Republican-supported law aroused strong opposition because of the combined impact of two requirements—that all children had to attend some public or private school and, most critically, that "no school shall be regarded as a school under this act unless there shall be taught therein, as part of the elementary education of children, reading, writing, arithmetic, and United States history in the English language."[47] Almost immediately, German Protestants and Catholics, long angry about Republican support for temperance, denounced the legislation as a tyrannical affront to their cultural and religious traditions. The consequence was a rise in the fortunes of Wisconsin Democrats, who swept the state elections in 1890.

The Bennett Law became so controversial, argues Kleppner, "because the educational question dealt not merely with external manifestations of conflicting values, but with the attempts on the part of each group to perpetuate [its] values."[48] What was at stake was the ability to mold the future of the region and the nation. In political terms, as the exacting work of Kleppner and Jensen demonstrates, the battle was between *pietistic* Republicans and *liturgical* Democrats. But on a deeper level the struggle was over the ability of middle-class, Protestant midwesterners to maintain their cultural hegemony.

Given the upsurge in working class consciousness in the mid-1880s, it is hardly surprising to find middle-class Republicans strenuously campaigning for temperance, blue laws, and the English language. What was surprising was that they were no longer winning elections. The Republican defeat in Wisconsin in 1890 was not isolated. Throughout the Midwest, Republicans were labeled as Puritanical and anti-libertarian. Even the Force Bill of 1890—legislation designed to give Congress the power to supervise congressional elections in the South—hurt Republican candidates as Democrats attacked them as "fanatics" and centralizers.[49] Ironically, the very issues on which the Republican bourgeoisie had ridden to power in the 1850s and 1860s—attacks on Southerners and immigrants—were now leading them to defeat. In 1890, thirty-three midwestern Republican congressmen lost their seats, and the Midwest, writes Jensen, "was now Democratic."[50]

The reasons for this shift are clear. First, it only took the movement of a few thousand votes to turn years of victory into defeat. But more crucial in the long run was the changing nature of midwestern economic and political structures. The changes wrought in the social structure by industrialism and urbanization required new ways of thinking and behaving. The bourgeoisie was thrown on the defensive, by what appeared to be a united working class. Big business may not have been heartless and cruel, but middle-class midwesterners recognized that old shibboleths about character and hard work did not make as much sense in the Chicago of the 1890s as they had in the Cincinnati of the 1850s. As John L. Thomas argues in his collective biography of Edward Bellamy, Henry George, and Henry Demarest Lloyd, the Haymarket tragedy convinced "liberals in all the professions" that "their most urgent task was educating middle-class Americans by helping them to adjust their preferences for the fluidity and individualism of an agrarian social order to an industrial one in which these values seemed dysfunctional."[51]

Although the crisis of the 1880s inspired a nostalgic utopianism and evocations of "traditional" bourgeois values, middle-class Americans gradually came to terms with new conditions. As they "searched for order" in the modern industrial world, Americans participated in an organizational revolution that created new national professional networks.[52] They enlisted the aid of science and statistics in analyzing and documenting the ills of industrialism, tempering bourgeois moralism with a new secular spirit. And the Republican party in the mid-1890s began to practice the politics of accommodation.

The heavily pietistic tenor of the GOP had long worried professional politicians such as Rutherford B. Hayes. But the defeats of 1890 enabled the party to shed its Puritanical image and to identify itself with progress and prosperity. Helped immeasurably by the great depression of the 1890s and divisions among Democrats, the Republicans recovered their political momentum and inaugurated nearly four decades of regional ascendancy with the presidential campaign of 1896.

The key to their success, typified by the victory of William McKinley of Ohio (with the support of businessmen such as Mark Hanna and Charles Dawes), was the acceptance of cultural pluralism. "They avoided identification with those cultural symbols with which the party had usually identified itself," notes Kleppner. The Republican party became instead "an integrative mechanism that sought to avoid subcoalitional conflicts by minimizing cultural questions and addressing itself to a commonly shared concern with 'prosperity.'"[53] In the 1896 campaign, Richard Jensen writes, the Republicans "promised every ethnic minority that, if they demonstrated their patriotism and good faith by voting for

McKinley, the new Republican administration would guarantee their security."[54]

In the cities, moreover, Republican businessmen such as Hazen Pingree of Detroit accommodated themselves to new political realities. They attempted to work with rather than against working-class communities; they campaigned for more *efficient*, rather than more *moral*, government. As Melvin G. Holli has written of Pingree, he "took Detroit's Republican party with its nativist and rural bias and its business-class orientation and transformed it into a useful instrument for social reform."[55] Detroit had long been a Democratic city when Pingree, a white Anglo-Saxon Protestant shoe manufacturer and a life-long Republican, ran for mayor in 1889. Republicans were suffering there as elsewhere from their identification with "Puritan" morality and cultural inflexibility. Pingree won by appealing to ethnic voters such as Germans and Poles. Significantly, given the Republicans' long support of temperance, he launched his campaign in a saloon. "He drank 'red-eye' whisky with the Irish voters, spoke to German societies, [and] flattered the Poles."[56] Bolstered by an ethnically balanced ticket, Pingree revitalized the Republican party by transforming it from an instrument of moral reform into one of social reform. In the end, Germans and Poles were the key to his victory, a debt Pingree recognized when it came time to make political appointments.[57]

In office, men such as Pingree stood for reorganization of city government and services, eschewing the moralistic postures of middle-class nativism for sound business practices and rational action. The idea, argues Zane Miller in *Boss Cox's Cincinnati*, was to "educate, discipline, organize, and coalesce without arousing the divisive, emotional, and hysterical responses which helped immobilize municipal statesmen in the 1880s."[58]

The Republican leadership's acceptance of pluralism and the rejection of pietism amounted to an acknowledgment of the changes wrought by industrialism and urbanization in the American Midwest. Republican leaders, according to Jensen, now "said that America had become an interdependent, industrial nation, and that farms, factories, shops, mines, and railroads, and yes, banks, offices, schools, stores, and wholesale houses all cooperated to produce genuine wealth; no sector of the society could be punished without harm to everyone."[59] The election of 1896 marked the accommodation of the middle class to the new industrial order. It "proved beyond question," concludes John L. Thomas, "that the forces of corporate capitalism that were revolutionizing the rest of American life had now triumphed at the polls."[60]

Of course, not all midwesterners embraced the new order. Popular political protest took the form of support for insurgent Progressives such as Robert M. LaFollette. Political defeat and the economic crises of the

1890s transformed the sturdy Republican congressman into a leader of what the historian David Thelen describes as a grassroots movement against large-scale industrialism. Despite the growing power of national corporations and institutions in their lives, many midwesterners longed for the restoration of a world in which, they believed, there had been economic opportunity for all. They continued to insist "that capitalism's basic virtue was its liberation of the individual to progress at his own speed and ability." Still, the growing gap between rich and poor, the monotony and drudgery of factory work convinced many that "the United States was no longer a middle-class democracy with unlimited opportunity for all."[61]

Even in the villages and towns that dotted the midwestern landscape, changes in economic and social structures challenged the values so aggressively asserted by the mid-nineteenth-century bourgeoisie. Most apparent was increasing dependence on the outside world. As Lewis Atherton noted in *Main Street on the Middle Border*, "declining independence had been the lot of country towns since Civil War days." Public utilities, for example, "made the individual aware that he was becoming part of a larger world."[62]

Consumerism played a crucial role in the trend toward national conformity and the loss of independence. Slowly but surely, a demand for brand-name products and for goods from mail-order houses transformed the mentality of small-town residents. Railroads, chain stores, and eventually the automobile brought midwesterners into a national marketplace. People purchased goods to fill their leisure time and to make themselves stylish.[63] For many midwesterners, the accumulation of material goods and labor or time-saving gadgets became the primary benefit of living in a modern society. "The American citizen's first importance to his country is no longer that of citizen but that of consumer," a Muncie newspaper proclaimed in the 1920s.[64] Midwesterners seemed increasingly job-oriented, accepting prosperity as the key issue in their lives.[65]

Along with consumerism came a growing toleration of alternative cultures. Middle-class citizens might still look askance at parochial schools or saloons, but they tended to ignore rather than fight them. Cultural pluralism was hardly celebrated in the small town, but it became an unspoken part of life. The fact is that many people were not "self-respecting" by bourgeois standards. Although the middle class "dominated education and fought hard to enforce its convictions," wrote Atherton, "it was never able to establish conformity on the part of all citizens." (Atherton identified four other groups in village life, an upper class, Catholics, immigrants, and a lower class.)[66]

Economic boosterism lay behind many of the calls for tolerance. In Muncie, Indiana, in the 1920s, the Lynds found "an organized, professional type of city-boosting" which insisted that the city must be kept to the fore and its shortcomings blanketed under the din of local boosting—or new business will not come to town. The result of this is the muzzling of self-criticism by hurling the term "knocker" at the head of a critic and the drowning of incipient social problems under a public mood of everything being "fine and dandy."[67]

Consumerism and boosterism brought to the small towns and cities of the Midwest a facade of conformity, a kind of general homage to "traditional" middle-class dogmas. The economic transformation of the region diluted the midwestern identification with commercial capitalism: what had once been vital became reflexive. People adhered to certain values without being sure of what they meant—and by consciously avoiding any discussion of their implications. The Lynds reported that many citizens of Muncie treated the question of what a Christian believes as a joke, "a condition reflecting the general tendency to accept 'being a Christian' as synonymous with being 'civilized' or 'an honest man' or 'a reputable citizen.'"[68]

The Lynds criticized the people of Muncie for failing to adapt their culture to a new set of economic realities.[69] They concluded that the city's residents were caught between the material attractions of a new world and the moral imperatives of an old one. Even as they succumbed to the allurements of mass consumerism, Muncie's residents generally employed "the psychology of the last century" in raising children, dealing with deviants, and seeking jobs; they continued to adhere to "a *laissez-faire* individualism" that seemed out of place in a modern society.[70]

While the Lynds tend at times to caricature their subjects, they are surely correct in pointing out that early twentieth-century midwesterners did not welcome changes in the social structures of their lives. But that reluctance stemmed less from stupidity than from the power of the society into which they were born. So enormous was the appeal of bourgeois values, so tightly intertwined were they with regional identity, that people would not let them go. They were not so much afraid of change as they were *proud* of their past. The "psychology of the last century" was their tradition; it organized their world; it had created, or so they thought, a society of unprecedented plenty and progress. It is not surprising that they clung to the values of the nineteenth-century bourgeoisie. In fact, it would be more surprising had not so many people held on so tenaciously to the powerful promise of bourgeois conceptions of individual behavior and society.

The economic and political changes we have been describing in this chapter had an impact throughout American society in the twentieth century. But they had particular resonance in the Midwest because the region had been settled and developed in tandem with the establishment of commercial capitalism in the United States. Unlike New England or the South or the Southwest, the Midwest had no prior existence—as a European community—before this great transformation. The rise of middle-class values and the institutions of capitalism were synonymous with the rise of the Midwest. Their triumph in the middle of the nineteenth century had been its triumph. The Midwest had been defined as the home of responsible, earnest, industrious citizens, free from all save voluntary ties with others. But industrialism brought different kinds of people to the region and created new forms of dependency that jeopardized the crucial link between production and citizenship at the foundation of the Republican, bourgeois ideology. Midwesterners had transformed their region into a showplace of commercial capitalism only to have their very success transform their society once again.

By the 1890s, moreover, the midwestern bourgeoisie had lost its initiative and surrendered its momentum. The acceptance of cultural pluralism by political and economic leaders in the last decade of the nineteenth century marked the end of the dynamic phase of midwestern culture. Accommodation to differences had never been part of that world. When Republican leaders accepted pluralism, when they accepted the social changes brought on by industrialism, when they sang the praises of consumers rather than producers, they were to a significant degree abandoning their origins.

Thus as industrialism, consumerism, and political pluralism transformed the world of small-scale capitalistic enterprise, they threatened the very identity of the American Midwest and its middle-class citizens. Could it be that their hegemony would be so short-lived? Could it be that what had amounted to revolutionary values in the 1850s had, by the 1890s, become traditional values to be defended against the forces of change?

3. The Middle-Class Frontier

At the end of the nineteenth century many middle-class midwesterners were interested in the origins and history of their culture or "civilization" as they called it. There was a veritable wave of nostalgia for the "good old days" of small-town life when "traditional" values had supposedly held sway. Countless local and county histories were produced, often consisting of little more than collections of biographies of the ancestors of respectable, leading citizens. Novelists and poets also turned to the past, celebrating the simple virtues of earlier days and condemning the materialism of the present.

Indeed, it is not coincidental that the Midwest produced its own version of an American literary renaissance at this time. As the middle-class world of commercial capitalism that had defined the region stagnated into ritualistic celebrations of progress and prosperity, and as the citizens of small towns seemed to lose their deep sense of engagement with conflicting cultures, intellectuals naturally enough began brooding on the origins and nature of midwestern culture. In the early twentieth century, they found little to praise, attacking small towns for their sterility and their repression, their lack of imagination and their parochialism. *Winesburg, Ohio* and *Main Street* became symbols of midwestern blandness and stagnation. The typical midwesterner was Sinclair Lewis's George Babbitt, a pathetic man going about the business of business, trying to conform, without any real sense of power or meaning in his life. The Midwest had lost its dynamism, its urgency.

When Babbitt rises to give the annual address to the Zenith Real Estate Board, he cannot resist, having begun with a joke at the expense of the Irish, to celebrate what he calls the "Ideal Citizen." That person is a caricature of the mid-nineteenth century middle-class citizen. He is decent, Christian, industrious, well-informed, a believer in progress and a lover of children. But he has lost the energy, the edge, the radical quality that he had possessed in the era of the Civil War. Bourgeois life has become routine. Babbitt speaks not of a new race of people but of "the specifications of the Standardized American Citizen!"[71]

While there are such men in all American cities, they predominate in the Midwest. Babbitt is proud of his region because it is the most fully American. With the exception of Chicago, it stands against "foreign ideas and communism." In his city of Zenith, there is

> the largest proportion of these Regular Guys, and that's what sets it in a class by itself; that's why Zenith will be remembered in history as having set the pace for a civilization that shall endure when the old time-killing ways are gone forever and the day of earnest efficient endeavor shall have dawned all round the world![72]

In the mouth of this stereotypical booster and conformist, the revolutionary ideas of commercial capitalism have become empty platitudes. Babbitt's only vision is of a time when

> our sons and daughters see that the ideal of American manhood and culture isn't a lot of cranks sitting around chewing the rag about their Rights and their Wrongs, but a God-fearing, hustling, successful, two-fisted Regular Guy, who belongs to some church with pep and piety to it, who belongs [to some voluntary organization] . . . who plays hard and works hard, and whose answer to his critics is a square-toed boot that'll teach the grouches and smart alecks to respect the He-man and get out and toot for Uncle Samuel, U.S.A.![73]

Babbitt is convinced that the origins of the "new type of civilization" he both embodies and celebrates lay in the spirit and determination of the

American people. His fervent hope is that someday "folks will quit hand-ing all the credit to a lot of moth-eaten, mildewed, out-of-date, old, Euro-pean dumps, and give proper credit to the famous Zenith spirit."[74] Freder-ick Jackson Turner may have put it more eloquently. But the sentiment of his frontier thesis was essentially the same.

If Lewis wrote with heavy-handed sarcasm, his concern with the nature of midwestern civilization was hardly unique. The region produced the leading American novelists of the era, including Theodore Dreiser of In-diana, Sinclair Lewis of Minnesota, Ernest Hemingway of Illinois, and Sherwood Anderson of Ohio. Their works reflected a number of styles and subjects, but what they had in common was a concern with the fate of middle-class values in a modern industrial society. Although this theme was not peculiar to midwestern writers, it had a particular signifi-cance for them. Above all, they betrayed an ambivalence about the soci-ety in which they had matured; they sensed that something was wrong and they looked to the past to find out what it was.

Sherwood Anderson's *Winesburg, Ohio* is, as the literary critic David D. Anderson has suggested, an excellent example of this genre.[75] In one of the stories that make up the book—"Godliness"—Anderson describes the fate of an Ohio farmer named Jesse Bentley, a man whose personal ambition was matched only by his piety. Born before the Civil War, Bent-ley thought of "himself as an extraordinary man, one set apart from his fellows. He wanted terribly to make his life a thing of great importance . . . and he wanted God to notice and to talk to him."[76] Bentley saw his prosperity as a sign of God's favor. He was, he believed, a chosen son of God and destined to be the progenitor of a new race of men. But Jesse fathers a girl, not a boy, and has to put his faith in his only grandson, David, whom he eventually alienates.

Although Sherwood Anderson was not a historian, he was profoundly aware of the social context that produced men such as Jesse Bentley. An-derson does not see him as unique. To the contrary, his Jesse is a man whose ambitions and zeal reflect a particular ethos. His godliness was born of an earlier era, Anderson suggests, one of ignorance and loneliness. But since that time a "revolution" has taken place.[77] Its cause is "modern industrialism" and what it engenders is greed and materialism. Jesse, like men all around him, finds the new technology and the new wealth irre-sistible. He begins to look for new ways to make money, and to partici-pate more fully in "the most materialistic age in the history of the world . . . when the will to power would replace the will to serve and beauty would be well-nigh forgotten in the terrible headlong rush of mankind toward the acquiring of possessions."[78]

Confused by his greed, confounded by the appeal of materialism, Jesse Bentley longs for escape from these new economic and social complexities. Like others, he looks for answers in the past, indeed, in a peculiarly midwestern kind of past.

> Sometimes he was altogether doubtful and thought that God had deserted the world. He regretted the fate that had not let him live in a simpler and sweeter time when at the beckoning of some strange cloud in the sky men left their lands and houses and went forth into the wilderness to create new races.[79]

The longing of Jesse Bentley for personal glory and for some larger meaning leads him back to the frontier, to a romanticized era when men seemed to have power over their environment, when, he imagined, they had transformed the world.

Bentley can no longer do such things, of course. His ambitions isolate him from reality, trap him in a world of possessions he craves but does not really want. By focusing on David, his grandson, Jesse seeks to rekindle the past, to find meaning, to be empowered. "For him the coming of the boy David did much to bring back with renewed force the old faith and it seemed to him that God had at last looked with favor upon him."[80] In the end, however, Jesse's faith terrifies the boy and drives him away. The old man is left alone, having created nothing but destroyed much.

Anderson's story is not a meditation on history, but his characterization of Jesse Bentley gives us insight into the midwestern mind at the turn of the twentieth century. The literature produced by its citizens suggests that something has gone terribly wrong. We could easily ascribe this malaise to a general sense of alienation from materialism among intellectuals in the early twentieth century. But what seems peculiar about the midwestern writers is their—or at least their characters'—sense of loss. They seem to be mourning the passing of some kind of golden age when the world made sense and people had the power to change it. The settlement of the Midwest had made something new, something vital, something important, but it had either disappeared or become ossified into sterile rituals and empty rhetoric.

David D. Anderson has written that midwestern writers did not, as early critics suggested, hate small-town life. Men such as Sherwood Anderson, Booth Tarkington, and Brand Whitlock were searching for the meaning of midwestern culture. The Northwest Ordinance, writes David Anderson, had "promised a new relationship between the individual and his peers. . . . It [had] promised an open society, plentiful, cheap land, and the opportunity to rise as far as one's talents and ability might take him."[81] The chance to succeed or fail on one's own merits in an open society was the essence of the midwestern myth that "together with faith in the Republican Party . . . , the sanctity of the agricultural way of life, and the virtue of life in the towns, was the foundation upon which society had been constructed."[82] In the novels of Sherwood Anderson, Tarkington, Whitlock, and others, the small towns of the Midwest are the last outposts of that culture against the rising industrial order. According to David Anderson, the message that dominates the Tarkington novels is that "success and fulfillment are the result of the movement Westward, to the arena in which the individual, his merits, his mettle, and his virtue are tested and judgement rendered by his peers."[83] In the realm of popular culture, in short, the frontier and middle-class values had become fused. To the midwestern bourgeoisie, they had always been one and inseparable. The wilderness had, after the inevitable demise of Indians, trappers, squatters, and soldiers, become the refuge of industrious, pious, decent people.

This interpretation of midwestern history was extremely powerful. And a major reason that it was so persuasive to so many people was that their loyalty to the economic and social structures of commercial capitalism was becoming increasingly tenuous. Industrialism and urbanization had significantly altered the environment in which citizens, *as individuals*, had tested themselves and achieved wealth and reputation. Now many ambitious young people left the small towns of the Midwest to find meaning as well as fame and fortune. They went to the cities, to the East, and to Europe. Or some followed Hemingway's Nick Adams into the woods—a kind of modern frontier—to test their individual mettle and to reenact the idealized exploits of their forebears.[84]

Yet, even in such places, these latter-day pioneers continued to be guided—or haunted?—by the values inculcated in the towns and villages of the Midwest. The ideology of the nineteenth-century middle class retained its hold on midwestern minds long after it had lost its urgency. The Midwest, after all, had been defined in its terms. Regional identity had grown out of the constant struggles of the middle class with different kinds of people and in the unyielding assertion of the supremacy of commercial capitalism. At the beginning of the twentieth century, a great many people continued to insist that the typical American was the white, middle-class, Republican businessman in a small town in the Midwest. The truth of this assertion was beside the point.

But more than a century after the writing of the Northwest Ordinance, many midwesterners no longer sought identity and meaning in the celebration of progress, or in wars against alternative cultures, or in the exercise of their own characters. Rather, midwestern culture expressed itself in the making of myth, imagining a frontier era in which people—middle-class, midwestern people—had once been the powerful progenitors of a new civilization. Having lost control of the present, they laid claim to the legitimacy conferred by history. In the early twentieth century, the rhetorical self-image of the Midwest was still, in the words of a sometime resident, F. Scott Fitzgerald, about "the richness of life," about "infinite possibilities," about "inexhaustible variety." But those who actually sought to inhabit that world were, like Fitzgerald's midwesterner, Nick Carraway, merely beating against the currents of history and thus condemned to be "borne back ceaselessly into the past."[85]

Typical of such midwesterners was the historian Frederick Jackson Turner. In the 1890s, at precisely the moment when industrialism and pluralism were coming to dominate the region, Turner emerged as the most powerful interpreter of its origins and culture. He provided the scholarly and theoretical basis for the growing celebration of the long-lost environment that had supposedly called forth the best in settlers as they laid the foundations of a new kind of civilization. Despite their concerns about the present (or perhaps because of them), the citizens of the Midwest could take pride in their glorious past. As Turner—the son of a Republican family in a small town in Wisconsin—began to tell the world, the people of the Midwest had done much more than create a prosperous and orderly civilization. They had recreated the United States of America in their own image.

Frederick Jackson Turner, Regional Historian

In a superb biography of Frederick Jackson Turner published in 1973, Ray Allen Billington suggested that the influential historian's views on the significance of the frontier owed much to "the environment in which he was reared."[1] Billington referred specifically to the "quasi-frontier community" of Portage, Wisconsin, in which Turner was born in November 1861.[2] The point was that Frederick Jackson Turner had come of age in a society that valued precisely the traits of "democratic egalitarianism" and "individualism" he would later associate with the settlement of the frontier. The Turner who delivered his famous paper on "The Significance of the Frontier in American History" at the 1893 meeting of the American Historical Association in Chicago was a product of the world he described.

Billington was surely right in pointing to the influence of Turner's early environment in shaping his scholarship. Midwesterners celebrated individualism and enterprise, championed economic development and moral certainty, and asserted the importance of their region in the progress of American culture. But Turner's world was shaped less by the frontier experience than by the middle-class milieu of his family.[3] In many ways, his life's work was dedicated to demonstrating the primacy of bourgeois values and commercial capitalism in American history. *If* Americans were individualistic, democratic, and enterprising, *if* they valued hard work, domestic morality, and material progress and believed in the efficacy of political parties and private initiative, it was because of their peculiar experience in creating new societies on the frontier.

While Turner tended to ascribe these characteristics to most Americans, his principal subjects were the residents of the Ohio and Mississippi valleys in the early nineteenth century. Little wonder that his work had its greatest influence on the history of the Old Northwest. Turner, above all, was a regional historian. It in no way diminishes his achievement to suggest that he provided a model for the history of the Midwest which reflected the values and aspirations of both his class and his section as well as his race and gender. Turner, of course, would never have described himself in this way. For like other midwesterners, he assumed that the history of his region was also essentially the history of the United States.

The significance of Turner's work, in fact, was to legitimize the hegemony of the nineteenth-century midwestern middle class. In the communities of the Old Northwest, the birth of bourgeois society had been natural and inevitable. The Midwest had been created and nurtured not by foreign or eastern influences but by the initiatives of thousands of individuals who, whatever their other differences, shared a commitment to material and moral progress. The society they built, however challenged by the impact of industrialization or immigration, was, in Turner's view, the seminal American society. His history, in other words, extended even as it defended the midwestern bourgeois perspective.

In the end, the genius of Frederick Jackson Turner lay less in his historical research than in his ability to fashion a particular story of the past that captured the imagination of a great many people who were very much like him. The fact that his celebration of the bourgeois world required what might seem to us a perversion of the history of the region is beside the point. (Turner would undoubtedly think the same of the preceding pages.) What does matter is that he provided a framework for debating the meaning of the past that has lasted for a century. If his story no longer makes as much sense now—if it sometimes seems ethnocentric, racist, sexist, dichotomous, or just plain superficial—it is only because our world is different from his.[4] We need our own story.

NOTES

Introduction

1. Frederick Jackson Turner, *The Frontier in American History* (New York, 1920), 3–4.

2. Turner was, of course, well aware of the significance of sectionalism in American history. See particularly his *The Rise of the New West, 1819–1829* (New York, 1906) and *The Significance of Sections in American History* (New York, 1932).

3. See Ray Allen Billington, *Frederick Jackson Turner: Historian, Scholar, Teacher* (New York, 1973). For further discussion of Turner see our epilogue.

4. Readers will need to know exactly what we mean by terms such as "commercial capitalism," "the market," "culture," "Old Northwest," and "Midwest." *Commercial capitalism* refers to an economic and social order in which the primary activity is the private, competitive production of goods for profit; it entails the widespread use of cash, banks, and cheap and efficient transportation and communication systems as well as the exaltation of private enterprise and profit. By *market* we mean the impersonal, trans-local system of exchange relationships linking producers and consumers in the regional, national, and world economies. *Culture* we define as the rules under which a community operates, the usually unspoken collection of values, assumptions, and social cues through which people understand and deal with one another. Finally, we use the terms *Old Northwest* and *Midwest* to refer to the region in two different periods of its history; the first is employed in discussions of the area before the 1850s and the second in our descriptions of it once its middle-class citizens had begun to give it some overall cultural cohesion. Although we realize that geographic definitions of the Midwest vary widely, we have concentrated on the history of the states—Ohio, Indiana, Illinois, Michigan, and Wisconsin—settled in the first half of the nineteenth century under the Ordinance of 1787.

Readers more interested in history than historiography should consult Malcolm J. Rohrbough's excellent survey, *The Trans-Appalachian Frontier: People, Societies, and Institutions, 1775–1850* (New York, 1978). The fullest introduction to the early history of the Midwest remains R. Carlyle Buley, *The Old Northwest: Pioneer Period, 1815–1840*, 2 vols. (Bloomington, Indiana, 1950). See also the recent brief histories of individual states collected in *Heartland: Comparative Histories of the Midwestern States*, ed. James H. Madison (Bloomington, Indiana, 1988).

I: The Significance of the Northwest Ordinance

1. Caleb Atwater, *The General Character, Present and Future Prospects of the People of Ohio* (Columbus, Ohio, 1827); Caleb Atwater, *A History of the State of Ohio, Natural and Civil* (Cincinnati, 1838); Jacob Burnet, *Notes on the Early Settlement of the North-Western Territory* (Cincinnati, 1847); Salmon P. Chase, ed., *The Statutes of Ohio and of the Northwestern Territory Adopted or Enacted from 1788 to 1833 Inclusive* (Cincinnati, 1833); and Timothy Walker, *Annual*

Discourse, Delivered before the Ohio Historical and Philosophical Society, at Columbus, on the 23d of December, 1837 (Cincinnati, 1838).

2. John D. Barnhart, *Valley of Democracy: The Frontier versus the Plantation in the Ohio Valley, 1775–1818* (Bloomington, Indiana, 1953); Beverley W. Bond, Jr., *The Civilization of the Old Northwest: A Study of Political, Social, and Economic Development, 1788–1812* (New York, 1934); and R. Carlyle Buley, *The Old Northwest: Pioneer Period, 1815–1840*, 2 vols. (Bloomington, Indiana, 1950).

3. Malcolm J. Rohrbough, *The Land Office Business: The Settlement and Administration of American Public Lands, 1789–1837* (New York, 1968), 3–25; Payson J. Treat, *The National Land System, 1785–1820* (New York, 1910), 15–40; Paul Wallace Gates, *History of Public Land Law Development* (Washington, D.C., 1968), 59–74; and William D. Pattison, *Beginnings of the American Rectangular Land Survey System, 1784–1800* (Chicago, 1957).

4. These developments are recounted at length in Thomas P. Abernethy, *Western Lands and the American Revolution* (New York, 1937); Merrill Jensen, *The New Nation: A History of the United States during the Confederation* (New York, 1950); Jack Ericson Eblen, *The First and Second United States Empires: Governors and Territorial Government, 1784–1912* (Pittsburgh, 1968); and Peter S. Onuf, *The Origins of the Federal Republic: Jurisdictional Controversies in the United States, 1775–1787* (Philadelphia, 1983).

5. Peter S. Onuf, "Toward Federalism: Virginia, Congress, and the Western Lands," *William and Mary Quarterly*, 3d ser., 39 (1977): 374.

6. Peter S. Onuf, "Maryland: The Small Republic in the New Nation," in *Ratifying the Constitution*, ed. Michael Gillespie and Michael Lienesch (Lawrence, Kansas, 1989), 171–200.

7. Norman K. Risjord, *Chesapeake Politics, 1781–1800* (New York, 1978), 240–47.

8. Peter S. Onuf, "Liberty, Development, and Union: Visions of the West in the 1780s," *William and Mary Quarterly*, 3d ser., 43 (1986): 179–213. See also William R. Willoughby, "Early American Interest in Waterway Connections between the East and the West," *Indiana Magazine of History* 52 (1956): 319–42.

9. George Washington to Henry Knox, December 5, 1784, *The Writings of George Washington*, ed. John C. Fitzpatrick, 39 vols. (Washington, D.C., 1931–1944), 28: 4.

10. Cathy Matson and Peter S. Onuf, "Toward a Republican Empire: Interest and Ideology in Revolutionary America," *American Quarterly* 37 (1985): 496–531.

11. Staughton Lynd, "The Compromise of 1787," in *Class Conflict, Slavery, and the United States Constitution: Ten Essays* (Indianapolis, 1967), 210.

12. Drew R. McCoy, "James Madison and Visions of National Identity in the Confederation Period: A Regional Perspective," in *Beyond Confederation: Origins of the Constitution and American National Identity*, ed. Richard Beeman, Stephen Botein, and Edward C. Carter, II (Chapel Hill, North Carolina, 1987), 245–46.

13. Onuf, "Liberty, Development, and Union," 181.

14. Frederick W. Marks III, *Independence on Trial: Foreign Affairs and the Making of the Constitution* (Baton Rouge, Louisiana, 1973). See also Charles R. Ritcheson, *Aftermath of Revolution: British Policy toward the United States, 1783–1795* (Dallas, Texas, 1968).

15. Gordon S. Wood, *The Creation of the American Republic, 1776–1787* (Chapel Hill, North Carolina, 1969).

16. Robert F. Berkhofer, Jr., "The Northwest Ordinance and the Principle of

Territorial Evolution," in *The American Territorial System,* ed. John P. Bloom (Athens, Ohio, 1973), 45–55; and Thomas P. Slaughter, *The Whiskey Rebellion: Frontier Epilogue to the American Revolution* (New York, 1986).

17. Berkhofer, "Northwest Ordinance and the Principle of Territorial Evolution." See also Peter S. Onuf, "Territories and Statehood," *Encyclopedia of American Political History,* ed. Jack P. Greene, 3 vols. (New York, 1984), 3: 1283–1304.

18. Peter S. Onuf, "The Founders' Vision: Education in the Development of the Old Northwest," in *"Schools and the Means of Education Shall Forever Be Encouraged": A History of Public Education in the Old Northwest, 1787–1880,* ed. Paul H. Mattingly and Edward W. Stevens (Athens, Ohio, 1987), 5–15.

19. Peter S. Onuf, *Statehood and Union: A History of the Northwest Ordinance* (Bloomington, Indiana, 1987).

20. Eblen, *First and Second United States Empires,* 47.

21. Robert F. Berkhofer, "Jefferson, the Ordinance of 1784, and the Origins of the American Territorial System," *William and Mary Quarterly,* 3d ser., 29 (1972): 231–62.

22. Berkhofer, "Northwest Ordinance and the Principle of Territorial Evolution."

23. See Albert Furtwangler, *The Authority of Publius: A Reading of the Federalist Papers* (Ithaca, New York, 1984).

24. Rosemarie Zagarri, *The Politics of Size: Representation in the United States, 1776–1812* (Ithaca, New York, 1987).

25. Drew R. McCoy, *The Elusive Republic: Political Economy in Jeffersonian America* (Chapel Hill, North Carolina, 1980); and McCoy, "James Madison and Visions of National Identity."

26. Onuf, "Liberty, Development, and Union," 180.

27. *Strader* v. *Graham,* 10 Howard 82 (1850). See the excellent discussion in Don E. Fehrenbacher, *The Dred Scott Case: Its Significance in American Law and Politics* (New York, 1978).

28. Walter C. Haight, "The Binding Effect of the Ordinance of 1787," *Publications of the Michigan Political Science Association* 2 (1896–1897): 343–402.

29. Phillip R. Shriver, "America's Other Bicentennial," *The Old Northwest* 9 (1983): 219–35.

30. Paul Finkelman, "Slavery and the Northwest Ordinance: A Study in Ambiguity," *Journal of the Early Republic* 7 (1986): 343–70.

31. Robert Ferguson, "'We Do Ordain and Establish': The Constitution as Literary Text," *William and Mary Law Review* 29 (1987): 3–25.

32. *Strader* v. *Graham,* 95–96.

33. Onuf, *Statehood and Union,* 89.

34. Todd B. Galloway, "The Ohio-Michigan Boundary Line Dispute," *Ohio Archaeological and Historical Quarterly* 4 (1895): 473–84; Carl Wittke, "The Ohio-Michigan Boundary Dispute Re-Examined," *Ohio Historical Quarterly* 45 (1936): 299–319; Alec R. Gilpin, *The Territory of Michigan* (East Lansing, Michigan, 1970); and Onuf, *Statehood and Union,* 94–108.

35. Eblen, *First and Second United States Empires,* 213–36. See also Burnet, *Notes on the Early Settlement,* 335–69; and Peter S. Onuf, "Territories and Statehood," 1283–1304.

36. Onuf, *Statehood and Union,* 108.

37. The petitions are collected in Jacob Piatt Dunn, Jr., "Slavery Petitions and Papers," *Indiana State Historical Society Publications* 2 (1894): 443–529. See also Richard Frederick O'Dell, "The Early Antislavery Movement in Ohio" (Ph.D. diss., University of Michigan, 1948); Jacob Piatt Dunn, Jr., *Indiana, A Redemp-*

tion from Slavery (Boston, 1890), 219–60; Emma Lou Thornbrough, *The Negro in Indiana before 1900: A Study of a Minority* (Indianapolis, 1957), 8–12; and Onuf, *Statehood and Union,* 109–32.

38. William A. Dunning, "Are the States Equal under the Constitution?" *Political Science Quarterly* 3 (1888): 425–53; and Peter S. Onuf, "New State Equality: The Ambiguous History of a Constitutional Principle," *Publius* 18 (1988): 53–69.

39. Finkelman, "Slavery and the Northwest Ordinance," 359.

40. Eugene H. Berwanger, *The Frontier against Slavery: Western Anti-Slavery Negro Prejudice and the Slavery Extension Controversy* (Urbana, Illinois, 1967); and Onuf, *Statehood and Union.* See also William H. Brown, *An Historical Sketch of the Early Movement in Illinois for the Legalization of Slavery* (Chicago, 1865); and Merton L. Dillon, "The Antislavery Movement in Illinois, 1809–1844" (Ph.D. diss., University of Michigan, 1950).

41. Onuf, *Statehood and Union,* 132.

42. Ibid.

43. Eblen, *First and Second United States Empires,* 14. An earlier version of this section appears in Andrew R. L. Cayton, "The Origins of Politics in the Old Northwest," in *Pathways to the Old Northwest: An Observance of the Bicentennial of the Northwest Ordinance* (Indianapolis, 1988), 59–70.

44. Ibid., 113.

45. Both men are lacking a modern biographer. On St. Clair, see William H. Smith, *The St. Clair Papers: The Life and Public Services of Arthur St. Clair,* 2 vols. (Cincinnati, 1882); Jeffrey P. Brown, "Arthur St. Clair and the Northwest Territory," *Northwest Ohio Quarterly* 59 (1988): 75–90; Patrick J. Furlong, "The Investigation of General Arthur St. Clair, 1792–1793," *Capital Studies* 5 (1977); Furlong, "Putting the Ordinance to Work in the Northwest," *The Northwest Ordinance: A Bicentennial Handbook,* ed. Robert M. Taylor, Jr. (Indianapolis, 1987), 79–104; Alfred B. Sears, "The Political Philosophy of Arthur St. Clair," *Ohio Historical Quarterly* 69 (1940): 41–57; and G. L. Wilson, "Arthur St. Clair and the Administration of the Old Northwest, 1788–1802" (Ph.D. diss., University of Southern California, 1957).

On Sargent, see Benjamin H. Pershing, "Winthrop Sargent: A Builder in the Old Northwest" (Ph.D. diss., University of Chicago, 1927). See also George B. Toulmin, "The Political Ideas of Winthrop Sargent, A New England Federalist on the Frontier," *Journal of Mississippi History* 15 (1953): 207–29; Robert V. Haynes, "The Formation of the Territory," in *A History of Mississippi,* ed. Richard Aubrey McLemore, 3 vols. (Hattiesburg, Mississippi, 1973) 1: 174–216; and John Wunder, "American Law and Order Comes to Mississippi Territory: The Making of Sargent's Code, 1798–1800," *Journal of Mississippi History* 38 (1976): 131–56.

46. Andrew R. L. Cayton, *The Frontier Republic: Ideology and Politics in the Ohio Country, 1780–1825* (Kent, Ohio, 1986), chaps. 2–3. See also Gordon S. Wood, "Interests and Disinterestedness in the Making of the Constitution," in Beeman, Botein, and Carter, eds., *Beyond Confederation,* 69–109.

47. Randolph C. Downes, *Frontier Ohio, 1788–1803* (Columbus, Ohio, 1935).

48. Barnhart, *Valley of Democracy,* 159.

49. Jeffrey P. Brown, "Frontier Politics: The Evolution of a Political Society in Ohio, 1788–1814" (Ph.D. diss., University of Illinois at Urbana, 1979); Brown, "The Ohio Federalists, 1803–1815," *Journal of the Early Republic* 2 (1982): 261–82; and Brown, "William McMillan and the Conservative Cincinnati Jeffersonians," *The Old Northwest* 12 (1986): 117–36. See also Jo Tice Bloom, "The Congressional Delegates from the Northwest Territory, 1799–1803," *The Old Northwest* 3 (1977): 3–22.

50. Donald J. Ratcliffe, "The Experience of Revolution and the Beginnings of Party Politics in Ohio, 1776–1816," *Ohio History* 85 (1976): 186–230.

51. Peter S. Onuf, "From Constitution to Higher Law: The Reinterpretation of the Northwest Ordinance," *Ohio History* 94 (1985): 5–33.

52. Ibid.

53. Cayton, *Frontier Republic*, chap. 5. See also Andrew R. L. Cayton, "Land, Reputation, and Power: The Cultural Dimension of Politics in the Ohio Country," *William and Mary Quarterly*, 3d ser., forthcoming, for a more recent treatment of the Virginia-born leaders of the opposition to St. Clair.

54. Onuf, *Statehood and Union*.

55. Barnhart, *Valley of Democracy*, 161–77. See also Jo Tice Bloom, "The Territorial Delegates of Indiana Territory, 1801–1816," *The Old Northwest* 12 (1986): 7–26; and Bloom, "Peaceful Politics: The Delegates from Illinois Territory, 1809–1818," *The Old Northwest* 6 (1980): 203–16.

56. Alec R. Gilpin, *The Territory of Michigan* (East Lansing, Michigan, 1970). See also Timothy Sherer, "The Resistance to Representative Government in Early Michigan Territory," *The Old Northwest* 5 (1979): 167–80; Clifford I. Tobias, "Herry D. Gilpin: 'Governor in and over the Territory of Michigan,'" *Michigan History* 59 (1975): 153–70.

57. Alice E. Smith, *From Exploration to Statehood*. Volume 1 of *The History of Wisconsin* (Madison, Wisconsin, 1973).

58. Kenneth R. Owens, "Pattern and Structure in Western Territorial Politics," in Bloom, ed., *American Territorial System*, 174. See also Earl Pomeroy, "The Territory as a Frontier Institution," *The Historian* 7 (1944): 29–41.

59. The key works are Lance Banning, *The Jeffersonian Persuasion: Evolution of a Party Ideology* (Ithaca, New York, 1978); and McCoy, *Elusive Republic*.

60. See Joyce Appleby, *Capitalism and a New Social Order: The Republican Vision of the 1790s* (New York, 1984); John R. Nelson, *Liberty and Property: Political Economy and Policymaking in the New Nation, 1789–1812* (Baltimore, 1987); and Steven Watts, *The Republic Reborn: War and the Making of Liberal America, 1790–1820* (Baltimore, 1987), 329–31.

61. Cayton, *Frontier Republic*, chap. 3; Onuf, *Statehood and Union*, chaps. 1–3. See also Wood, *Creation of the American Republic*.

62. Ratcliffe, "Experience of Revolution," 192. See Cayton, "Land, Reputation, and Power."

63. See Charles Royster, *Light-Horse Harry Lee and the Legacy of the American Revolution* (New York, 1981).

64. See Ratcliffe, "Experience of Revolution."

65. Cayton, *Frontier Republic*.

66. See Onuf, *Statehood and Union*, 151, and passim for a fuller discussion of many of the themes developed in this chapter.

II: The Peopling of the Old Northwest

1. Peter H. Wood, *Black Majority: Negroes in Colonial South Carolina from 1670 through the Stono Rebellion* (New York, 1974).

2. Among the most important of these works are Eugene D. Genovese, *Roll, Jordan, Roll: The World the Slaves Made* (New York, 1972, 1974); and Lawrence W. Levine, *Black Culture and Black Consciousness: Afro-American Folk Thought from Slavery to Freedom* (New York, 1977).

3. David Grayson Allen, *In English Ways: The Movement of Societies and the Transferral of English Local Law and Custom to Massachusetts Bay in the Seven-*

teenth Century (Chapel Hill, North Carolina, 1981); T. H. Breen, *Puritans and Adventurers: Change and Persistence in Early America* (New York, 1980), 3–67; Virginia DeJohn Anderson, "Migrants and Motives: Religion and the Settlement of New England, 1630–1640," *New England Quarterly* 58 (1985): 339–83; and David Cressy, *Coming Over: Migration and Communication between England and New England in the Seventeenth Century* (Cambridge, England, 1987).

4. Kathleen Conzen, *Immigrant Milwaukee, 1836–1860: Accommodation and Community in a Frontier City* (Cambridge, Massachusetts, 1976); Kathleen Conzen, "Peasant Pioneers: Generational Succession among German Farmers in Frontier Minnesota," in *The Countryside in the Age of Capitalist Transformation*, ed. Steven Hahn and Jonathan Prude (Chapel Hill, North Carolina, 1985), 259–92; and Jon Gjerde, *From Peasants to Farmers: The Migration from Balestrand Norway to the Upper Middle West* (Cambridge, England, 1985).

5. Gjerde, *From Peasants to Farmers*, 239.

6. The best examples of supporters of Turner are Stanley Elkins and Eric McKitrick, "A Meaning for Turner's Frontier: Democracy in the Old Northwest," *Political Science Quarterly* 69 (1954): 321–53; and Merle Curti, *The Making of an American Community: A Case Study of Democracy in a Frontier Community* (Stanford, California, 1959). The most persuasive critics are Allan Bogue, *Money at Interest: The Farm Mortgage on the Middle Border* (Ithaca, New York, 1955); Allan Bogue and Margaret Beattie Bogue, "'Profits' and the Frontier Land Speculator," *Journal of Economic History* 17 (1957): 1–24; Robert P. Swierenga, *Pioneers and Profits: Land Speculation on the Iowa Frontier* (Ames, Iowa, 1968); and Swierenga, *Acres for Cents: Delinquent Tax Auctions in Frontier Iowa* (Westport, Connecticut, 1976). See the discussion in Reginald Horsman, "Changing Images of the Public Domain: Historians and the Shaping of Midwest Frontiers," in *This Land of Ours: The Acquisition and Disposition of the Public Domain* (Indianapolis, 1978), 60–86.

7. Paul W. Gates, *Landlords and Tenants on the Prairie Frontier: Studies in American Land Policy* (Ithaca, New York, 1973).

8. Susan E. Gray, "Family, Land, and Credit: Yankee Communities on the Michigan Frontier, 1830–1860" (Ph.D. diss., University of Chicago, 1985).

9. D. W. Meinig, *The Shaping of America: A Geographical Perspective on 500 Years of History. Volume 1: Atlantic America, 1492–1800* (New Haven, Connecticut, 1986), 349. See also James E. Davis, "'New Aspects of Men and New Forms of Society': The Old Northwest, 1790–1820," *Journal of the Illinois State Historical Society* 69 (1976): 164–72; and Malcolm J. Rohrbough, "Diversity and Unity in the Old Northwest, 1790–1850: Several Peoples Fashion a Single Region," in *Pathways to the Old Northwest: An Observance of the Bicentennial of the Northwest Ordinance* (Indianapolis, 1988), 71–88.

10. Gregory Steven Rose, "Hoosier Origins: The Nativity of Indiana's United States–Born Population in 1850," *Indiana Magazine of History* 81 (1985): 201–32. See also Gregory S. Rose, "Upland Southerners: The County Origins of Southern Migrants to Indiana by 1850," *Indiana Magazine of History* 82 (1986): 242–63.

11. Richard Lyle Power, *Planting Corn Belt Culture: The Impress of the Upland Southerner and Yankee in the Old Northwest* (Indianapolis, 1953). See also James M. Berquist, "Tracing the Origins of a Midwestern Culture: The Case of Central Indiana," *Indiana Magazine of History* 77 (1981): 1–32. Other specialized studies include Robert Bray and Paul Bushnell, "From New England to the Old Northwest: The American Odyssey of the Jeremiah Greenman Family," *Journal of the Illinois State Historical Society* 69 (1976): 201–12; Thomas J. Schlereth,

"The New England Presence on the Midwestern Landscape," *The Old Northwest* 9 (1983): 125–42; and Morris C. Taber, "New England Influence in Southeastern Michigan," *Michigan History* 45 (1961): 305–36.

12. Henry Glassie, *Pattern in the Material Folk Culture of the Eastern United States* (Philadelphia, 1968); John R. Stilgoe, *Common Landscape of America, 1580 to 1845* (New Haven, Connecticut, 1982).

13. Donald A. Hutslar, *The Architecture of Migration: Log Construction in the Ohio Country, 1750–1850* (Athens, Ohio, 1986).

14. Meinig, *Atlantic America*, 448–49.

15. William N. Parker, "From Northwest to Mid-West: Social Bases of a Regional History," in *Essays in Nineteenth Century Economic History: The Old Northwest* ed. David C. Klingaman and Richard K. Vedder (Athens, Ohio, 1975), 11.

16. Bernard Bailyn, *The Peopling of British North America* (New York, 1986), 7–8.

17. See Peter D. McClelland and Richard J. Zeckhauser, *Demographic Dimensions of the New Republic: American Internal Migration, Vital Statistics, and Manumissions, 1800–1860* (Cambridge, England, 1982); and Morton Owen Schapiro, *Filling Up America: An Economic-Demographic Model of Population Growth and Distribution in the Nineteenth-Century United States* (Greenwich, Connecticut, 1986).

18. Richard K. Vedder and Lowell E. Gallaway, "Migration and the Old Northwest," in Klingaman and Vedder, eds., *Essays in Nineteenth Century Economic History* 159.

19. Ibid., 162.

20. Malcolm J. Rohrbough, *The Trans-Appalachian Frontier: People, Societies, and Institutions, 1775–1850* (New York, 1978), 163, 285, 322.

21. Vedder and Gallaway, "Migration and the Old Northwest," 162–63, 161.

22. Ibid., 164.

23. Ibid., 170.

24. Ibid., 173.

25. James Henretta, "Families and Farms: *Mentalité* in Pre-Industrial America," *William and Mary Quarterly*, 3d ser., 35 (1978): 9.

26. See Rowland Berthoff, "A Country Open for Neighborhood," *Indiana Magazine of History* 84 (1988): 25–45; and Richard Jensen, "Midwestern Transformation: From Traditional Pioneers to Modern Society," *Local History Today: Papers Presented at Four Regional Workshops for Local Historical Organizations in Indiana, June, 1978-April, 1979* (Indianapolis, 1979): 1–12. A useful, general survey of recent work by historians of early America on this issue is Allan Kulikoff, "The Transition to Capitalism in Rural America," *William and Mary Quarterly*, 3d ser., 46 (1989): 120–44.

Unfortunately, we were unable to read J. Sanford Rikoon, *Threshing in the Midwest: A Study of Traditional Culture and Technological Change* (Bloomington, Indiana, 1988), before completing our study.

27. John Mack Faragher, *Sugar Creek: Life on the Illinois Prairie* (New Haven, Connecticut, 1986), 237.

28. Gray, "Family, Land, and Credit."

29. George Fredrickson, Review, *The New York Review of Books* 24 (1987): 37–39.

30. Juliet E. K. Walker, *Free Frank: A Black Pioneer on the Antebellum Frontier* (Lexington, Kentucky, 1983).

31. Faragher, *Sugar Creek* 181.

32. Steven J. Ross, *Workers on the Edge: Work, Leisure, and Politics in Industrializing Cincinnati, 1788–1890* (New York, 1985), 3. See also Sean Wilentz, *Chants Democratic: New York City and the Rise of the American Working Class, 1788–1850* (New York, 1984).

33. See Curti, *Making of an American Community*; and Elkins and McKitrick, "A Meaning for Turner's Frontier."

34. Ross, *Workers on the Edge*, 59.

35. Ibid., xvii.

36. Faragher, *Sugar Creek*, 204.

37. Ibid., 237.

38. William Cronon, *Changes in the Land: Indians, Colonists, and the Ecology of New England* (New York, 1983).

39. Ibid., 160–61.

40. Ibid., 126.

41. David C. Klingaman and Richard K. Vedder, "Introduction," in Klingaman and Vedder, eds., *Essays in Nineteenth Century Economic History*, ix. See also Jeremy Atack and Fred Bateman, "Self-Sufficiency and the Origins of the Marketable Surplus in the Rural North, 1860," *Agricultural History* 58 (1984): 296–313.

42. Andrew R. L. Cayton, "The Northwest Ordinance from the Perspective of the Frontier," in *The Northwest Ordinance, 1787: A Bicentennial Handbook*, ed. Robert M. Taylor, Jr. (Indianapolis, 1987), 1–23.

43. Rohrbough, *Trans-Appalachian Frontier* 93–114; Randolph C. Downes, "Trade in Frontier Ohio," *Mississippi Valley Historical Review* 16 (1929–1930): 467–94. See also John Lauritz Larson and David Vanderstel, "Agent of Empire: William Conner on the Indiana Frontier, 1800–1855," *Indiana Magazine of History* 80 (1984): 301–28.

44. George Rogers Taylor, "Agrarian Discontent in the Mississippi Valley Preceding the War of 1812," *Journal of Political Economy* 39 (1931): 471–505.

45. Carville Earle, "Regional Economic Development West of the Appalachians, 1815–1860," in *North America: The Historical Geography of a Changing Continent*, ed. Robert D. Mitchell and Paul A. Groves (Totowa, New Jersey, 1982), 174–80. For a model of economic growth in the Old Northwest in the first half of the nineteenth century, see Edward K. Muller, "Selective Urban Growth in the Middle Ohio Valley, 1800–1860," *Geographical Review* 66 (1976): 178–99. See also Timothy R. Mahoney, "Urban History in a Regional Context: River Towns on the Upper Mississippi, 1840–1860," *Journal of American History* 72 (1985): 318–39. More specialized studies of economic growth include Robert E. Ankli, "Agricultural Growth in Antebellum Illinois," *Journal of the Illinois State Historical Society* 63 (1970): 387–98; Victor Bogle, "New Albany: Mid-Nineteenth Century Economic Expansion," *Indiana Magazine of History* 53 (1957): 127–46; Thomas J. Brown, "The Age of Ambition in Quincy, Illinois," *Journal of the Illinois State Historical Society* 75 (1982): 242–61; William J. Cronon, "To Be the Center City: Chicago, 1848–1857," *Chicago History* 10 no. 3 (1981): 130–40; Michael H. Ebner, "'In the Suburbes of Town,' Chicago's North Shore to 1871," *Chicago History* 11 no. 2 (1982): 66–77; Charles N. Glaab, "Jesup W. Scott and a West of Cities," *Ohio History* 73 (1964): 3–12; John Denis Haeger, "Eastern Money and the Urban Frontier: Chicago, 1833–1842," *Journal of the Illinois State Historical Society* 64 (1971): 267–84; John D. Haeger, "The American Fur Company and the Chicago of 1812–1835," *Journal of the Illinois State Historical Society* 61 (1968): 117–39; John D. Haeger, "Capital Mobilization and the Urban Center: The Wisconsin Lakeport," *Mid-America* 60 (1978): 75–94; John D. Haeger, "The Aban-

doned Townsite on the Midwestern Frontier: A Case Study of Rockwell, Illinois," *Journal of the Early Republic* 3 (1983): 165–84; John D. Haeger, "A Time of Change: Green Bay, 1815–1834," *Wisconsin Magazine of History* 54 (1970): 285–98; Glen E. Holt, "The Birth of Chicago: An Example of Economic Patronage," *Journal of the Illinois State Historical Society* 76 (1983): 82–94; R. Douglas Hurt, "Dairying in Nineteenth-Century Ohio," *The Old Northwest* 5 (1979): 387–400; R. Douglas Hurt, "The Sheep Industry in Ohio, 1807–1900," *The Old Northwest* 7 (1981): 237–54; Shirley A. Leckie, "Toledo, Ohio: A Study in the Process and Problems of Nineteenth-Century Urbanization," *The Old Northwest* 10 (1984): 319–38; Donald R. MacKenzie, "Collections and Exhibits: The Itinerant Artist in Early Ohio," *Ohio History* 73 (1964): 41–46; Patrick E. McLear, "Speculation, Promotion, and the Panic of 1837 in Chicago," *Journal of the Illinois State Historical Society* 62 (1969): 135–46; Patrick E. McLear, "Land Speculation and Urban and Regional Development: Chicago in the 1830s," *The Old Northwest* 6 (1980): 137–52; James Mak, "Intraregional Trade in the Antebellum West: Ohio, A Case Study," *Agricultural History* 46 (1972): 489–97; Ronald E. Seavoy, "Borrowed Laws to Speed Development: Michigan, 1835–1863," *Michigan History* 59 (1975): 39–68; Alice E. Smith, "Banking without Banks: George Smith and the Wisconsin Marine and Fire Insurance Company," *Wisconsin Magazine of History* 48 (1965): 268–81; Harry R. Stevens, "Samuel Watts Davies and the Industrial Revolution in Cincinnati," *Ohio History* 70 (1961): 95–127; William A. White, "Tradition and Urban Development: A Contrast of Chicago and Toronto in the Nineteenth Century," *The Old Northwest* 8 (1982): 247–72; and Thomas R. Winpenny, "Perils in Transferring Technology to the Frontier: A Case Study," *Journal of the Early Republic* 5 (1985): 503–22.

46. Malcolm J. Rohrbough, *The Land Office Business: The Settlement and Administration of American Public Lands, 1789–1837* (New York, 1968).

47. Bogue, *Money at Interest*; Bogues, "'Profits'"; Curti, *Making of an American Community*; Terry L. Anderson, "The First Privatization Movement," in *Essays on the Economy of the Old Northwest* ed., David C. Klingaman and Richard K. Vedder (Athens, Ohio, 1987), 59–76; Jay Ladin, "Mortgage Credit in Tippecanoe County, Indiana, 1865–1880," *Agricultural History* 41 (1967): 37–44; Stanley Lebergott, "'O Pioneers': Land Speculation and the Growth of the Midwest," in Klingaman and Vedder, eds., *Essays on the Economy* 19–36; Jonathan Lurie, "Speculation and Profits: The Ambivalent Agrarian in the Late Nineteenth Century," *Agricultural History* 46 (1972): 269–78; Edward H. Rastatter, "Nineteenth-Century Land Policy: The Case for the Speculator," in Klingaman and Vedder, eds., *Essays in Nineteenth Century Economic History*, 118–37; Park Siyoing, "Land Speculation in Western Illinois: Pike County, 1821–1835," *Journal of the Illinois State Historical Society* 77 (1984): 115–28; Donald L. Winters, *Farmers without Farms: Agricultural Tenancy in Nineteenth-Century Iowa* (Westport, Connecticut, 1978); and Winters, "Agricultural Tenancy in the Nineteenth-Century Middle West: The Historiographical Debate," *Indiana Magazine of History* 78 (1982): 128–53.

48. Eric F. Haites, James Mak, and Gary M. Walton, *Western River Transportation: The Era of Early Internal Development, 1810–1860* (Baltimore, 1975), 113. See also Lawrence E. Larsen, "New Orleans and the River Trade: Reinterpreting the Role of the Business Community," *Wisconsin Magazine of History* 61 (1977): 112–24; Gary M. Walton, "River Transportation and the Old Northwest Territory," in Klingaman and Vedder, eds., *Essays on the Economy* 225–42; and Donald T. Zimmer, "The Ohio River: Pathway to Settlement," in *Transportation and the Early Nation: Papers Presented at an Indiana American Revolution Bi-*

centennial Symposium (Indianapolis, 1982): 61–88. For efforts to build roads, see Carl Abbott, "The Plank Road Enthusiasm in the Antebellum Middle West," *Indiana Magazine of History* 67 (1971): 95–116; Richard D. Durbin and Elizabeth Durbin, "Wisconsin's Old Military Road: Its Genesis and Construction," *Wisconsin Magazine of History* 68 (1984): 3–42; and Thomas L. Hardin, "The National Road in Illinois," *Journal of the Illinois State Historical Society* 60 (1967): 5–22.

49. Haites, Mak, and Walton, *Western River Transportation.*

50. John G. Clark, *The Grain Trade in the Old Northwest* (Urbana, Illinois, 1966), 79.

51. Harry N. Scheiber, *Ohio Canal Era: A Case Study of Government and the Economy, 1820–1861* (Athens, Ohio, 1969), 355. See also Douglas E. Clanin, "Internal Improvements in National Politics, 1816–1830," in *Transportation and the Early Nation*, 30–60; Ralph D. Gray, "The Canal Era in Indiana," in *Transportation and the Early Nation*, 113–34; John Lauritz Larson, " 'Bind the Republic Together': The National Union and the Struggle for a System of Internal Improvements," *Journal of American History* 74 (1987): 363–87; Ronald E. Shaw, "The Canal Era in the Old Northwest," in *Transportation and the Early Nation*, 89–112; Ronald E. Shaw, "Canals in the Early Republic: A Review of Recent Literature," *Journal of the Early Republic* 4 (1984): 117–42; and Harry N. Scheiber, "The Transportation Revolution and American Law: Constitutionalism and Public Policy," in *Transportation and the Early Nation*, 1–29.

For specialized studies of the relationship between government support and internal improvements, see Daniel J. Elazar, "Gubernatorial Power and the Illinois and Michigan Canal, A Study of Political Development in the Nineteenth Century," *Journal of the Illinois State Historical Society* 58 (1965): 396–423; Richard T. Farrell, "Internal-Improvement Projects in Southwestern Ohio, 1815–1834," *Ohio History* 75 (1966): 10–25; Harry N. Scheiber, "Urban Rivalry and Internal Improvements, 1820–1860," *Ohio History* 7 (1962): 227–39; Harry N. Scheiber, "The Pennsylvania and Ohio Canal: Transport Innovation, Mixed Enterprise, and Urban Commercial Rivalry, 1825–1861," *The Old Northwest* 6 (1980): 105–36; and John S. Still, "Ethan Allen Brown and Ohio's Canal System," *Ohio History* 66 (1957): 22–56.

52. Scheiber, *Ohio Canal Era* 355–56.

53. Ibid., 356.

54. Earle, "Regional Economic Development," 181.

55. Clark, *Grain Trade*, 286–87.

56. Earle, "Regional Economic Development," 183.

57. John Lauritz Larson, *The Bonds of Enterprise: John Murray Forbes and Western Development in America's Railway Age* (Cambridge, Massachusetts, 1984), xv.

For studies of other entrepreneurs and the development of railroads, cities, and industry in the mid-nineteenth century Midwest, see Victor Bogle, "Railroad Building in Indiana, 1850–1855," *Indiana Magazine of History* 58 (1962): 21–32; Craig Buettinger, "The Rise and Fall of Hiram Pearson: Mobility on the Urban Frontier," *Chicago History* 9 no. 2 (1980): 112–17; William L. Downard, "William Butler Ogden and the Growth of Chicago," *Journal of the Illinois State Historical Society* 75 (1982): 47–60; Patrick E. McLear, "John Stephen Wright and Urban and Regional Promotion in the Nineteenth Century," *Journal of the Illinois State Historical Society* 68 (1975): 407–20; Patrick E. McLear, "The Galena and Chicago Union Railroad: A Symbol of Chicago's Economic Maturity," *Journal of the*

Illinois State Historical Society 73 (1980): 17–26; Walter Rumsey Marvin, "The Steubenville and Indiana Railroad: The Pennsylvania's Middle Route to the Middle West," *Ohio History* 66 (1957): 11–21; Grant Morrison, "Interregional Entrepreneurship in the 1830s: The Role of New Yorkers in the Founding of an Ohio Cooperation," *The Old Northwest* 7 (1981): 23–40; John E. Pixton, Jr., "Faith v. Economics: The Marietta and Cincinnati Railroad, 1845–1883," *Ohio History* 6 (1957): 1–10; Stuart M. Rich, "John E. Holmes: An Early Wisconsin Leader," *Wisconsin Magazine of History* 56 (1972–1973): 127–39; John D. Sover, "Iron Roads in the Old Northwest: The Railroads and the Growing Nation," *Transportation and the Early Nation*, 135–56; Ivan M. Tribe, "Dream and Reality in Southern Ohio: The Development of the Columbus and Hocking Valley Railroad," *The Old Northwest* 4 (1978): 337–57; Margaret Walsh, "Business Success and Capital Availability in the New West: Milwaukee Ironmasters in the Middle Nineteenth Century," *The Old Northwest* 1 (1975): 159–80; and Elizabeth Pearson White, "Captain Benjamin Godfrey and the Alton and Sangamon Railroad," *Journal of the Illinois State Historical Society* 67 (1974): 466–86.

For evidence that not everyone welcomed canals, see James E. Feckle, "The 'People' versus 'Progress' in the Old Northwest: Local Opposition to the Construction of the Wabash and Erie Canal," *The Old Northwest* 8 (1982): 309–28.

58. Larson, *Bonds of Enterprise*, 82.

59. Earle, "Regional Economic Development," 176.

60. Clark, *Grain Trade*, 4.

61. Ibid., 8, 178–80.

62. Earle, "Regional Economic Development," 184.

63. Allan Bogue, *From Prairie to Cornbelt: Farming in the Illinois and Iowa Prairies in the Nineteenth Century* (Chicago, 1963), 185.

64. See Nicholas P. Hardeman, *Shucks, Shocks, and Hominy Blocks: Corn as a Way of Life in Pioneer America* (Baton Rouge, Louisiana, 1981).

65. Paul C. Henlein, *Cattle Kingdom in the Ohio Valley, 1783–1860* (Lexington, Kentucky, 1959), 3–12.

66. Ibid., 71–72.

67. Earle, "Regional Economic Development," 190–91. See also David E. Schob, *Hired Hands and Plowboys: Farm Labor in the Midwest, 1815–1860* (Urbana, Illinois, 1975).

68. Earle, "Regional Economic Development," 190.

69. Ibid., 194.

70. Robert Leslie Jones, *History of Agriculture in Ohio to 1880* (Kent, Ohio, 1983), 7.

71. Ibid., 38.

72. Power, *Planting Corn Belt Culture*, 137.

73. Henlein, *Cattle Kingdom*, 21.

74. Forrest McDonald and Grady McWhiney, "The Antebellum Southern Herdsman: A Reinterpretation," *Journal of Southern History* 41 (1975), 73.

75. Ibid. See also John Solomon Otto, "The Migration of the Southern Plain Folk: An Interdisciplinary Synthesis," *Journal of Southern History* 51 (1985), 183–201.

76. Sam Powers Hilliard, *Hog Meat and Hoecake: Food Supply in the Old South, 1840–1860* (Carbondale, Illinois, 1972), 68.

77. Jeremy Atack and Fred Bateman, "Yankee Farming and Settlement in the Old Northwest: A Comparative Analysis," in Klingaman and Vedder, eds., *Essays on the Economy*, 92, 93, 92.

III: The Origins of Community in the Old Northwest

1. The most important studies are Stanley Elkins and Eric McKitrick, "A Meaning for Turner's Frontier: Democracy in the Old Northwest," *Political Science Quarterly* 69 (1954): 321–54; George Blackburn and Sherman L. Richards, Jr., "A Democratic History of the West: Manistie County, Michigan, 1860," *Journal of American History* 57 (1970–1971): 600–18; Allan Bogue, "Social Theory and the Pioneer," *Agricultural History* 34 (1960): 21–34; Merle Curti, *The Making of an American Community: A Case Study of Democracy in a Frontier County* (Stanford, California, 1959); Don Harrison Doyle, *The Social Order of a Frontier Community: Jacksonville, Illinois, 1825–1870* (Urbana, Illinois, 1978); and Robert R. Dykstra, *The Cattle Towns* (New York, 1968). See also Robert R. Dykstra and William Silag, "Doing Local History: Monographic Approaches to the Small Community," *American Quarterly* 37 (1985): 411–25.

Exhaustive statistical analyses of land ownership through tax records have convinced economic historian Lee Soltow that, while severe inequalities existed on the frontier of the Old Northwest, they were far from oppressive. The distribution of wealth compares favorably with that in the eastern United States and particularly well with that in European countries. See Soltow, "The Growth of Wealth in Ohio, 1800–1969," in *Essays in Nineteenth Century Economic History: The Old Northwest*, ed. David C. Klingaman and Richard K. Vedder (Athens, Ohio, 1975), 191–207; Soltow, "Inequality amidst Abundance: Land Ownership in Early Nineteenth-Century Ohio," *Ohio History* 88 (1979): 133–51; Soltow, "Progress and Mobility among Ohio Propertyholders, 1810–1825," *Social Science History* 7 (1983): 405–26; and Soltow, "Tocqueville's View of the Northwest in 1835: Ohio a Generation after Settlement," in *Essays on the Economy of the Old Northwest*, ed. David C. Klingaman and Richard K. Vedder (Athens, Ohio, 1987), 131–56. See also Craig Buettinger, "Economic Inequality in Early Chicago, 1849–1850," *Journal of Social History* 11 (1978): 413–18. Buettinger found that the wealthiest 1 percent of Chicago's males owned 52 percent of the city's wealth, while 74.6 percent (7,226 adult males) were "destitute" (414). On the other hand, Gordon W. Kirk, Jr., *The Promise of American Life: Social Mobility in a Nineteenth-Century Immigrant Community, Holland, Michigan, 1847–1894* (Philadelphia, 1978), argues that frontier settlements offered more economic opportunities and upward mobility than eastern cities.

2. See, for example, Bogue, "Social Theory and the Pioneer." For a different point of view, see Jane Marie Pederson, "The Country Visitor: Patterns of Hospitality in Rural Wisconsin, 1880–1925," *Agricultural History* 58 (1984): 347–64.

Historians of the Old Northwest also think of utopian enterprises when invoking the term community. See, for example, Arthur Bestor, *Backwoods Utopias: The Sectarian and Owenite Phases of Communitarian Socialism in America, 1663–1829* (Philadelphia, 1950); Arthur Bestor, "Patent-Office Models of the Good Society: Some Relationships between Social Reform and Westward Expansion," *American Historical Review* 54 (1953): 502–26; Donald F. Carmony and Josephine M. Elliott, "New Harmony, Indiana: Robert Owen's Seedbed for Utopia," *Indiana Magazine of History* 76 (1980): 161–261; Donald E. Pitzer and Josephine M. Elliott, "New Harmony's First Utopians, 1814–1824," *Indiana Magazine of History* 75 (1979): 225–302; and Robert P. Weeks, "A Utopian Kingdom in the American Grain," *Wisconsin Magazine of History* 61 (1977): 3–20.

3. Thomas Bender, *Community and Social Change in America* (New Brunswick, New Jersey, 1978). See also Richard R. Beeman, "The New Social History and the Search for 'Community' in Colonial America," *American Quarterly* 29

(1977): 422–43. According to Beeman, community is created by "communication and not simply physical space." Thus historians need to study "those patterns of association that occurred among groups within the locality and individuals and institutions that were a part of the larger civilization beyond the geographical locale" (422). Both Bender and Beeman rely heavily on the work of Robert Redfield.

The significance of trans-local community is also suggested by the high rates of mobility in the region. See Kenneth J. Winkle, *The Politics of Community: Migration and Politics in Antebellum Ohio* (Cambridge, England, 1988).

4. On the diversity of community pressures on free blacks, for example, see Herbert B. Fields, "Free Negroes in Case County before the Civil War," *Michigan History* 44 (1960): 375–83; David A. Gerber, *Black Ohio and the Color Line, 1860–1915* (Urbana, Illinois, 1976), 15–23; David M. Katzman, *Before the Ghetto: Black Detroit in the Nineteenth Century* (Urbana, Illinois, 1973), 5–55, 135; Richard W. Pih, "Negro Self-Improvement Efforts in Ante-bellum Cincinnati, 1836–1850," *Ohio History* 78 (1969): 179–87; Joe William Trotter, Jr., *Black Milwaukee: The Making of an Industrial Proletariat, 1915–1945* (Urbana, Illinois, 1985), 26–33; and Juliet E. K. Walker, *Free Frank: A Black Pioneer on the Antebellum Frontier* (Lexington, Kentucky, 1983).

5. See Jack E. Eblen, "An Analysis of Nineteenth-Century Frontier Populations," *Demography* 2 (1965): 399–413; John Modell, "Family and Fertility on the Indiana Frontier," *American Quarterly* 23 (1971): 615–34; and G. Alexander Ross, "Fertility Change on the Michigan Frontier: Saginaw County, 1840–1850," *Michigan Historical Review* 12 (1986): 69–86. For the second half of the nineteenth century, see Susan E. Bloomberg, Mary Frank Fox, Robert M. Warner, Sam Bass Warner, Jr., "A Census Probe into Nineteenth-Century Family History: Southern Michigan, 1850–1880," *Journal of Social History* 5 (1971): 26–45.

6. James E. Davis, *Frontier America, 1800–1840: A Comparative Demographic Analysis of the Settlement Process* (Glendale, California, 1977), 180.

7. Ibid., 181.

8. Michael Conzen, *Frontier Farming in an Urban Shadow* (Madison, Wisconsin, 1971), 60–62.

9. Kathleen Neils Conzen, *Immigrant Milwaukee: Accommodation and Community in a Frontier City* (Cambridge, Massachusetts, 1976), 48.

10. Doyle, *Social Order* 111–12.

11. Donald Leet, "Human Fertility and Agricultural Opportunities in Ohio Counties from Frontier to Maturity, 1810–1860," in Klingaman and Vedder, eds., *Essays in Nineteenth Century Economic History*, 142. See also Peter J. Coleman, "Restless Grant County: Americans on the Move," *Wisconsin Magazine of History* 46 (1962): 16–20; and Kirk, *Promise of American Life*. Disease also had an impact on settlement patterns. See Peter H. Harstad, "Sickness and Disease on the Wisconsin Frontier: Malaria, 1820–1850," *Wisconsin Magazine of History* 43 (1959–1960): 83–96; and Peter H. Harstad, "Disease and Sickness on the Wisconsin Frontier: Cholera," *Wisconsin Magazine of History* 43 (1959–1960): 220–30.

12. John Mack Faragher, *Sugar Creek: Life on the Illinois Prairie* (New Haven, Connecticut, 1986), 56. See also Susan Gray, "Family, Land, and Credit: Yankee Communities on the Michigan Frontier, 1830–1860" (Ph.D. diss., University of Chicago, 1985).

13. Mary P. Ryan, *Cradle of the Middle Class: The Family in Oneida County, New York, 1790–1865* (Cambridge, England, 1981), 13.

14. See the discussions in Kathleen Neils Conzen, "Historical Approaches to the Study of Rural Ethnic Communities," in *Ethnicity on the Great Plains* ed.

Frederick C. Luebke (Lincoln, Nebraska, 1980), 1–18; and Robert P. Swierenga, "Theoretical Perspectives on the New Rural History: From Environmentalism to Modernization," *Agricultural History* 56 (1982): 495–503. See also Robert E. Bieder, "Kinship as a Factor in Migration," *Journal of Marriage and the Family* 35 (1973): 429–39; and the articles by Yda Sauerssig-Schreuder and David G. Vanderstel in *The Dutch in America: Immigration, Settlement, and Cultural Change,* ed. Robert P. Swierenga (New Brunswick, New Jersey, 1985).

15. Faragher, *Sugar Creek* 13.

16. Elliott J. Gorn, "'Gouge and Bite, Pull Hair and Scratch': The Social Significance of Fighting in the Southern Backcountry," *American Historical Review* 90 (1985): 18–43; and George M. Fredrickson, *The Inner Civil War: Northern Intellectuals and the Crisis of the Union* (New York, 1965).

17. John Mack Faragher, *Women and Men on the Overland Trail* (New Haven, Connecticut, 1979), 47–57. See also John Mack Faragher, "History from the Inside-Out: Writing the History of Women in Rural America," *American Quarterly* 33 (1981): 537–57. For a somewhat different perspective on this topic, see Joan M. Jensen, *Loosening the Bonds: Mid-Atlantic Farm Women, 1750–1850* (New Haven, Connecticut, 1986).

18. *Women and Men on the Overland Trail,* 65.

19. Conzen, *Immigrant Milwaukee,* 92–94.

20. See Peter Williams, "Religion and the Old Northwest: A Bibliographical Essay," *The Old Northwest* 5 (1979): 57–73.

Studies of specific sects include Mary Farrell Bednarowski, "Spiritualism in Wisconsin in the Nineteenth Century," *Wisconsin Magazine of History* 59 (1975): 3–19; James L. Burke and Donald E. Bensch, "Mount Pleasant and the Early Quakers of Ohio," *Ohio History* 83 (1974): 220–55; David B. Eller, "Hoosier Brethren and the Origins of the Restoration Movement," *Indiana Magazine of History* 76 (1980): 1–20; David B. Eller, "The Pietistic Origins of Sectarian Universalism in the Midwest," *The Old Northwest* 12 (1986): 41–64; F. Gerald Ham, "The Prophet and the Mumaygums: Isaac Bullard and the Vermont Pilgrims of 1817," *Wisconsin Magazine of History* 56 (1973): 290–99; Alan I. Marcus, "Am I My Brother's Keeper?: Reform Judaism in the American West, Cincinnati, 1840–1870," *Queen City Heritage* 44 (1986): 3–19; Ann Deborah Michael, "The Origins of the Jewish Community of Cincinnati, 1817–1860," *Cincinnati Historical Society Bulletin* 30 (1972): 155–82; N. Gordon Thomas, "The Millerite Movement in Ohio," *Ohio History* 81 (1972): 95–107; and the essays in the special issue on "The Mormons in Illinois, 1838–1846," *Journal of the Illinois State Historical Society* 64 (1971): 4–90.

21. John B. Boles, *The Great Revival, 1787–1805: The Origins of the Southern Evangelical Mind* (Lexington, Kentucky, 1972).

22. William Warren Sweet, *Religion in the Development of American Culture* (New York, 1952); Sweet, *Religion on the Frontier,* 4 vols. (Chicago, 1931–46); and Peter G. Mode, *The Frontier Spirit in American Christianity* (New York, 1923).

Specialized studies of camp meetings and circuit riders include Paul H. Bouse, "The Fortunes of a Circuit Rider," *Ohio History* 72 (1963): 91–115; Robert Bray, "Camp-Meeting Revivalism and the Idea of Western Community: Three Generations of Early Ohio Writers," *The Old Northwest* 10 (1984): 257–84; Robert A. Brunger, "Methodist Circuit Riders," *Michigan History* 51 (1967): 252–67; Almer M. Pennewell, "John Scripps, Methodist Circuit Rider Extraordinary," *Journal of the Illinois State Historical Society* 58 (1965): 265–78; and Charles Townsend, "Peter Cartwright's Circuit Riding Days in Ohio," *Ohio History* 74 (1965): 90–98.

23. T. Scott Miyakawa, *Protestants and Pioneers: Individualism and Conformity on the American Frontier* (Chicago, 1964).

24. Donald G. Mathews, "The Second Great Awakening as an Organizing Process, 1780–1830: An Hypothesis," *American Quarterly* 21 (1969): 23–43.

25. Nathan O. Hatch, "The Christian Movement and the Demand for a Theology of the People," *Journal of American History* 67 (1980): 545–67; Gordon S. Wood, "Evangelical America and Early Mormonism," *New York History* 61 (1980): 359–86.

26. Williams, "Religion and the Old Northwest," 73.

27. Donald G. Mathews, *Religion in the Old South* (Chicago, 1977), 40.

28. Ibid., 41.

29. Ibid., 49–55.

30. Andrew R. L. Cayton, *The Frontier Republic: Ideology and Politics in the Ohio Country, 1780–1825* (Kent, Ohio, 1986), 12–32.

31. Ibid., 33–50.

32. Stuart Blumin, *The Urban Threshold: Growth and Change in a Nineteenth-Century American Community* (Chicago, 1964); John S. Gilkeson, Jr., *Middle-Class Providence* (Princeton, New Jersey, 1986); Karen Halttunen, *Confidence Men and Painted Women: A Study of Middle Class Culture in America, 1830–1870* (New Haven, Connecticut, 1983); Paul Johnson, *A Shopkeeper's Millennium: Society and Revivals in Rochester, New York, 1815–1837* (New York, 1978); Ryan, *Cradle of the Middle Class*; and Carroll Smith-Rosenberg, *Disorderly Conduct: Visions of Gender in Victorian America* (New York, 1985). Stuart Blumin reviews much of this literature in "The Hypothesis of Middle-Class Formation in Nineteenth-Century America: A Critique and Some Proposals," *American Historical Review* 90 (1985): 292–338.

33. Halttunen, *Confidence Men* 10–55; and Smith-Rosenberg, *Disorderly Conduct* 79–89, summarize these developments. On masculine culture, see Elliott J. Gorn, *The Manly Art: Bare-Knuckle Prize Fighting in America* (Ithaca, New York, 1986).

34. Ryan, *Cradle of the Middle Class*, 15.

35. Ibid., 64, 105–106, 145, 234.

36. Halttunen, *Confidence Men*, 59–61.

37. Kathryn Kish Sklar, *Catharine Beecher: A Study in American Domesticity* (New Haven, Connecticut, 1973), xiii, xii, 113, 128.

38. Lawrence Friedman, *Gregarious Saints: Self and Community in American Abolitionism, 1830–1870* (Cambridge, England, 1982), 12.

39. See Carolyn R. Shine, "Hunting Shirts and Silk Stockings: Clothing Early Cincinnati," *Cincinnati Historical Society Bulletin* 45 (1987): 23–48; and Donna L. Streifthau, "Fancy Chairs and Finials: Cincinnati Furniture Industry, 1819–1830," *Cincinnati Historical Society Bulletin* 29 (1971): 171–200.

On early Cincinnati, see Daniel Aaron, "Cincinnati, 1818–1838: A Study of Attitudes in the Urban West" (Ph.D. diss., Harvard University, 1942); M. H. Dunlop, "Curiosities Too Numerous to Mention: Early Regionalism and Cincinnati's Western Museum," *American Quarterly* 36 (1984): 524–48; Richard T. Farrell, "Cincinnati in the Early Jacksonian Period, 1816–1834: An Economic and Political Study" (Ph.D. diss., Indiana University, 1967); Richard T. Farrell, "Cincinnati, 1800–1830: Economic Development through Trade and Industry," *Ohio History* 77 (1968): 111–29; Alan L. Marcus, "The Strange Career of Municipal Health Initiatives: Cincinnati and City Government in the Early Nineteenth Century," *Journal of Urban History* 7 (1980): 3–30; Louis Leonard Tucker, "Cincinnati: Athens of the West, 1830–1861," *Ohio History* 75 (1966): 10–25; Richard C. Wade,

The Urban Frontier: Pioneer Life in Early Pittsburgh, Cincinnati, Lexington, Louisville, and St. Louis (Cambridge, Massachusetts, 1959); and Earl Irvin West, "Early Cincinnati's Unprecedented Spectacle," *Ohio History* 79 (1970): 5–17 [describes a debate between Robert Dale Owen and Alexander Campbell].

40. Steven J. Ross, *Workers on the Edge: Work, Leisure, and Politics in Industrializing Cincinnati, 1788–1890* (New York, 1985), 9.

41. Ibid., 16, 30, 55, 31.

42. Ibid., 57.

43. James H. Madison, *The Indiana Way: A State History* (Bloomington and Indianapolis, 1986), 87.

44. See, for example, Harry N. Scheiber, "Entrepreneurship and Western Development: The Case of Micajah T. Williams," *Business History Review* 37 (1963): 345–68; Scheiber, "Alfred Kelley and the Ohio Business Elite, 1822–1859," *Ohio History* 87 (1978): 365–92.

45. See, for example, Richard S. Alcorn, "Leadership and Stability in Mid-Nineteenth Century America: A Case Study of an Illinois Town," *Journal of American History* 61 (1974): 685–702; Victor Bogle, "A View of New Albany Society at Mid-Nineteenth Century," *Indiana Magazine of History* 54 (1958): 93–118; Buettinger, "Economic Inequality in Early Chicago, 1849–1850"; Doyle, *Social Order*; Kirk, *Promise of American Life*, especially 131; and Walter Glazer, "Voluntary Associations in Cincinnati," *Historical Methods Newsletter* 5 (1972): 151–68.

46. Glazer, "Voluntary Associations," 152, 162.

47. Lewis Atherton, *Main Street on the Middle Border* (Bloomington, Indiana, 1954), 23, 65–108.

48. Winkle, *Politics of Community*, 77.

49. Ibid., 176.

50. Doyle, *Social Order*, 3, 15.

51. Ibid., 92.

52. Ibid., 101, 107, 111–12.

53. Ibid., 192.

54. The key work is David Brion Davis, *The Problem of Slavery in the Age of Revolution, 1770–1823* (Ithaca, New York, 1975).

55. Ryan, *Cradle of the Middle Class*, chaps. 2–4; Smith-Rosenberg, *Disorderly Conduct*, 129–64; and Ann Douglas, *The Feminization of American Culture* (New York, 1977). See also Linda K. Kerber, "Separate Spheres, Female Worlds, Woman's Place: The Rhetoric of Women's History," *Journal of American History* 75 (1988): 9–39.

56. Nancy Cott, *The Bonds of Womanhood: "Woman's Sphere" in New England, 1780–1835* (New Haven, Connecticut, 1977). See also the valuable account of a Connecticut woman in Lois Scharf, "'I Would Go Wherever Fortune Would Direct': Hannah Huntington and the Frontier of the Western Reserve," *Ohio History* 97 (1988): 5–28.

57. Ellen Carol DuBois, *Feminism and Suffrage: The Emergence of an Independent Women's Movement in America, 1848–1869* (Ithaca, New York, 1978); and Barbara Leslie Epstein, *The Politics of Domesticity: Women, Evangelism and Temperance in Nineteenth-Century America* (Middletown, Connecticut, 1981).

58. Nancy Hewitt, *Women's Activism and Social Change: Rochester, New York, 1822–1872* (Ithaca, New York, 1984), 22. See also Lori D. Ginzberg, "'Moral Suasion is Moral Balderdash': Women, Politics, and Social Activism in the 1850s," *Journal of American History* 73 (1986): 601–22.

59. Hewitt, *Women's Activism*, 23.

60. See especially Smith-Rosenberg, *Disorderly Conduct,* 53–76; and Lee Virginia Chambers-Schiller, *Liberty, A Better Husband: Single Women in America: The Generations of 1780–1840* (New Haven, Connecticut, 1984).

61. Marilyn Ferris Motz, *True Sisterhood: Michigan Women and Their Kin, 1820–1920* (Albany, New York, 1983), 14.

62. Ibid., 36.

63. See Donald M. Scott, "The Popular Lecture and the Creation of a Public in Mid-Nineteenth-Century America," *Journal of American History* 66 (1980): 791–819; Carl Bode, *The American Lyceum: Town Meeting of the Mind* (New York, 1956); John C. Colson, "'Public Spirit' at Work: Philanthropy and Public Libraries in Nineteenth-Century Wisconsin," *Wisconsin Magazine of History* 59 (1976): 192–209; E. Bruce Kirkham, "Harriet Beecher Stowe's Western Tour," *The Old Northwest* 1 (1975): 35–50; David Mead, *Yankee Eloquence in the Middle West: The Ohio Lyceum, 1850–1870* (East Lansing, Michigan, 1951); John Neufeld, "The Associated Western Literary Societies in the Midwest," *Michigan History* 51 (1967): 154–61; and Rita S. Saslaw, "Student Societies in Nineteenth Century Ohio: Misconceptions and Realities," *Ohio History* 88 (1979): 198–210.

64. Mary Kupiec Cayton, "The Making of an American Prophet: Emerson, His Audiences, and the Rise of the Culture Industry in America," *American Historical Review* 92 (1987), 605–606.

65. Ibid., 614.

66. Faragher, *Sugar Creek.*

67. Peter S. Onuf, "The Founders' Vision: Education in the Development of the Old Northwest," in *"Schools and the Means of Education Shall Forever Be Encouraged": A History of Education in the Old Northwest, 1787–1880,* ed. Paul H. Mattingly and Edward W. Stevens (Athens, Ohio, 1987), 5–15.

68. Carl F. Kaestle, "Public Education in the Old Northwest: 'Necessary to Good Government and the Happiness of Mankind,'" *Indiana Magazine of History* 84 (1988): 65.

Studies of private and public education efforts include Mauck Brammer, "Winthrop B. Smith: Creator of the Eclectic Educational Series," *Ohio History* 80 (1971): 45–59; Robert A. Brunger, "Albion College: The Founding of a Frontier School," *Michigan History* 51 (1967): 130–53; David L. Calkins, "Black Education in Nineteenth Century Cincinnati," *Cincinnati Historical Society Bulletin* 38 (1980): 115–28; James T. Herget, "Democracy Revisited: The Land and School Districts in Illinois," *Journal of the Illinois State Historical Society* 72 (1979): 123–38; Daniel T. Johnson, "Financing the Western Colleges, 1844–1862," *Journal of the Illinois State Historical Society* 65 (1972): 43–53; John Lankford, "'Culture and Business': The Founding of the Fourth Normal School at River Falls," *Wisconsin Magazine of History* 47 (1963): 26–34; Charles E. Peterson, Jr., "The Common School Advocate: Molder of the Public Mind," *Journal of the Illinois State Historical Society* 57 (1964): 261–69; William C. Ringenberg, "The Oberlin College Influence in Early Michigan," *The Old Northwest* 3 (1977): 111–32; and Richard S. Taylor, "Western Colleges as Securities of Intelligence and Virtue: The Towne-Eddy Report of 1846," *The Old Northwest* 7 (1981): 41–66.

69. Kaestle, "Public Education in the Old Northwest," 68.

70. Doyle, *Social Order,* 207.

71. Wayne Edison Fuller, *The Old Country School: The Story of Rural Education in the Middle West* (Chicago, 1982), 38.

72. Bender, *Community* 138–41; Richard Jensen, "Midwestern Transformation: From Traditional Pioneers to Modern Society," *Local History Today: Papers Presented at Four Regional Workshops for Local Historical Organizations in Indi-*

ana, June 1978–April 1979 (Indianapolis, 1979), 8–12; and Edward W. Stevens, Jr., "Structural and Ideological Dimensions of Literacy and Education in the Old Northwest," in Klingaman and Vedder, eds., *Essays on the Economic History* 157–86.

73. See Julia P. Cutler, *Life and Times of Ephraim Cutler* (Cincinnati, 1890).

74. Fuller, *Old Country School*, 30, 48.

75. Ibid., 48.

76. Kaestle, "Public Education in the Old Northwest," 67–68. See also Carl F. Kaestle, "The Development of Common School Systems in the States of the Old Northwest," in Mattingly and Stevens, eds., *"Schools and the Means of Education"* 67–68; Carl F. Kaestle, *Pillars of the Republic: Common Schools and American Society, 1780–1860* (New York, 1983).

77. Atherton, *Main Street on the Middle Border*, 76–88.

78. Kaestle, "Public Education in the Old Northwest," 68–69.

79. Polly Welts Kaufman, *Women Teachers on the Frontier* (New Haven, Connecticut, 1984). See also Marie A. Vinovskis and Richard M. Bernard, "Beyond Catharine Beecher: Female Education in the Antebellum Period," *Signs* 3 (1978): 856–69. In "Coeducation of the Sexes at Oberlin College: A Study of Social Ideas in Mid-Nineteenth Century America," *Journal of Social History* 6 (1972–1973): 160–76, Ronald W. Hogeland argues that the introduction of coeducation was "conceived of and implemented with men's priorities in mind" (160). Women were "expected to be catalysts for cultivation, reservoirs for wifedom, and redemptive agents for male sensuality. In each case they were to give unselfishly of themselves in order to assist in the mission of the church, which ultimately was dependent upon the leading sex" (172).

80. Kathryn Kish Sklar, "Female Teachers: 'Firm Pillars' of the West," in Mattingly and Stevens, *"Schools and the Means of Education,"* 62.

81. Kaestle, "Public Education in the Old Northwest," 69–73. See also Jack Nortrup, "The Troubles of an Itinerant Teacher [Frances Willard] in the Early Nineteenth Century," *Journal of the Illinois State Historical Society* 71 (1978): 279–87.

82. Ibid., 68–69. See also Atherton, *Main Street* 72–76.

83. Jed Dannenbaum, *Drink and Disorder: Temperance Reform in Cincinnati from the Washingtonian Revival to the WCTU* (Urbana, Illinois, 1984), 9. See also Joseph F. Kett, "Review Essay: Temperance and Intemperance as Historical Problems," *Journal of American History* 67 (1981): 878–85; and Joseph R. Gusfield, *Symbolic Crusade: Status Politics and the American Temperance Movement* (Urbana, Illinois, 1970).

Valuable local studies include David M. Fahey, "Who Joined the Sons of Temperance? Livelihood and Age in the Black Book and Minutes, Phoenix Division, Dexter, Michigan, 1848–1851," *The Old Northwest* 11 (1985–1986): 221–26; and Marc L. Harris, "The Process of Voluntary Association: Organizing the Ravenna Temperance Society, 1830," *Ohio History* 94 (1985): 158–70.

84. Gorn, *Manly Art*. See also Herbert G. Gutman, *Work, Culture and Society in Industrializing America* (New York, 1976), 19–21. We do not mean to suggest that all working-class and rural peoples opposed or ignored temperance reform. Public schools, temperance, and antislavery were not exclusively middle-class issues; nevertheless all had the effect of promoting middle-class values. See Eric Foner, *Politics and Ideology in the Age of the Civil War* (New York, 1980), esp. 22–27.

85. W. J. Rorabaugh, *The Alcoholic Republic: An American Tradition* (New

York, 1979), 232–33, and passim. See also Thomas P. Slaughter, *The Whiskey Rebellion: Frontier Epilogue to the American Revolution* (New York, 1986).

86. Dannenbaum, *Drink and Disorder*, 22.

87. Ibid., 8. See also Doyle, *Social Order*, 212–17.

88. Friedman, *Gregarious Saints*, 79.

89. Stanley Harrold, *Gamaliel Bailey and Antislavery Union* (Kent, Ohio, 1986); Frederick J. Blue, *Salmon P. Chase: A Life in Politics* (Kent, Ohio, 1987); James Brewer Stewart, *Joshua R. Giddings and the Tactics of Radical Politics* (Cleveland, Ohio, 1970); Douglas H. Gamble, "Joshua Giddings and the Ohio Abolitionists: A Study in Radical Politics," *Ohio History* 88 (1979): 37–56; Edward Magdol, *Owen Lovejoy: Abolitionist in Congress* (New Brunswick, New Jersey, 1967); Hans L. Trefousse, *Benjamin Franklin Wade: Radical Republican from Ohio* (New York, 1963).

See also David French, "Elizur Wright, Jr. and the Emergence of Anti-Colonization Sentiment on the Connecticut Western Reserve," *Ohio History* 85 (1976): 49–66; John R. McKivigan, "The Christian Anti-Slavery Convention Movement of the Northwest," *The Old Northwest* 5 (1979): 345–66; Thomas D. Matijasic, "Abolition vs. Colonization: The Battle for Ohio," *Queen City Heritage* 45 (1987): 27–40; Edgar F. Raines, Jr., "The American Missionary Association in Southern Illinois, 1856–1862: A Case Study in the Abolition Movement," *Journal of the Illinois State Historical Society* 65 (1977): 246–68; and Donald J. Ratcliffe, "Captain James Riley and Antislavery Sentiment in Ohio, 1819–1824," *Ohio History* 81 (1972): 76–94.

90. Peter F. Walker, *Moral Choices: Memory, Desire, and Imagination in Nineteenth-Century American Abolitionism* (Baton Rouge, Louisiana, 1978), 304. See also Louis Gerteis, *Morality and Utility in American Anti-Slavery Reform* (Chapel Hill, North Carolina, 1987).

91. Bertram Wyatt-Brown, "Conscience and Career: Young Abolitionists and Missionaries Compared," in *Yankee Saints and Southern Sinners* (Baton Rouge, Louisiana, 1985), 68.

92. Walker, *Moral Choices*, 303–304. See also John L. Hammond, "Revival, Religion and Antislavery Politics," *American Sociological Review* 39 (1974): 175–86; and Ronald G. Walters, *The Antislavery Appeal: American Abolitionism after 1830* (Baltimore, 1976).

93. Leonard Richards, *"Gentlemen of Property and Standing": Anti-Abolition Mobs in Jacksonian America* (New York, 1970), 155.

IV: The Origins of Politics in the Old Northwest

1. The standard Turnerian accounts include John D. Barnhart, *Valley of Democracy: The Frontier versus the Plantation in the Ohio Valley, 1775–1818* (Bloomington, Indiana, 1953); Solon J. Buck, *Illinois in 1818* (Urbana, Illinois, 1967); John D. Barnhart and Dorothy L. Riker, *Indiana to 1816: The Colonial Period* (Indianapolis, 1971); Randolph C. Downes, *Frontier Ohio, 1788–1803* (Columbus, Ohio, 1935); Floyd Streeter, *Political Parties in Michigan, 1837–1860* (Lansing, Michigan, 1918).

2. Peter S. Onuf, *Statehood and Union: A History of the Northwest Ordinance* (Bloomington, Indiana, 1987); Onuf, "From Constitution to Higher Law: The Reinterpretation of the Northwest Ordinance," *Ohio History* 94 (1985): 5–33; and Andrew R. L. Cayton, "The Origins of Politics in the Old Northwest," in *Pathways to the Old Northwest* (Indianapolis, 1988), 59–70.

3. Ronald Formisano, "Deferential-Participant Politics: The Early Republic's Political Culture, 1789–1840," *American Political Science Review* 68 (1974): 473–84; Richard Hofstadter, *The Idea of a Party System* (Berkeley, California, 1970); and Ralph L. Ketcham, *Presidents above Party: The First American Presidency, 1789–1829* (Chapel Hill, North Carolina, 1984).

4. Ronald Formisano, *The Birth of Mass Political Parties: Michigan, 1827–1861* (Princeton, New Jersey, 1971); and Michael F. Holt, *The Political Crisis of the 1850s* (New York, 1978).

5. Onuf, "From Constitution to Higher Law."

6. See Bernard Bailyn, *The Origins of American Politics* (New York, 1967); Patricia Bonomi, *A Factious People: Politics and Society in Colonial New York* (New York, 1971); Richard L. Bushman, *King and People in Provincial Massachusetts* (Chapel Hill, North Carolina, 1985); Jack P. Greene, *The Quest for Power: The Lower Houses of Assembly in the Southern Royal Colonies, 1689–1776* (Chapel Hill, North Carolina, 1963); and John Murrin, "Political Development," in *Colonial British America: Essays in the New History of the Early Modern Era*, ed. Jack P. Greene and J. R. Pole (Baltimore, 1984), 408–56.

7. Andrew R. L. Cayton, "Land, Reputation, and Power: The Cultural Dimension of Politics in the Ohio Country," *William and Mary Quarterly*, 3d ser., forthcoming.

8. Andrew R. L. Cayton, *The Frontier Republic: Ideology and Politics in the Ohio Country, 1780–1825* (Kent, Ohio, 1986).

9. Donald J. Ratcliffe, "The Experience of Revolution and the Beginnings of Party Politics in Ohio, 1776–1816," *Ohio History* 85 (1976): 197.

10. Ibid., 201.

11. Ibid., 216.

12. For a comparison with New York, see Michael Wallace, "Changing Concepts of Party in the United States: New York, 1815–1828," *American Historical Review* 74 (1968): 453–91; and with Massachusetts, Ronald P. Formisano, *The Transformation of Political Culture: Massachusetts Parties, 1790s–1840s* (New York, 1983).

13. Donald J. Ratcliffe, "Voter Turnout in Early Ohio," *Journal of the Early Republic* 7 (1987): 233. See also Ray Myles Shortridge, "An Assessment of the Frontier's Influence on Voter Turnout," *Agricultural History* 50 (1976): 445–59. In analyzing voting patterns in the 1840s and 1850s, Shortridge concluded that the frontier had no impact on turnout.

14. Ibid., 234–35.

15. Ibid., 246.

16. Ibid., 247.

17. Ratcliffe, "Experience of Revolution," 217. See also Jeffrey P. Brown, "The Ohio Federalists, 1803–1815," *Journal of the Early Republic* 2 (1982): 261–82.

18. Cayton, *Frontier Republic*, 81–109.

19. Ibid.

20. Ibid., 33–50.

21. Ibid., 81–83.

22. Brown, "Ohio Federalists."

23. Cayton, *Frontier Republic*, 68–80.

24. James H. Madison, *The Indiana Way: A State History* (Bloomington and Indianapolis, 1986), 133. On Illinois, see John W. McNulty, "Sidney Breese: His Early Career in Law and Politics in Illinois," *Journal of the Illinois State Historical Society* 61 (1968): 164–81; and Donald S. Spencer, "Edward Coles: Virginia

Gentleman in Frontier Politics," *Journal of the Illinois State Historical Society* 61 (1968): 150–63.

25. Elliott J. Gorn, "'Gouge and Bite, Pull Hair and Scratch': The Social Significance of Fighting in the Southern Backcountry," *American Historical Review* 90 (1985): 38. See also Cayton, "Land, Power, and Reputation"; Edward L. Ayers, *Vengeance and Justice: Crime and Punishment in the Nineteenth Century American South* (New York, 1984), chap. 1; and Bertram Wyatt-Brown, *Southern Honor: Ethics and Behavior in the Old South* (New York, 1982).

26. Ibid., 41.

27. See, for example, Beverley W. Bond, Jr., *The Civilization of the Old Northwest, 1788–1812* (New York, 1934); and R. Carlyle Buley, *The Old Northwest: Pioneer Period, 1815–1840*, 2 vols. (Bloomington, Indiana, 1950).

28. Gorn, "'Gouge and Bite.'"

29. Ibid.

30. For discussions of Indian-white relations in this period, see Burt Anson, *The Miami Indians* (Norman, Oklahoma, 1970); Colin G. Calloway, *Crown and Calumet: British-Indian Relations, 1783–1815* (Norman, Oklahoma, 1987); Randolph C. Downes, *Council Fires on the Upper Ohio* (Pittsburgh, 1940); R. David Edmunds, *The Shawnee Prophet* (Lincoln, Nebraska, 1983); Edmunds, *Tecumseh and the Quest for Indian Leadership* (Boston, 1984); Reginald Horsman, *Expansion and American Indian Policy, 1783–1812* (East Lansing, Michigan, 1967); and Francis Paul Prucha, *The Great Father: The United States Government and the American Indians*, 2 vols. (Lincoln, Nebraska, 1984).

31. C. S. Weslager, *The Delaware Indians: A History* (New Brunswick, New Jersey, 1972).

32. Cayton, *Frontier Republic*, chaps. 1 and 2; and Onuf, *Statehood and Union*, chaps. 1 and 2.

33. Andrew R. L. Cayton, "The Northwest Ordinance from the Perspective of the Frontier," in *The Northwest Ordinance: A Bicentennial Handbook*, ed. Robert M. Taylor, Jr. (Indianapolis, 1987), 1–23.

34. Cayton, *Frontier Republic*, 74.

35. Buley, *The Old Northwest* 2, 477; Reginald Horsman, *The Frontier in the Formative Years, 1783–1815* (New York, 1970), 137.

36. W. Eugene Hollon, *Frontier Violence: Another Look* (New York, 1974), 32–33.

37. Pauline Maier, *From Resistance to Revolution: Colonial Radicals and the Development of American Opposition to Britain, 1765–1776* (New York, 1972), 3–48; Paul A. Gilje, "The Baltimore Riot of 1812 and the Breakdown of the Anglo-American Mob Tradition," *Journal of Social History* 13 (1980): 547–64; Paul A. Gilje, *The Road to Mobocracy: Popular Disorder in New York City, 1763–1834* (Chapel Hill, North Carolina, 1987), chap. 1; and Leonard L. Richards, *"Gentlemen of Property and Standing": Anti-Abolition Mobs in Jacksonian America* (New York, 1970).

38. On the role of the courts, see David J. Bodenhamer, "Law and Disorder on the Early Frontier: Marion County, Indiana, 1823–1850," *Western Historical Quarterly* 10 (1979): 323–36; David J. Bodenhamer, "Criminal Punishment in Antebellum Indiana: The Limits of Reform," *Indiana Magazine of History* 82 (1986): 358–403; David J. Bodenhamer, "The Democratic Impulse and Legal Change in the Age of Jackson: The Example of Criminal Juries in Antebellum Indiana," *The Historian* 45 (1983): 206–19; Howard Fergenbaum, "The Lawyer in Wisconsin, 1836–1860: A Profile," *Wisconsin Magazine of History* 55

(1971–1972): 100–106; M. Paul Holsinger, "Timothy Walker: Blackstone for the New Republic," *Ohio History* 84 (1975): 145–57; Alice E. Smith, "Courts and Judges in Wisconsin Territory," *Wisconsin Magazine of History* 56 (1973): 179–88; and Richard D. Younger, "The Grand Jury on the Frontier," *Wisconsin Magazine of History* 40 (1956–1957): 3–12. For a discussion of the legal system on a different frontier, see Michael Bellesiles, "The Establishment of Legal Structures on the Frontier: The Case of Revolutionary Vermont," *Journal of American History* 73 (1987): 895–915. See also Mary K. Bonsteel Tachau, *Federal Courts in the Early Republic: Kentucky, 1789–1816* (Princeton, New Jersey, 1978).

39. Harry T. Watson, *Jacksonian Politics and Community Conflict: The Emergence of the Second American Party System in Cumberland County, North Carolina* (Baton Rouge, Louisiana, 1981), 3.

40. Frederick Jackson Turner, *Rise of the New West, 1818–1829* (New York, 1906); Harry Stevens, *The Early Jackson Party in Ohio* (Durham, North Carolina, 1957); and Donald J. Ratcliffe, "The Role of Voters and Issues in Party Formation: Ohio, 1824," *Journal of American History* 59 (1972): 847–71.

41. Watson, *Jacksonian Politics*, 14.

42. Ronald P. Formisano, *The Birth of Mass Political Parties: Michigan, 1827–1861* (Princeton, New Jersey, 1971); Stephen Carey Fox, "The Group Bases of Ohio Political Behavior, 1804–1848" (Ph.D. diss., University of Cincinnati, 1973); Fox, "Politicians, Issues and Voter Preference in Jacksonian Ohio: A Critique of an Interpretation," *Ohio History* 87 (1977): 155–70; Fox, "The Bank War, the Idea of 'Party,' and the Division of the Electorate in Jacksonian Ohio," *Ohio History* 88 (1979): 253–76; Donald J. Ratcliffe, "Politics in Jacksonian Ohio: Reflections on the Ethnocultural Interpretation," *Ohio History* 88 (1979): 5–36; and James Roger Sharp, *The Jacksonians versus the Banks: Politics in the States after the Panic of 1837* (New York, 1970). See also Thomas A. Flinn, "Continuity and Change in Ohio Politics," *Journal of Politics* 20 (1962): 521–44.

43. See Holt, *The Political Crisis of the 1850s*, vii-x, chaps. 1 and 2. For general reviews of the literature on the Jacksonian party system, see Ronald P. Formisano, "Toward a Reorientation of Jacksonian Politics: A Review of the Literature, 1959–1975," *Journal of American History* 63 (1976): 42–65; Richard B. Latner, "A New Look at Jacksonian Politics," *Journal of American History* 61 (1975): 943–69; Latner and Peter D. Levine, "Perspectives on Antebellum Pietistic Politics," *Reviews in American History* 4 (1976): 15–24; and Richard L. McCormick, "Ethno-Cultural Interpretations of Nineteenth-Century American Voting Behavior," *Political Science Quarterly* 89 (1974): 351–77.

44. Kenneth J. Winkle, *The Politics of Community: Migration and Politics in Antebellum Ohio* (Cambridge, England, 1988), 47.

45. Ibid., 51.

46. Ibid., 63.

47. Watson, *Jacksonian Politics*, 322.

48. On the role of banks in the early nineteenth-century Midwest, see Buley, *The Old Northwest* 1, 565–632; Donald R. Adams, "The Role of Banks in the Economic Development of the Old Northwest," in *Essays in Nineteenth Century Economic History: The Old Northwest* ed. David C. Klingaman and Richard K. Vedder (Athens, Ohio, 1975), 208–45; Fred R. Marckhoff, "Currency and Banking in Illinois before 1865," *Journal of the Illinois State Historical Society* 52 (1959): 365–418; James H. Madison, "Business and Politics in Indianapolis: The Branch Bank and the Junto, 1837–1846," *Indiana Magazine of History* 71 (1975): 1–20; and Harry N. Scheiber, "Bancroft and the Bank of Michigan," *Michigan History* 44 (1960): 82–90.

49. On the Panic of 1819, see Thomas H. Greer, "Economic and Social Effects of the Depression of 1819 in the Old Northwest," *Indiana Magazine of History* 44 (1948): 227–43; and Stevens, *Early Jackson Party*, 9–14.

50. William G. Shade, *Banks or No Banks: The Money Issue in Western Politics, 1832–1865* (Detroit, 1972). See also Erling Erickson, *Banking in Frontier Iowa, 1836–1865* (Ames, Iowa, 1971).

51. Shade, *Banks or No Banks*, 111. See also Herbert Ershkowitz and William G. Shade, "Consensus or Conflict? Political Behavior in the State Legislatures during the Jacksonian Era," *Journal of American History* 58 (1971): 591–622; Rodney O. Davis, "Partisanship in Jacksonian State Politics: Party Divisions in the Illinois Legislature, 1834–1841," in *Quantification in American History: Theory and Research*, ed. Robert P. Swierenga (New York, 1970), 149–62; and Arnold Shankman, "Partisan Conflicts, 1839–1841, and the Illinois Constitution," *Journal of the Illinois State Historical Society* 63 (1970): 336–67.

52. Ibid., 110.

53. Richard Hofstadter, *The American Political Tradition and the Men Who Made It* (New York, 1948); and Bray Hammond, *Banks and Politics in America: From the Revolution to the Civil War* (Princeton, New Jersey, 1957).

54. Marvin Meyers, *The Jacksonian Persuasion: Politics and Belief* (Stanford, California, 1957).

55. Lee Benson, *The Concept of Jacksonian Democracy: New York as a Test Case* (Princeton, New Jersey, 1961).

56. See, among many other writings, Edward Pessen, *Jacksonian America: Society, Personality, and Politics* (Homewood, Illinois, 1969).

57. Watson, *Jacksonian Politics*; and J. Mills Thornton, *Power and Politics in a Slave Society: Alabama, 1806–1860* (Baton Rouge, Louisiana, 1978). See John Ashworth, *"Agrarians" v. "Aristocrats": Party Political Ideology in the United States, 1837–1848* (Cambridge, England, 1983).

58. Daniel Walker Howe, *The Political Culture of the American Whigs* (Chicago, 1979), 56. See also Thomas Brown, *Politics and Statesmanship: Essays on the American Whig Party* (New York, 1985); and Lynn Marshall, "The Strange Still-Birth of the Whig Party," *American Historical Review* 72 (1967): 445–68.

Studies of the Whigs in the Old Northwest include Leonard Erickson, "Politics and Repeal of Ohio's Black Laws, 1837–1849," *Ohio History* 82 (1973): 154–75; Thomas D. Matijasic, "Whig Support for African Colonization: Ohio as a Test Case," *Mid-America* 66 (1984): 79–92; James Stegemoeller, "That Contemptible Bauble: The Birth of the Cincinnati Whig Party," *Cincinnati Historical Society Bulletin* 39 (1981): 201–23.

59. Sharp, *Jacksonians versus the Banks*, 188. See also David J. Bodenhamer, "Criminal Justice and Democratic Theory in Antebellum America: The Grand Jury Debate in Indiana," *Journal of the Early Republic* 5 (1985): 481–502, for a discussion of a Whig-Jacksonian split over the role of grand juries. While Whigs tended to support them, Jacksonians denounced them as infringements of individual liberty.

60. Shade, *Banks or No Banks*, 136.

61. Ibid., 137–41.

62. Ibid., 141.

63. Ibid., 144.

64. Formisano, *Birth of Mass Political Parties*, 54.

65. Ibid., 10.

66. Ibid., 101.

67. Shade, *Banks or No Banks*, 144.

68. Formisano, *Birth of Mass Political Parties*, 20.
69. Sharp, *The Jacksonians versus the Banks*, 206.
70. Formisano, *Birth of Mass Political Parties*, 16.
71. Ibid.; Fox, "The Bank War." See also Marshall, "Strange Still-Birth."
72. Howe, *Political Culture*, 32–33.
73. Sharp, *Jacksonians versus the Banks*, 168; McCoy cited in Formisano, *Birth of Mass Political Parties*, 44.
74. John Mack Faragher, *Sugar Creek: Life on the Illinois Prairie* (New Haven, Connecticut, 1986), 192, 194.
75. Don Harrison Doyle, *The Social Order of a Frontier Community: Jacksonville, Illinois, 1825–1870* (Urbana, Illinois, 1978), 171.
76. Winkle, *Politics of Community*, 79.
77. Stephen E. Maizlish, *The Triumph of Sectionalism: The Transformation of Ohio Politics, 1844–1856* (Kent, Ohio, 1983), chap. 1.
78. Robert W. Johannsen, *Stephen A. Douglas* (New York, 1973), 27.
79. Ibid., 79, 137, 79.

V: The Politics of Cultural Definition

1. Eric Foner, *Free Soil, Free Labor, Free Men: The Ideology of the Republican Party before the Civil War* (New York, 1970); and Foner, *Politics and Ideology in the Age of the Civil War* (New York, 1980).
2. Eric Hobsbawm, *The Age of Capital, 1848–1875* (London, 1975).
3. For discussions of the Midwest as a region in the nineteenth century, see William N. Parker, "Native Origins of Modern Industry: Heavy Industrialization in the Old Northwest," in *Essays on the Economy of the Old Northwest*, ed. David C. Klingaman and Richard K. Vedder (Athens, Ohio, 1987), 252–54, 258–60; Parker, "From Northwest to Mid-West: Social Bases of a Regional History," in *Essays in Nineteenth Century Economic History: The Old Northwest*, ed. David C. Klingaman and Richard K. Vedder (Athens, Ohio, 1975), 3–34; and Harry N. Scheiber, "Preface: On the Concepts of 'Regionalism' and 'Frontier,'" in *The Old Northwest: Studies in Regional History, 1787–1910*, ed. Harry N. Scheiber (Lincoln, Nebraska, 1969), vii-xix.
4. See Peter S. Onuf, *Statehood and Union: A History of the Northwest Ordinance* (Bloomington, Indiana, 1987), 133–52.
5. The argument of this chapter was influenced by Chantal Mouffe, "Hegemony and New Political Subjects: Toward a New Concept of Democracy," in *Marxism and the Interpretation of Culture*, ed. Cary Nelson and Lawrence Grossberg (Urbana, Illinois, 1988), 89–101.
6. Michael F. Holt, *The Political Crisis of the 1850s* (New York, 1978), 121.
7. Jed Dannenbaum, *Drink and Disorder: Temperance Reform in Cincinnati from the Washingtonian Revival to the WCTU* (Urbana, Illinois, 1984), 7.
8. Ibid., 72.
9. Kathleen Neils Conzen, *Immigrant Milwaukee, 1836–1860: Accommodation and Community in a Frontier City* (Cambridge, Massachusetts, 1976), 42, 124.
10. Ibid., 191. See also Robert E. Cazden, "The German Book Trade in Ohio before 1848," *Ohio History* 84 (1974): 57–77; La Vern J. Rippley, "The Chillicothe Germans," *Ohio History* 75 (1966): 212–25; Carl Wittke, "Ohio's Germans, 1840–1875," *Ohio History* 66 (1957): 339–54; and the special issue on the Germans in Cincinnati, *Queen City Heritage* 42 (1984), no. 3.
11. Ibid.

12. Ibid., 227.

13. Studies of other European immigrants in the nineteenth-century Midwest include Joseph J. Barton, *Peasants and Strangers: Italians, Rumanians, and Slovaks in an American City, 1890–1950* (Cambridge, Massachusetts, 1975); Karel D. Bicha, "The Czechs in Wisconsin History," *Wisconsin Magazine of History* 53 (1969–1970): 194–203; Philip S. Friedman, "The Americanization of Chicago's Danish Community, 1850–1920," *Chicago History* 9 no. 1 (1980): 30–41; Lawrence McCaffrey, Ellen Skerrett, Michael F. Funchion, and Charles Fanning, *The Irish in Chicago* (Urbana, Illinois, 1987); Frederick Hale, "The Americanization of a Danish Immigrant in Wisconsin, 1847–1872," *Wisconsin Magazine of History* 64 (1980): 202–15; Gary Ross Mormino, *Immigrants on the Hill: Italian-Americans in St. Louis, 1882–1982* (Urbana, Illinois, 1986); Humbert S. Nelli, *Italians in Chicago, 1880–1930: A Study in Ethnic Mobility* (New York, 1970); William J. Orr, "Rasmus Sorensen and the Beginning of Danish Settlement in Wisconsin," *Wisconsin Magazine of History* 65 (1981–1982): 195–213; Theodore Salutos, "The Greeks of Milwaukee," *Wisconsin Magazine of History* 53 (1969–1970): 175–93; and Jo Ellen Vinyard, "Inland Urban Immigrants: The Detroit Irish, 1850," *Michigan History* 57 (1973): 121–39.

14. Holt, *Political Crisis*, 160–61.

15. Ibid., 159–61. See also Michael F. Holt, "The Politics of Impatience: The Origins of Know-Nothingism," *Journal of American History* 55 (1973): 309–31; and John B. Weaver, "Ohio Republican Attitudes Towards Nativism, 1854–1855," *The Old Northwest* 9 (1983): 289–306.

16. Ibid., 166–69.

17. Dannenbaum, *Drink and Disorder*, 77. See also Joseph R. Gusfield, *Symbolic Crusade: Status Politics and the American Temperance Movement* (Urbana, Illinois, 1970), 1–86. For discussions of urban disorder, see John C. Schneider, "Urbanization and the Maintenance of Order: Detroit, 1824–1847," *Michigan History* 60 (1976): 260–90; and John C. Schneider, "Public Order and the Geography of the City: Crime, Violence, and the Police in Detroit, 1845–1875," *Journal of Urban History* 4 (1978): 183–208.

18. Ibid., 83.

19. Ibid., 146. For a discussion of a parallel split over the question of public education, see F. Michael Perko, "The Building Up of Zion: Religion and Education in Nineteenth Century Cincinnati," *Cincinnati Historical Society Bulletin* 38 (1980): 97–114.

20. Ibid., 147.

21. David Brion Davis, *The Slave Power Conspiracy and the Paranoid Style* (Baton Rouge, Louisiana, 1969). See also Frederick Blue, *The Free Soilers: Third Party Politics, 1848–1851* (Urbana, Illinois, 1973); Frederick J. Blue, *Salmon P. Chase: A Life in Politics* (Kent, Ohio, 1987); Stanley Harrold, *Gamaliel Bailey and Antislavery Union* (Kent, Ohio, 1986); and especially, Richard Sewell, *The House Divided: Sectionalism and Civil War, 1848–1865* (Baltimore, 1988).

22. Onuf, *Statehood and Union*, 146–52; Foner, *Free Soil, Free Labor, Free Men*.

23. Holt, *Political Crisis*; and William E. Gienapp, *The Origins of the Republican Party, 1852–1856* (New York, 1987).

24. Bruce W. Collins, "The Ideology of Ante-Bellum Northern Democrats," *American Studies* 11 (1977): 103–21. See also Jean H. Baker, *Affairs of Party: The Political Culture of Northern Democrats in the Mid-Nineteenth Century* (Ithaca, New York, 1983).

25. Holt, *Political Crisis*, 101–38.

26. Foner, *Free Soil, Free Labor, Free Men.*

27. See Holt, *Political Crisis*; and Gienapp, *Origins of the Republican Party.* Holt suggests that "in some ways" his "whole book is an extended dialog with Foner's work."(xi)

28. Ronald P. Formisano, *The Birth of Mass Political Parties: Michigan, 1827–1861* (Princeton, New Jersey, 1971), 328–31.

29. Eric Foner, "Abolitionism and the Labor Movement in Ante-bellum America," in *Politics and Ideology*, 76.

30. Eric Foner, "The Causes of the American Civil War: Recent Interpretations and New Directions," in *Politics and Ideology*, 26.

31. Collins, "Ideology of the Ante-Bellum Northern Democrats," 118, 119.

32. Gienapp, *Origins of the Republican Party*, 429.

33. Stephen E. Maizlish, *The Triumph of Sectionalism: The Transformation of Ohio Politics, 1844–1856* (Kent, Ohio, 1983), xiii.

34. Ibid., 203.

35. Onuf, *Statehood and Union*, 151.

36. Ibid., 149.

37. Vallandigham quoted in Frank L. Klement, "Middle Western Copperheadism and the Genesis of the Granger Movement," in Scheiber, ed., *The Old Northwest*, 326.

38. Formisano, *Birth of Mass Political Parties*, 324.

39. Gienapp, *Origins of the Republican Party*, 435.

40. Ibid., 437.

41. Ibid., 438. See also Don Harrison Doyle, *The Social Order of a Frontier Community: Jacksonville, Illinois, 1825–1870* (Urbana, Illinois, 1978), 135; Merle Curti, *The Making of an American Community: A Case Study of Democracy in a Frontier County* (Stanford, California, 1959), 327–28.

42. Sound studies of the politics of the 1850s in individual states include Eric J. Cardinal, "Antislavery Sentiment and the Political Transformation in the 1850s: Portage County, Ohio," *The Old Northwest* 1 (1975): 223–38; Eric J. Cardinal, "The Ohio Democracy and the Crisis of Disunion, 1860–1861," *Ohio History* 86 (1977): 19–39; Victor B. Howard, "The 1856 Election in Ohio: Moral Issues in Politics," *Ohio History* 80 (1971): 24–44; Maizlish, *Triumph of Sectionalism*; Lorle A. Porter, "The Lecompton Issue in Knox County Politics: Division of the Democracy, 1858," *Ohio History* 81 (1972): 157–92; E. Duane Elbert, "Southern Indiana in the Election of 1860: The Leadership and the Electorate," *Indiana Magazine of History* 70 (1974): 1–24; Patrick W. Riddleberger, "The Making of a Political Abolitionist: George W. Julian and the Free Soilers, 1848," *Indiana Magazine of History* 51 (1955): 221–336; Emma Lou Thornbrough, *Indiana in the Civil War Era, 1850–1880* (Indianapolis, 1965); Roger H. Van Bolt, "The Rise of the Republican Party in Indiana, 1855–1856," *Indiana Magazine of History* 51 (1955): 185–220; Don E. Fehrenbacher, *Prelude to Greatness: Lincoln in the 1850s* (Stanford, California, 1962); Fehrenbacher, *Chicago Giant: A Biography of 'Long John' Wentworth* (Madison, Wisconsin, 1957); Victor B. Howard, "The Illinois Republican Party," *Journal of the Illinois State Historical Society* 64 (1971): 125–60, 285–311; Formisano, *Birth of Mass Political Parties*; John F. Reynolds, "Piety and Politics: Evangelism in the Michigan Legislature, 1837–1861," *Michigan History* 61 (1977): 323–52; Ronald E. Seavoy, "The Organization of the Republican Party in Michigan, 1846–1854," *The Old Northwest* 6 (1980): 343–76; Norton Wesley, "Methodist Episcopal Church in Michigan and the Politics of Slavery, 1850–1860," *Michigan History* 48 (1964): 193–213; Richard N. Current, *The Civil War Era, 1848–1873* (Madison,

Wisconsin, 1976); Frank L. Byrne, "Maine Law Versus Lager Beer: A Dilemma of Wisconsin's Young Republican Party," *Wisconsin Magazine of History* 42 (1958–1959): 115–23; George H. Daniels "Immigrant Vote in the 1860 Election: The Case of Iowa," *Mid-America* 44 (1962): 146–62; and Morton M. Rosenberg, *Iowa on the Eve of the Civil War: A Decade of Frontier Politics* (Norman, Oklahoma, 1972).

See also Ray M. Shortridge, "Voting for Minor Parties in the Antebellum Midwest," *Indiana Magazine of History* 74 (1978): 117–34; and Shortridge, "Voting Patterns in the American Midwest, 1840–1872" (Ph.D. diss., University of Michigan, 1974).

43. John Lauritz Larson, *Bonds of Enterprise: John Murray Forbes and Western Development in America's Railway Age* (Cambridge, Massachusetts, 1984), 91. See also Walter S. Glazer, "Wisconsin Goes to War: April, 1861," *Wisconsin Magazine of History* 50 (1966–1967): 147–64.

44. Steven J. Ross, *Workers on the Edge: Work, Leisure, and Politics in Industrializing Cincinnati, 1788–1890* (New York, 1985), 133–34.

45. Current, *Civil War Era*, 376–78.

46. Ibid., 480–82.

47. Eric Foner, *Reconstruction: America's Unfinished Revolution, 1863–1877* (New York, 1988), 464.

48. John H. Keiser, *Building for the Centuries: Illinois, 1865 to 1898* (Urbana, Illinois, 1977), xiii.

49. Peter Dobkin Hall, *The Organization of American Culture: Private Institutions, Elites, and the Origins of American Nationality* (New York, 1982), 220–39; and George M. Fredrickson, *The Inner Civil War: Northern Intellectuals and the Crisis of the Union* (New York, 1965).

50. Larson, *Bonds of Enterprise*, 91–102. See David Thelen, *Paths of Resistance: Tradition and Dignity in Industrializing Missouri* (New York, 1986), a book that helped shape the arguments of this chapter.

Local studies include Peter H. Argersinger and Jo Ann E. Argersinger, "The Machine Breakers: Farmworkers and Social Change in the Rural Midwest of the 1870s," *Agricultural History* 58 (1984): 393–410; D. Balasabramanian, "Wisconsin Foreign Trade in the Civil War Era," *Wisconsin Magazine of History* 46 (1963): 257–62; Jack S. Blocker, Jr., "Market Integration, Urban Growth and Economic Change in an Ohio County, 1850–1880," *Ohio History* 89 (1980): 298–316; Douglas E. Booth, "Transportation, City Building, and Financial Crisis: Milwaukee, 1852–1868," *Journal of Urban History* 9 (1983): 335–64; Herbert Brinks, "The Effect of the Civil War in 1861 on Michigan Lumbering and Mining Industries," *Michigan History* 44 (1960): 101–107; Dorothy J. Ernst, "Wheat Speculation in the Civil War Era: Daniel Wells and the Grain Trade," *Wisconsin Magazine of History* 47 (1963–1964): 125–35; Charles K. Hyde, "From 'Subterranean Lotteries' to Orderly Investment: Michigan Copper and Eastern Dollars, 1841–1865," *Mid-America* 66 (1984): 3–20; Gordon W. Kirk, Jr., *The Promise of American Life: Social Mobility in a Nineteenth-Century Immigrant Community, Holland, Michigan, 1847–1894* (Philadelphia, 1978); Byron H. Levene, "Lincoln and McCormick: Two American Emancipators," *Wisconsin Magazine of History* 42 (1958–1959): 97–101; Wayne D. Rasmussen, "The Civil War: A Catalyst of Agricultural Revolution," *Agricultural History* 39 (1965): 187–95; Richard H. Sewell, "Michigan Farmers and the Civil War," *Michigan History* 44 (1960): 353–74; Thomas S. Ulen, "The Regulation of Grain Warehousing and Its Economic Effects: The Competitive Position of Chicago in the 1870s and 1880s," *Agricultural History* 56 (1982): 194–210; Margaret Walsh, "Industrial Opportunity on the Urban Frontier: 'Rags to Riches' and Milwaukee Clothing Manufacturers, 1840–1880," *Wisconsin Magazine of History* 57 (1974): 175–94; Margaret Walsh, "The Dynamics of Industrial Growth in the Old Northwest, 1830–1870: An Interdisciplinary Approach," in *Business and Economic History: Papers Presented at the Twenty-first Annual Meeting of the Business History Conference,* ed. Paul Uselding (Urbana, Illinois, 1975), 12–29; and Margaret Walsh, "From Pork Merchant to Meat Packer: The Midwestern Meat Industry in the Mid-Nineteenth Century," *Agricultural History* 56 (1982): 127–37.

51. Eric Foner, "Politics, Ideology, and the Origins of the American Civil War," in *Politics and Ideology,* 48.

52. Yates quoted in Philip D. Swenson, "Illinois: Disillusionment with State Activism," in *Radical Republicans in the North: State Politics during Reconstruction,* ed. James C. Mohr (Baltimore, 1976), 105.

53. Swenson, "Illinois," 104, 106, 105–109; George M. Blackburn, "Michigan: Quickening Government in a Developing State," in Mohr, ed., *Radical Republicans,* 139, 119–43; Blackburn, "Radical Republican Motivation: A Case History," *Journal of Negro History* 54 (1969): 109–26; Richard N. Current, "Wisconsin: Shifting Strategies to Stay on Top," in Mohr, ed., *Radical Republicans,* 144–66.

54. Robert R. Dykstra, "Iowa: 'Bright Radical Star,'" in Mohr, ed., *Radical Republicans,* 187.

55. Ibid., 167–93.

56. Stephen L. Hansen, *The Making of the Third Party System: Voters and Parties in Illinois, 1850–1876* (Ann Arbor, Michigan, 1980), 127, 141. See also Paul Kleppner, *The Third Electoral System, 1853–1892: Parties, Voters, and Political Cultures* (Chapel Hill, North Carolina, 1979).

57. Felice A. Bonadio, "Ohio: A 'Perfect Contempt of All Unity,'" in Mohr, ed., *Radical Republicans* 82–103. See also Bonadio, *North of Reconstruction, Ohio Politics, 1865–1870* (New York, 1970).

58. Foner, *Reconstruction,* 471.

59. Emma Lou Thornbrough, *The Negro in Indiana* (Indianapolis, 1957), ix. See also Darrel E. Bigham, "The Black Family in Evansville and Vanderburgh County, Indiana, in 1866," *Indiana Magazine of History* 75 (1979): 117–46; Darrel E. Bigham, "Work, Residence, and the Emergence of the Black Ghetto in Evansville, Indiana, 1865–1900," *Indiana Magazine of History* 76 (1980): 287–318; Darrel E. Bigham, "The Black Family in Evansville and Vanderburgh County, Indiana: A 1900 Postscript," *Indiana Magazine of History* 78 (1982): 154–92; and Frederick A. Karst, "A Rural Black Settlement in St. Joseph County, Indiana, Before 1900," *Indiana Magazine of History* 74 (1978): 252–92.

60. David A. Gerber, *Black Ohio and the Color Line, 1860–1915* (Urbana, Illinois, 1976), 26, 44. See also Erving E. Beauregard, "Ohio's First Black College Graduate," *Queen City Heritage* 45 (1987): 3–18; Geoffrey Blodgett, "John Mercer Langston and the Case of Edmonia Lewis: Oberlin, 1862," *Journal of Negro History* 53 (1968): 201–18; David L. Calkins, "Black Education and the Nineteenth Century City: An Institutional Analysis of Cincinnati's Colored Schools, 1850–1887," *Cincinnati Historical Society Bulletin* 33 (1975): 161–74; Leonard Erickson, "Toledo Desegregates, 1871," *Northwest Ohio Quarterly* 41 (1968–1969): 4–12; Lawrence Grossman, "'In His Veins Coursed No Bootlicking Blood': The Career of Peter H. Clark," *Ohio History* 86 (1977): 79–95; W. Sherman Jackson, "Emancipation, Negrophobia, and Civil War Politics in Ohio, 1863–1865," *Journal of Negro History* 65 (1980): 250–60; Samuel Matthews, "John Isom Gaines: The Architect of Black Public Education," *Queen City Heritage* 45 (1987): 41–48; Percy E. Murray, "Harry C. Smith–Joseph B. Foraker Alli-

ance: Coalition Politics in Ohio," *Journal of Negro History* 68 (1983): 171–84;
and Edgar A. Toppin, "Humbly They Served: The Black Brigade in the Defense
of Cincinnati," *Journal of Negro History* 48 (1963): 75–97.

61. Foner, *Reconstruction*, 471. For ample documentation of racism, see V.
Jacque Voegeli, *Free But Not Equal: The Midwest and the Negro during the Civil
War* (Chicago, 1967). See also Frank R. Levstik, "The Toledo Riot of 1862: A Study
of Midwest Negrophobia," *Northwest Ohio Quarterly* 44 (1972): 100–106.

62. Roger D. Bridges, "Equality Deferred: Civil Rights for Illinois Blacks,
1865–1885," *Journal of the Illinois State Historical Society* 74 (1981): 108. See
also Larry Gara, "The Underground Railroad in Illinois," *Journal of the Illinois
State Historical Society* 56 (1963): 508–28; Elmer Gertz, "The Black Laws of Illinois," *Journal of the Illinois State Historical Society* 56 (1963): 454–73; and Syl-
vester C. Watkins, Sr., "Some of Early Illinois' Free Negroes," *Journal of the Illinois State Historical Society* 56 (1963): 495–507.

63. Foner, *Reconstruction*, 472.

64. Joe William Trotter, Jr., *Black Milwaukee: The Making of an Industrial
Proletariat, 1915–1945* (Urbana, Illinois, 1985), 9.

65. Ibid., 33.

66. David M. Katzman, *Before the Ghetto: Black Detroit in the Nineteenth
Century* (Urbana, Illinois, 1973), 75–121. On blacks in nineteenth-century Michigan, see also Willis F. Dunbar with William G. Shade, "The Black Man Gains
the Vote: The Centennial of Impartial Suffrage in Michigan," *Michigan History*
56 (1972): 42–57; Ronald P. Formisano, "The Edge of Caste: Colored Suffrage in
Michigan, 1827–1861," *Michigan History* 56 (1972): 19–41; and John C. Schneider, "Detroit and the Problem of Disorder: The Riot of 1863," *Michigan History*
58 (1974): 4–24.

67. Juliet E. K. Walker, *Free Frank: A Black Pioneer on the Antebellum Frontier* (Lexington, Kentucky, 1983).

68. Peases quoted in Katzman, *Before the Ghetto*, 210. See also Kenneth L.
Kusmer, *A Ghetto Takes Shape: Black Cleveland, 1870–1930* (Urbana, Illinois,
1976).

69. The basic work is John G. Sproat, *"The Best Men": Liberal Reformers in
the Gilded Age* (New York, 1968). But see also Richard Allen Gerber, "The Liberal
Republicans of 1872 in Historiographical Perspective," *Journal of American History* 62 (1975–1976): 40–73.

70. See Foner, *Reconstruction*, 461–534.

71. Quoted in Herbert G. Gutman, "An Iron Workers' Strike in the Ohio Valley, 1873–1874," *Ohio History* 68 (1959): 353–70. For discussions of labor unrest
in the Midwest, see Andrew Birtle, "Governor George Hoadly's Use of the Ohio
National Guard in the Hocking Valley Coal Strike of 1884," *Ohio History* 91
(1982): 37–57; Jerry M. Cooper, "The Wisconsin National Guard in the Milwaukee Riots of 1886," *Wisconsin Magazine of History* 55 (1971): 31–48; George B.
Cotkin, "Strikebreakers, Evictions and Violence: Industrial Conflict in the Hocking Valley, 1884–1885," *Ohio History* 87 (1978): 140–50; and Elizabeth and
Kenneth Fones-Wolf, "The War at Mingo Junction: The Autonomous Workman
and the Decline of the Knights of Labor," *Ohio History* 92 (1983): 37–51; Herbert
G. Gutman, "The Braidwood Lockout of 1874," *Journal of the Illinois State Historical Society* 53 (1960): 5–28; Henry B. Leonard, "Ethnic Cleavage and Industrial
Conflict in Late Nineteenth Century America: The Cleveland Rolling Mills
Company Strikes of 1882 and 1885," *Labor History* 20 (1979): 524–48; and Richard Schneirov, "Chicago's Great Upheaval of 1877," *Chicago History* 9 no. 2
(1980): 2–17.

72. Michael E. McGerr, "The Meaning of Liberal Republicanism: The Case of Ohio," *Civil War History* 28 (1982): 307. See also David P. Thelen, "Rutherford B. Hayes and the Reform Tradition in the Gilded Age," *American Quarterly* 22 (1970): 150–65. Thelen argues that Hayes's "passion for social harmony" (152), his faith in public education, religion, and family, and his emphasis on individualism demonstrates a "strong continuity between the antebellum and progressive traditions"(151).

73. Ibid., 308, 315.

74. Larson, *Bonds of Enterprise*, 135.

75. Ibid.

76. George H. Miller, *Railroads and the Granger Laws* (Madison, Wisconsin, 1971), 197. See also Denise E. Nordin, "A Revisionist Interpretation of the Patrons of Husbandry, 1867–1900," *The Historian* 32 (1969): 630–43; Gerald Prescott, "Gentlemen Farmers in the Gilded Age," *Wisconsin Magazine of History* 55 (1971–1972): 197–212; Ray V. Scott, "Grangerism in Champaign County, Illinois, 1873–1877," *Mid-America* 43 (1961): 139–63; and Dale E. Treleven, "Railroads, Elevators, and Grain Dealers: The Genesis of Antimonopolism in Milwaukee," *Wisconsin Magazine of History* 52 (1969): 205–33.

77. See Lawrence Goodwyn, *Democratic Promise: The Populist Movement in America* (New York, 1976). See also Graham A. Cosmas, "The Democracy in Search of Issues: The Wisconsin Reform Party, 1873–1877," *Wisconsin Magazine of History* 46 (1962–1963): 93–108; and Richard M. Doolen, "The National Greenback Party in Michigan Politics, 1876–1888," *Michigan History* 47 (1963): 161–92.

78. Ross, *Workers on the Edge*, 235. The seminal study is David Montgomery, *Beyond Equality: Labor and the Radical Republicans, 1862–1872* (New York, 1967). See also Eric Foner, "Abolitionism and the Labor Movement in Antebellum America," *Politics and Ideology*, 57–76.

79. Ibid., 199.

80. Bruce Carlan Levine, "Free Soil, Free Labor, and Freimanner: German Chicago in the Civil War Era," in *German Workers in Industrial Chicago, 1850–1910: A Comparative Perspective*, ed. Hartmut Keil and John B. Jentz (DeKalb, Illinois, 1983), 167.

81. Ibid., 178.

82. Richard Jules Oestreicher, *Solidarity and Fragmentation: Working People and Class Consciousness in Detroit, 1875–1900* (Urbana, Illinois, 1986), 89. See also Leon Fink, *Workingmen's Democracy: The Knights of Labor and American Politics* (Urbana, Illinois, 1983); Michael J. Cassity, "Modernization and Social Crisis: The Knights of Labor and a Midwest Community [Sedalia, Missouri], 1885–1886," *Journal of American History* 66 (1979): 41–61; and Susan Levine, *Labor's True Woman: Carpet Weavers, Industrialization, and Labor Reform in the Gilded Age* (Philadelphia, 1984).

83. Ross, *Workers on the Edge*, 263. See also Oestreicher, *Solidarity and Fragmentation*, 30–143.

84. Ibid., 221.

85. Nick Salvatore, *Eugene V. Debs: Citizen and Socialist* (Urbana, Illinois, 1982), 7.

86. Ibid., 19.

87. Ibid., 8.

88. Ibid., 25.

89. Ellen Carol DuBois, *Feminism and Suffrage: The Emergence of an Independent Women's Movement in America, 1848–1869* (Ithaca, New York, 1978), 22.

90. For the history of the suffrage movement in a midwestern state, see Steven M. Buechler, *The Transformation of the Woman Suffrage Movement: The Case of Illinois, 1850–1920* (New Brunswick, New Jersey, 1986), especially his interesting comments on the differences between the movement in the Midwest and the Northeast, pp. 200–201, 217–28. "The movement in the Midwest started later, progressed more slowly, and remained less organized throughout the entire antebellum period than the movement in the Northeast"(217). The midwestern movement, however, "matured" more quickly, and by the late 1860s, the two regions were "synchronized"(219).

See also Carol J. Blum, "The Cincinnati Women's Christian Association: A Study of Innovation and Change, 1868–1880," *Queen City Heritage* 41 (1983): 56–64; Lyle Koehler, "Women's Rights, Society and the Schools: Feminist Activities in Cincinnati, Ohio, 1864–1880," *Queen City Heritage* 42 (1984): 3–17; and Pat Creech Scholten, "A Public 'Jollification': The 1859 Women's Rights Petition before the Indiana Legislature," *Indiana Magazine of History* 72 (1976): 347–59.

91. Charles A. Isetts, "A Social Profile of the Women's Temperance Crusade: Hillsboro, Ohio," in *Alcoholism, Reform, and Society: The Liquor Issue in Social Context,* ed. Jack S. Blocker (Westport, Connecticut, 1979), 101–10. See also Ruth Bordin, "'A Baptism of Power and Liberty': The Women's Crusade in 1873–1874," *Ohio History* 87 (1978): 393–404; Gusfield, *Symbolic Crusade,* 61–110; Marian J. Morton, "Temperance Benevolence and the City: The Cleveland Non-Partisan Women's Christian Temperance Union, 1874–1900," *Ohio History* 91 (1982): 58–73; and F. M. Whitaker, "Ohio WCTU and the Prohibition Amendment Campaign of 1883," *Ohio History* 83 (1974): 84–102.

92. Dannenbaum, *Drink and Disorder,* 220.

93. Barbara Leslie Epstein, *The Politics of Domesticity: Women, Evangelism, and Temperance in Nineteenth-Century America* (Middletown, Connecticut, 1981), 101.

94. Ibid., 114. See also Carroll Smith-Rosenberg, *Disorderly Conduct: Visions of Gender in Victorian America* (New York, 1985), 167–81, 217–96. The result was what Smith-Rosenberg calls the "New Woman," who, in the late 1800s, "rejecting conventional female roles and asserting their right to a career, to a public voice, to visible power, laid claim to the rights and privileges customarily accorded bourgeois men"(176).

VI: The Politics of Accommodation and the Significance of the Frontier

1. Richard J. Jensen, *The Winning of the Midwest: Social and Political Conflict, 1888–1896* (Chicago, 1971), 178.

2. Richard Jules Oestreicher, *Solidarity and Fragmentation: Working People and Class Consciousness in Detroit, 1875–1900* (Urbana, Illinois, 1986), 4.

3. David F. Burg, *Chicago's White City of 1893* (Lexington, Kentucky, 1976), 3, 47.

4. David Montgomery, *The Fall of the House of Labor: The Workplace, the State, and American Labor Activism, 1865–1925* (Cambridge, England, 1987).

5. Steven J. Ross, *Workers on the Edge: Work, Leisure, and Politics in Industrializing Cincinnati, 1788–1890* (New York, 1985), 230.

6. Ibid., 232.

7. Robert S. Lynd and Helen Merrell Lynd, *Middletown: A Study in Modern American Culture* (New York, 1929), 21.

8. Ibid., 39.

9. Ibid., 39–40.

10. Ibid., 76.

11. Montgomery, *Fall of the House of Labor*, 49.

12. Ross, *Workers on the Edge*, 256. See also Zane L. Miller, *Boss Cox's Cincinnati: Urban Politics in the Progressive Era* (Chicago, 1968), 14.

13. Oestreicher, *Solidarity and Fragmentation*, 3. See also Melvin G. Holli, *Reform in Detroit: Hazen S. Pingree and Urban Politics* (New York, 1969), 11.

14. Oestreicher, *Solidarity and Fragmentation*, 39. See also Richard Oestreicher, "Urban Working-Class Political Behavior and Theories of American Electoral Politics, 1870–1940," *Journal of American History* 74 (1988): 1257–86. The seminal work here is Herbert G. Gutman, *Work, Culture and Society in Industrializing America: Essays in American Working Class and Social History* (New York, 1976), esp. the essay "Work, Culture and Society in Industrializing America, (1815–1919)," 3–78. See also Eric Foner, "Class, Ethnicity, and Radicalism in the Gilded Age: The Land League and Irish-America," in *Politics and Ideology*, 150–200; John J. Patrick, "The Cleveland Fenians: A Study in Ethnic Leadership," *The Old Northwest* 9 (1983): 307–30; and Oliver Zunz, "The Organization of the American City in the Late Nineteenth Century: Ethnic Structure and Spatial Arrangement in Detroit," *Journal of Urban History* 3 (1977): 443–66.

15. Kathleen Neils Conzen, "Historical Approaches to the Study of Rural Ethnic Communities," in *Ethnicity on the Great Plains*, ed. Frederick C. Luebke (Lincoln, Nebraska, 1980), 9. See also Kathleen Neils Conzen, "Peasant Pioneers: Generational Succession among German Farmers in Frontier Minnesota," in *The Countryside in the Age of Capitalist Transformation: Essays in the Social History of Rural America*, ed. Steven Hahn and Jonathan Prude (Chapel Hill, North Carolina, 1985), 259–92; and Dorothy O. Johansen, "A Working Hypothesis for the Study of Migration," *Pacific Historical Review* 36 (1967): 1–12.

16. Jon Gjerde, *From Peasants to Farmers: The Migration from Balestrand, Norway to the Upper Middle West* (Cambridge, England, 1985), 168–209. See also Robert C. Ostergren, *A Community Transplanted: The Trans-Atlantic Experience of a Swedish Immigrant Settlement in the Upper Middle West, 1835–1915* (Madison, Wisconsin, 1988).

17. Oestreicher, *Solidarity and Fragmentation*, xv.

18. Ibid., 211.

19. Ibid., 89.

20. Ibid., 128.

21. Quoted in Paul Avrich, *The Haymarket Tragedy* (Princeton, New Jersey, 1984), 216. See also James M. Morris, "No Haymarket for Cincinnati," *Ohio History* 83 (1974): 17–32; the essays in the special issue on the Haymarket in *Chicago History* 15 no. 2 (1986), and Bruce C. Nelson, *Beyond the Martyrs: A Social History of Chicago's Anarchists, 1870–1900* (New Brunswick, New Jersey, 1988).

22. *The [Chicago] Times* quoted in Avrich, *Haymarket Tragedy*, 219.

23. Roy Rosenzweig, *Eight Hours for What We Will: Workers and Leisure in an Industrial City, 1870–1920* (Cambridge, England, 1983), 58. See also Elliott J. Gorn, "'Good-Bye Boys, I Die a True American': Homicide, Nativism, and Working-Class Culture in Antebellum New York City," *Journal of American History* 74 (1987): 388–410; and Jon M. Kingsdale, "The 'Poor Man's Club': Social Functions of the Urban Working-Class Saloon," *American Quarterly* 25 (1973): 472–92. Valuable local studies include Perry Duis, "The Saloon in a Changing Chicago," *Chicago History* 4 no. 4 (1975–1976): 214–24; Perry Duis, "Whose City? Public and Private Places in Nineteenth-Century Chicago," *Chicago History* 12 nos. 1 and 2 (1983): 2–27, 2–23; and Richard Wilson Renner, "'In a Perfect

Ferment': Chicago, the Know-Nothings, and the Riot for Lager Beer," *Chicago History* 5 no. 3 (1976): 161–70.

24. Ibid., 61–64.

25. Williams quoted in ibid., 64.

26. Kathy Peiss, *Cheap Amusements: Working Women and Leisure in Turn-of-the-Century New York* (Philadelphia, 1986), 4.

27. Joanne J. Meyerowitz, *Women Adrift: Independent Wage Earners in Chicago, 1880–1930* (Chicago, 1988), xviii, xix.

28. Ibid., 141.

29. Jensen, *Winning of the Midwest*, 15.

30. Horace Merrill, *Bourbon Democracy of the Middle-West, 1865–1896* (Baton Rouge, Louisiana, 1953).

31. Jensen, *Winning of the Midwest*, 19.

32. Ibid., 16.

33. Ibid., 18. See also Paul Kleppner, *The Cross of Culture: A Social Analysis of Midwestern Politics, 1850–1900* (New York, 1970); and Robert S. Salisbury, "The Republican Party and Positive Government, 1869–1890," *Mid-America* 68 (1986): 15–34. Salisbury contends that Republicans on the national level advocated "positive action on behalf of economic development, a propensity to expend public monies, assistance to various underprivileged groups, regulation of private behavior, and the supremacy of national authority over that of the several states"(18).

34. Ibid., 52–88.

35. Ibid., 7.

36. Ibid., 11.

37. Melvyn Hammarberg, *The Indiana Voter: The Historical Dynamics of Party Allegiance during the 1870s* (Chicago, 1977), 86. See also Michael Les Benedict, "Numbers, Science, and History: A Review Essay of *The Indiana Voter*," *Indiana Magazine of History* 74 (1978): 48–68.

38. Merle Curti, *The Making of an American Community: A Case Study of Democracy in a Frontier County* (Stanford, California, 1959), 327.

39. Don Harrison Doyle, *The Social Order of a Frontier Community: Jacksonville, Illinois, 1825–1870* (Urbana, Illinois, 1978), 135.

40. Ronald P. Formisano, *The Birth of Mass Political Parties: Michigan, 1827–1861* (Princeton, New Jersey, 1971), 328.

41. Lewis Atherton, *Main Street on the Middle Border* (Bloomington, Indiana, 1954), 65–108. See also Daniel Walker Howe, "American Victorianism as a Culture," *American Quarterly* 27 (1975): 507–32.

General studies of local areas include Peter J. Coleman, "The Woodhouse Family: Grant County Pioneers," *Wisconsin Magazine of History* 42 (1959): 267–74; Jan Coombs, "The Health of Central Wisconsin Residents in 1880: A New View of Midwestern Rural Life," *Wisconsin Magazine of History* 68 (1985): 284–311; Lawrence H. Larsen, "Pierce County in 1860," *Wisconsin Magazine of History* 42 (1959): 175–81; and Lawrence H. Larsen, "Urban Services in Gilded Age Wisconsin," *Wisconsin Magazine of History* 71 (1987–1988): 83–117.

42. Brand Whitlock quoted in Stephen L. Hansen, *The Making of the Third Party System: Voters and Parties in Illinois, 1850–1876* (Ann Arbor, Michigan, 1980), 204.

43. Patrick F. Palermo, "The Rules of the Game: Local Republican Political Culture in the Gilded Age," *The Historian* 47 (1984–1985): 480, 483, 486.

44. David P. Thelen, *Robert M. LaFollette and the Insurgent Spirit* (Boston, 1976), 111.

45. Jensen, *Winning of the Midwest,* 58–88.

46. Frank L. Klement, "Middle Western Copperheadism and the Genesis of the Granger Movement," *The Old Northwest: Studies in Regional History, 1787–1910,* ed. Harry N. Scheiber (Lincoln, Nebraska, 1969), 323–40. For fuller discussions, see Frank L. Klement, *The Copperheads in the Middle West* (Chicago, 1960); and Frank L. Klement, *The Limits of Dissent: Clement L. Vallandigham and the Civil War* (Lexington, Kentucky, 1970). See the criticism of this argument in Ronald P. Formisano and William G. Shade, "The Concept of Agrarian Radicalism," *Mid-America* 52 (1970): 3–30. But see also Robert H. Abzug, "The Copperheads: Historical Approaches to Civil War Dissent in the Midwest," *Indiana Magazine of History* 66 (1970): 40–55. Abzug sees Copperheads as "very traditional people" who did not want "their prejudices and liberties falling prey to the Republicans"(54). On Ohio, see Thomas H. Scott, "Crawford County 'Ez Trooly Dimecratic': A Study of Midwestern Copperheadism," *Ohio History* 76 (1967): 33–53. On Illinois, see Robert E. Sterling, "Civil War Draft Resistance in Illinois," *Journal of the Illinois State Historical Society* 64 (1971): 244–66.

47. Kleppner, *Cross of Culture,* 158.

48. Ibid., 167.

49. Ibid., 154–55.

50. Jensen, *Winning of the Midwest,* 142.

51. John L. Thomas, *Alternative America: Henry George, Edward Bellamy, Henry Demarest Lloyd and the Adversary Tradition* (Cambridge, Massachusetts, 1983), 217–18.

52. The classic study is Robert Wiebe, *The Search for Order, 1877–1920* (New York, 1967).

53. Kleppner, *Cross of Culture,* 367, 368.

54. Jensen, *Winning of the Midwest,* 291.

55. Holli, *Reform in Detroit,* xiii.

56. Ibid., 18.

57. Ibid., 21.

58. Miller, *Boss Cox's Cincinnati,* 239.

59. Jensen, *Winning of the Midwest,* 305.

60. Thomas, *Alternative America,* 334.

61. Thelen, *LaFollette,* 22, 23.

62. Atherton, *Main Street on the Middle Border,* 217, 221.

63. Ibid., 217–42.

64. Lynds, *Middletown,* 88.

65. Thelen, *LaFollette,* esp. 155–78.

66. Atherton, *Main Street on the Middle Border,* 72–76 (quotation on 72).

67. Lynds, *Middletown,* 222.

68. Ibid., 315.

69. Ibid., 498.

70. Ibid., 497–98.

71. Sinclair Lewis, *Babbitt* (New York, 1922), 183.

72. Ibid., 184.

73. Ibid., 188.

74. Ibid., 184.

75. David D. Anderson, "The Midwestern Town in Midwestern Fiction," *Midamerica: The Yearbook of the Society for the Study of Midwestern Literature* 6 (1979): 27–43.

76. Sherwood Anderson, *Winesburg, Ohio* (New York, 1960), 69.

77. Ibid., 70.
78. Ibid., 81.
79. Ibid., 80.
80. Ibid., 82.
81. David D. Anderson, "Midwestern Town in Midwestern Fiction," 29.
82. Ibid., 30.
83. Ibid., 36.
84. See Ernest Hemingway, *In Our Time: Stories* (New York, 1925), especially the "The Big-Two Hearted River."
85. The quotations are from *The Great Gatsby* and are cited in Barry Gross, "Fitzgerald's Midwest: 'Something Gorgeous Somewhere'–Somewhere Else," *Midamerica: The Yearbook of the Society for the Study of Midwestern Literature* 6 (1979): 126.

Epilogue: Frederick Jackson Turner, Regional Historian

1. Ray Allen Billington, *Frederick Jackson Turner: Historian, Scholar, Teacher* (New York, 1973), 5. Turner's major writings include Frederick Jackson Turner, *The Rise of the New West, 1819–1829* (New York, 1906); *The Frontier in American History* (New York, 1920); *The Significance of Sections in American History* (New York, 1932); and *The United States, 1830–1850: The Nation and Its Sections* (New York, 1935).
2. Ibid., 15. Billington argues that had Turner "been city born and bred he would almost certainly not have evolved his frontier thesis" (17). Other especially insightful discussions of Turner include Lee Benson, *Turner and Beard: American Historical Writing Reconsidered* (Glencoe, Illinois, 1960); and Richard Hofstadter, *The Progressive Historians: Turner, Beard and Parrington* (New York, 1968).
3. For a valuable sketch of Turner's father's life and values, see Donald J. Berthrong, "Andrew Jackson Turner: 'Work Horse' of the Republican Party," *Wisconsin Magazine of History* 38 (1954–1955): 77–86.
4. See William Cronon, "Revisiting the Vanishing Frontier: The Legacy of Frederick Jackson Turner," *Western Historical Quarterly* 18 (1987): 157–71; Howard Lamar and Leonard Thompson, eds., *The Frontier in History: North America and Southern Africa Compared* (New Haven, Connecticut, 1981); and Patricia N. Limerick, *The Legacy of Conquest: The Unbroken Past of the American West* (New York, 1987).

INDEX

Adams, Nick: fictional character, 122
Allen, David Grayson: on migration to New England, 25
Alton, Illinois: anti-abolitionist mob in, 72
American Historical Association: Frederick Jackson Turner delivers paper before, 125
American Revolution: mentioned, 19; legacy of, 22–23
Anderson, David D.: on literature of Midwest, 121–22
Anderson, Sherwood: and *Winesburg, Ohio*, 120–21, 122
Anderson, Virginia DeJohn: on migration to New England, 25
Antiabolitionism, 72
Antimasons, 80
Antislavery: middle class and, 53, 62–63
Atack, Jeremy: on New Englanders as farmers, 41
Atherton, Lewis: on middle-class cores, 54–55; on values in McGuffey readers, 60; on Republican party, 111; on decline in independence of small towns, 116
Atwater, Caleb: historian of the Old Northwest, 1

Babbitt, George: fictional character, 119–20
Bailey, Gamaliel: antislavery leader, 62
Bailyn, Bernard: on the study of migration, 28
Balestrand, Norway: immigrants from, 26
Bank of the United States (Second): as political issue, 73, 74, 75–76
Banks: debate over, 75–76, 78, 90
Barnhart, John D.: historian of the Old Northwest, 1; on Ohio statehood controversy, 19
Bateman, Fred: on New Englanders as farmers, 41
Beecher, Catharine: on domesticity and Cincinnati, 52–53
Beecher family: and middle-class values, 52–53, 57
Beeman, Richard: and definition of community, 139
Bellamy, Edward: John L. Thomas biography of, 114
Bender, Thomas: and definition of community, 43

Bennett Law: public education as political issue in Wisconsin, 113
Benson, Lee: and interpretation of Jacksonian politics, 77
Bentley, Jesse: fictional character in *Winesburg, Ohio*, 120
Berkhofer, Robert F., Jr.: on development of national land policy in 1780s, 6, 8, 9
Berwanger, Eugene H.: on the frontier and slavery, 16
Billington, Ray Allen: and biography of Frederick Jackson Turner, 125
Blackburn, George M.: and Reconstruction politics in Michigan, 95
Blacks: and Reconstruction legislation, 95; after Civil War in midwestern cities, 96; mentioned, 85
Blumin, Stuart: and middle-class culture, 51
Bogue, Allan: on land speculators, 36; on environment and crop selection, 39
Bogue, Margaret: on land speculators, 36
Bond, Beverley W. Jr.: historian of the Old Northwest, 1
Boosterism: midwestern, 55, 111, 116–23
Breen, T. H.: on migration to New England, 25
Brown, Jeffrey P.: on Ohio statehood controversy, 19
Buechler, Steven M.: on women's suffrage movement, 157
Buley, R. Carlyle: historian of the Old Northwest, 1
Burnet, Jacob: historian of the Old Northwest, 1
Burr Conspiracy, 68

Canals, construction of, 36–37; debate over, 38; lack of in Michigan, 78
Cane Ridge, Kentucky: and Second Great Awakening, 48
Carraway, Nick: fictional character, 123
Carthage, Illinois: and anti-Mormon riot, 72
Cartwright, Peter: itinerant preacher, 48
Catholics: hostility toward, 72, 87–88, 90, 92; and politics, 81, 92, 111–12, 113; mentioned, 86, 116
Cayton, Andrew: on government of Northwest Territory, 18; on politics in early Ohio, 66